GOOD
LEADERS

THOUGHTS, WORDS, ACTIONS
IMPACTING OUR HISTORY

JAMES SYVER

Copyright © 2024 James Syver.

All rights reserved. No part of this book may be reproduced, stored, or transmitted by any means—whether auditory, graphic, mechanical, or electronic—without written permission of both publisher and author, except in the case of brief excerpts used in critical articles and reviews. Unauthorized reproduction of any part of this work is illegal and is punishable by law.

This book is a work of non-fiction. Unless otherwise noted, the author and the publisher make no explicit guarantees as to the accuracy of the information contained in this book and in some cases, names of people and places have been altered to protect their privacy.

Scripture quotations taken from The Holy Bible, New International Version® NIV® Copyright © 1973 1978 1984 2011 by Biblica, Inc. TM. Used by permission. All rights reserved worldwide.

Scripture texts in this work are taken from the New American Bible, revised edition © 2010, 1991, 1986, 1970 Confraternity of Christian Doctrine, Washington, D.C. and are used by permission of the copyright owner. All Rights Reserved. No part of the New American Bible may be reproduced in any form without permission in writing from the copyright owner.

ISBN: 979-8-89419-407-3 (sc)
ISBN: 979-8-89419-408-0 (hc)
ISBN: 979-8-89419-409-7 (e)

Because of the dynamic nature of the Internet, any web addresses or links contained in this book may have changed since publication and may no longer be valid. The views expressed in this work are solely those of the author and do not necessarily reflect the views of the publisher, and the publisher hereby disclaims any responsibility for them.

THE EWINGS PUBLISHING

One Galleria Blvd., Suite 1900, Metairie, LA 70001
(504) 702-6708

In memory of Sister Francesco, one of the founding members of the Missionaries of Charity, who worked with Mother Teresa in Calcutta and who died from the COVID-19 pandemic while serving in the New York borough of the Bronx.

To all, of our brothers, including my brother Richard, a sibling dedicated to his family, who would be honored with a twenty-one-gun salute. To all, of our neighbors, including Richard Krumm, who died defending his country.

Among so many willing to give, this book is in memory, too, of Paul Drexler, a friend and classmate. Shortly after graduating from the US Air Force Academy, Paul turned his vehicle in an auto accident in order, to save others, giving his own life. This book is in memory, then, of good thoughts, words, and deeds.

Jesus did many other things as well. If every one of them were written down, I suppose that even the whole world would not have room for the books that would be written.

—John 21:25 NIV

This writing is dedicated to Mother and Father and to all those good souls who labored to make a better life for themselves and their posterity—all those whose untold and unrecorded deeds have made each of our lives better. Each, then, may have received some favorite admonition to carry forward into their lives. "Judge ye not lest ye be judged" is but one.

More than this, this writing is dedicated to children, grandchildren, and those generations yet unborn, that their lives may be touched by love sent forward, just as we have received from those brave souls who have preceded us.

CONTENTS

Acknowledgments xi
Introduction xiii

Christian Führer 1
Introduction 2 6
John Paul II...7
William Booth 20
Alexander Hamilton..29
Thomas Jefferson 36
An Early Reflection...50
A Prelude To A Civil War...53
    A Song From John Newton 54
    A Note and Warning from the Last Living Framer
    of the Constitution, James Madison 56
    A Debate Always and Henry Clay 57
    A Whisper from Benjamin Franklin to You and I......59
Abraham Lincoln 63
Reverend Martin Luther King Jr. 94
John Quincy Adams... 116
Booker T. Washington 131
George Washington Carver 151
Mother Teresa 163

Francis S. Collins 186

George Frideric Handel 194

Monsignor Georges Lemaitre 205

Afterglow 215

Edith Stein 217

Florence Nightingale 237

Lin Zhao 256

William Wilberforce 276

Frederick Douglass 303

Eric Liddell 335

Works Cited 359

ACKNOWLEDGMENTS

This writer is indebted to all the various writers who have undertaken their extensive individual research of each of the individuals highlighted in this writing.

These brief writings may hopefully prove an encouragement to the mind for further understandings and appreciations.

INTRODUCTION

Can we forget those individuals that have written our history by their lives? Can we forget their inspirations and the Maker who inspired them?

The writings contained herein are introductions to some of the most profound personages who have set their footprints into history.

What is it that propelled them forward, so, as to define not only themselves but also a world to which we ourselves aspire? What character allowed theirs to inspire ours?

It is the author's belief that the twenty personages represented in this brief writing are best represented when the reader may take a step or two into their shoes and walk beside them as they follow their destinies. World histories have been impacted by the living of their lives. What made that possible? The twenty figures represented in these pages bring forward lives of brilliance and light. Some are known and some are not, but all are related. These personages have their own stories to tell. Ah, but if we could only be there!

These individual and unique histories, then, introduce thoughts developed in many and varied moments throughout time. What were the worlds into which these brave men and women were born, and how did they affect their times for the better?

Perhaps their stories are not yet finished. Perhaps these stories live on into our futures, inspiring the generations to follow.

Writing this book has been a most profound privilege and honor. I should like the pages of the persons written of be able to convey the included individuals' stories as they would like to have them told.

The lives of those written of in these pages have impacted, in some measure, each of our lives. Here, in history, as in life, we remain persons and individuals—subjects not only to kings and princes and movements and forces of politics and wars and the persuasions of our times, but also intrinsically, in each life, lived, to our own very Creator. We will understand our lives, then, as being on a plane, lifting us above ourselves alone.

Without this understanding, is a room without light. A day without the sun. A world without love, our country without a constitution to guide it, histories written with malice unforgiving, and shepherds never visited while watching their flocks.

Creation without the Creator. Emptiness without praise. Life without Christ.

This book is a collection of a few stories consequential to individuals and peoples—Christ-inspired histories. These true stories are but a very few of too many to be written showing the ways in which Christ has inspired individual lives—the ways in which humanity has been inspired.

Let us begin.

CHRISTIAN FÜHRER

A Pastor

The first story could be written about the Reverend Christian Führer, the pastor of St. Nicholas Church in what was Leipzig, East Germany, at the fall of the Berlin Wall. But, of course, it should not be. The pastor would credit Jesus.

Pastor Christian Führer's ministry began in the early 1980s. It was a time of tension between East Germany and West Germany. The Cold War's trench cut Germany in half. Would Germany again be the battleground of a third world war in the twentieth century? East Germany's police state controlled the population with the secret police (the Stasi) and kept tabs on possible opponents or dissidents. Suspicion and mistrust reigned amid the oppression.

The pastor began "prayers for peace" on Monday evenings. Atheism was the official belief construct of the East German communist regime, and the government strongly discouraged its citizens becoming involved in religious activities. Oftentimes, fewer than a dozen attended.

The weekly peace prayer meetings began in September of 1982, in St. Nikolai Church, at the request of young people. The slandered, the imprisoned, and those forced into silence, were able to feel liberation from the proscriptions of a repressive society. Some, for the first time, began to understand the Spirit of God. The pastor put out a sign in 1985 that read "Open to all." He reflected: "Open to all, people understood what that meant. The threshold of our church is low both for wheelchair users and atheists. To me, the open doors of the church are like the open arms of Jesus." A spiritual church guide for St. Nikolai written by the pastor evinces further understandings.

A particular moment of tension occurred in May of 1989, when the Socialist Unity Party of Germany (SED) claimed to have received 98 percent of the votes cast in a blatantly fraudulent election. Calls for reform grew in volume.

Pastor Führer recalled the following: "On May 1989, the authorities barricaded the streets leading to the church, hoping to put people off, but it had the opposite effect, and our congregation grew." In the past, these prayer meetings had been largely ignored. As their numbers grew, they were threatened, and pressure was put on them to stop the meetings.

On Saturday, October 7, the celebration of the fortieth anniversary of the German Democratic Republic occurred. On that day, police showed force and battered defenseless demonstrators. Then soldiers and tanks were mobilized. The police had their guns loaded with live ammunition. Extra beds and blood plasma were allocated to the Leipzig hospitals. Rumors from reliable sources circulated that the government intended to use the "Chinese solution" and repeat the massacre of Tiananmen Square in Beijing.

Tensions had run high for weeks. The authorities had made it clear that what they called the counterrevolution would be crushed once and for all. Water cannons, riot gear, and fists pounding shields awaited any who would assemble that night. A thousand SED members were ordered to occupy the church that Monday evening. As the pastor knew many of them, he told them they were welcome and that the church was open to all. The pastor said, "They had a job to perform. What had not been considered was the fact that these people were exposed to the Word, the gospel, and its impact! I was always glad the Stasi agents heard the Beatitudes from the Sermon on the Mount every Monday. Where else would they hear these?"

On Monday, October 9, 1989, about six thousand attended prayers in other churches, and seventy thousand altogether waited outside St. Nikolai—many holding candles. Pastor Führer said, "This was our first revolution in which the church played a decisive role, and we were part of it. It was the revolution that came out of the church and was truly, unique. "Our fear was not as big as our faith." As one SPD official said, "We'd been planning everything. We were prepared for everything—but not candles and prayers." One month after this miraculous gathering, the Berlin Wall would fall. The iron curtain that had divided the East from the West dissolved after a year.

Pastor Christian Führer said, "What moved me most was the people who had grown up in two atheistic tank ships—first the Nazi Regime and then the Communist's—were able to distill the message of Jesus into two words: no violence. Not one shop window was smashed, and no one was shot dead. For me, that means that God has had mercy on our city and the whole of Germany. We must never forget that politics is not just about money or business or the army or the media, but that faith can move mountains and help us win revolutions."

And one may ask, If, not for the influence of the church and church leadership, what would have happened? Pastor Führer reflected on the many conversations he had in that regard: "There is a very clear answer. It would have been like all other revolutions before—bloody and unsuccessful. Just look at previous uprisings in the communist bloc. There were several between 1953 and 1989. The church wasn't involved in any of them, and they ended in violence. The non-violence we saw here in Leipzig didn't start in the schools or the newspapers or politics. It came from Jesus and the church."

Home to this peaceful revolution for freedom—known also as the velvet revolution—was the church of St. Nikolai. It was established as a citizen's church in 1165 and a center of the Protestant Reformation in 1539. Today's divine services include the local Lutheran services, other Christian services, as well as Roman-Catholic services.

Blessed are the poor in spirit,
for theirs is the kingdom of heaven.

Blessed are those who mourn,
for they will be comforted.

Blessed are the meek,
for they will inherit the earth.

Blessed are those who hunger and thirst
for righteousness,
for they will be filled.

Blessed are the merciful,
for they will be shown mercy.

Blessed are the pure of heart,
for they will see God.

Blessed are the peacemakers,
for they will be called children of God.

Blessed are those who are persecuted
because of righteousness,
for theirs is the kingdom of heaven.

Blessed are you when people insult you,
persecute you and falsely say all kinds of
evil against you because of me. Rejoice
and be glad, because great is your reward
in heaven, for in the same way they persecuted
the prophets who were before you.
(Matthew 5:1–12 NIV)

As we leave the church of St. Nikolai, Pastor Christian Fuhrer leaves us with these words: "May you also be infused with the spirit of Jesus as a force of nonviolence and renewal. May something of the peace—stronger than all our reasoning and deeper than our fears— and some of the positive force emanating from this space dedicated to faith and freedom and humanity accompany you in your future life and work. Our Lord Jesus Christ blesses you."

INTRODUCTION 2

And so, there is a universe: from unfathomable distances and dimensions to the swirling nuclear particles within our own bodies. And so, there is life. Easy. Nothing to it. But just maybe there *is* something to it.

The author of these pages will offer examples of an unseen Creator at work within creation. It is at our level and within the human frame, even here, that creation itself can be perfected. The subjects to be mentioned in this brief annal have names and faces and places. Their inspirations reflect a greater good and unseen grace, put-to-use, in the world we live in.

JOHN PAUL II

A Pope

The unseen heroism of the faithful. Those everyday moments unsupported by a tyranny on high—a communist tyranny. The record of the millions sacrificed to attain some human ideal had been witnessed firsthand, close-up, by every living Pole. It was internalized, visceral—a part of everyday life. And it could be you who would be the neighbor missing without explanation—except for the explanation every man, woman, and child knew.

Under communist suppression there grew a temper, a silence, of character to the core that may, pray to God, enable these people to bring forward to faith the love they had for one another that they may see liberty in their day, that they may freely express their faith and realize a better way for their children, and that once again surrounded by the evils of Nazism and communism, they might breathe freely.

They would pray. And Karol Wojtyla prayed. Karol Jozef Wojtyla was born May 18, 1920, in the small town of Wadowice in southern Poland, the very day the Polish people were celebrating a newly independent Poland with a parade of victory in the capitol of Warsaw.

Marshal Jozef Pilsudski was being paraded as the hero of the "Polish Miracle"—Poland's first major military victory in over two centuries. The marshal and his young army had defeated no less an enemy than Lenin's Red Army of the Soviet Union when they captured the city of Kiev of the Soviet Ukraine.

Would that be the end? Lenin and Stalin had devised a plan to advance toward the defeated and war-shattered Germany, in order, to plant their communist rule there and then move on to the whole of Europe. The Soviets had already occupied Lithuania, Byelorussia, and other territories on their westward offensive.

No, this would not be the end—as it is never the end, it seems, when facing evil. Just three months later, on August 15, on the Feast of the Assumption of Our Lady, these same Polish forces would once again meet, and this time they would repulse a powerful Soviet counterattack at the city gates of Warsaw. This victory was to be known as the "Miracle on the Vistula," referring to the river bisecting the capital.

The young Karol grew up in a loving family and rural community peaceably centered on the Skawa River in the foothills of the Beskidy Mountains. Wadowice was established in 1325. It was incorporated into Poland in 1564. Wadowice's traditional orientation was toward the literature and theatre of Krakow and Vienna rather than to Warsaw. Traditional dress was worn by the peasants, and the mode of transport was the horse and wagon in pre-WWII Wadowice. There were very few automobiles in use.

On another level, Karol Wojtyla was the product of personal tragedy and suffering, having lost his entire family at a young age. A baby sister had died in infancy; his dear mother when he was nine; his oldest brother, a doctor, when he was twelve; and his loving father before his twenty-first birthday.

Karol was a rather strong athletic type, and he excelled in sports, such as soccer. His hometown also had a Jewish population. Wojtyla was also neighborly friends with one of the most beautiful girls in town and the best student at the girls' high school, Regina Beer. His first appearance on the Wadowice amateur stage was at age fifteen, as her leading man. The schools were excellent.

Before and after Wojtylas's graduation, hundreds of graduates would die in each of the world wars, including scores of Catholics and Jews in the Oswiecim concentration camp, just west of Wadowice, during World War II.

Later, in a papal pilgrimage, John Paul would speak to the remaining Jewish Community of Warsaw. He said, "Man lives on the basis, of his own experiences. I belong to the generation for which relationships with Jews was a daily occurrence." He referred to the 147th psalm, which was sung during the evening mass of his youth. It begins, "Praise ye the Lord: for it is good to sing praises unto our God." He further said, "I still have in my ears these words and this melody which I have remembered all my life. And then came the terrible experience of World War II and the [Nazi] occupation, the Holocaust, which was the extermination of Jews only for the reason, that they were Jews. It was a terrible upheaval that has remained in the memory of all the people who were close to these events."

Whether Wadowice was too remote or whether its citizens, like much of Poland, simply could not believe that war was approaching once more, the impression is that the people there ignored the signs of the gathering storm.

Then the Nazis occupied Poland. Karol Wojtyla labored in a quarry and in a chemical plant. He came to learn of a transpiring Holocaust and assisted in a broad-based resistance trying to save Jews. In the fall of 1942, he entered an underground seminary under the guidance of Adam Sapieha, archbishop of Krakow. He was also a key player in an underground cultural resistance theatre, which, if found, would have been his ticket to Oswiecim.

In time, the Nazis would eventually retreat. In August of 1944, Karol Wojtyla was living in an apartment in Krakow. The Nazi gestapo swept the city, seizing every young man they could find; they gathered eight thousand in total. Their purpose was to prevent an uprising. The action became known as Black Sunday. Karol Wojtyla was kneeling and praying in his basement apartment. For some reason, the gestapo raiders did not search the apartment of Karol Wojtyla. The Soviets then "liberated" Poland, and this would prove to mean no less than the suppression of all opposition to atheistic totalitarian rule. Karol, early on, in the war, had warned against the "red banner and the unreal international humanism."

Karol was correct, whether, or not, he knew or had read in *The Communist Manifesto* that "communism abolishes external truths, it abolishes all religion, and all morality." Marx, the manifesto's author, succinctly stated, "Communism begins where atheism begins." Within the Soviet Union, religious instruction was forbidden to those under the age of eighteen. Children were encouraged to turn in parents. "Church watchers" watched churches, reporting anyone who came to pray. Clergy were executed or sent to forced-labor camps in Siberia. In fact, Lenin himself wrote on Christmas Day, 1919, that "there can be nothing more abominable than religion." He ordered anyone observing Christmas rather than showing up for work to be killed. This trite and succinct phrase shows just an inkling of the challenge and chaos to be wrought and the tens of millions of lives to be sacrificed on behalf of this imposing superficial ideal.

It was in September of 1939 that Hitler and Stalin had invaded Poland—Hitler from the west and Stalin from the east. Only one snippet of an example of the horrors to be unleashed—250 men per night would be murdered in a velvet-covered (so, as to muffle sounds) Polish prison cell room each night for an entire month, and the same numbers in two other Soviet camps. This secret remained for decades inside the Kremlin. It would be many years later that the young Karol Wojtyla, as pope, would refer to the many examples of "the culture of death." Perhaps C. S. Lewis provides a glimpse within "The Screwtape Letters."

Now, back to reality. On November 1, 1946, the Day of All Saints, Cardinal Sapieha would ordain Karol Wojtyla as a priest of the Roman Catholic Church. Father Wojtyla would spend the next two years in study in Rome, Italy. Father Wojtyla's depth of understanding of the beginnings of Christianity was increased. He visited the catacombs, prayed with Padre Pio, and learned. The living conditions were rudimentary, without electricity or running water.

Defeated, postwar Italy did not possess political stability and nearly fell to communist rule. Karol would begin to further understand the dimension of the political realm. Fr. Wojtyla would be assigned to a rural area in his homeland. As he traveled by horse cart, reading books across the countryside, he would return greetings of "Praise Him,"—a reference to Jesus Christ. Fr. Wojtyla would later be assigned to St. Florian's University, one of few allowed in Poland.

The close-knit and traditional Polish Catholic culture was of help in ensuring some deference from repressive edicts, as evidenced in other surrounding Eastern European countries. However, life under communist rule would not be made easy, as it never is. Fr. Wotjyla would continue to write with reflection, but his writings would no longer appear in state-run newspapers. Instead, the Fr. participated in youth activities. When traveling with a youth group, he would dress informally. As one of the youths would say, "You could go to jail for celebrating Mass in a forest." As Fr. Wojtyla said: "As the communists suppressed all Catholic youth associations, a way had to be found to remedy the situation."

Later, when pope, His Holiness spoke of Jesus: "He spoke of the fact that God is at work in the world." His Holiness also spoke of Christianity: "Christianity is not only a religion of knowledge, of contemplation. It is a religion of God's action and of man's action." And he, spoke of God: "His is an action which passes through the heart of man and through the history of humanity."

In these times, both Winston Churchill and Pope Pius XII saw America as a beacon of hope. They offered that international communism's denials of liberties produced, in effect, its own slavery and thereby posed no less than a mortal threat to Christianity and to civilization. The absence of the recognition of the laws of nature and nature's God and the unalienable rights endowed by the Creator to each, individual, became, in every essence then, stultifyingly morbid.

As pope, John Paul wrote of this dark period in Polish history and the communist regime. He noted a Marian devotion and a bishop who initiated a national pilgrimage with the Black Madonna, setting off from Czestochowa to visit every parish and community in Poland: "… the communist authorities did all in their power to stop it. When the icon was 'arrested' by the police, the pilgrimage continued with the empty frame, and the message became even more eloquent. The frame with no picture was a silent sign of the lack of religious freedom in Poland. The nation knew it had a right to regain religious freedom and prayed fervently for it."

Fr. Wotjyla would witness tens of thousands of workers singing patriotic songs and religious hymns while marching to Freedom Square in Krakow for better working conditions. On June 28, 1956, the Polish People's Army fired, killing fifty-four.

On August 26, a million faithful, gathered for prayer at the annual celebration at the shrine of the Black Madonna. Imprisoned priests and bishops were freed from prison. The authorities agreed to refrain from the practice of both nominating and appointing bishops.

Father Wojtyla would remain publicly silent on matters of politics. He was named chairman of ethics at Catholic University in Lublin. He continued his writing. September 28, 1958, Karol Wojtyla was ordained as a bishop. From then on, he signed his letters and documents with the phrase: *"Totus Tuus,"* which is Latin for "Totally Yours"—or, in the Roman tradition, Jesus's via Mary.

The following year, Pope John XXIII unveiled plans for the Second Vatican Council on June 25. Bishop Karol Wojtyla was invited to attend. Karol Wojtyla attended every session of the Second Vatican Council. He said, "During the first session, the universality of the Church was brought home to me in an extraordinary way by my contact with a number of bishops from Africa."

As Bishop Wojtyla's dedication grew, his work schedule became busier and busier. The Polish communist regime began to see in Bishop Wojtyla an "evil influence" on Polish Society. The bishop must have been doing something right. On the other hand, during Karol Wojtyla's brilliant participation in Vatican II, he had also negotiated directly with the regime over a matter of seminary concern.

The bishop's outward view of the church would seem less directly politically hostile and more apolitical. And so, his nomination as archbishop was accepted by the regime. He would be installed March of 1964 at the age of forty-three. Archbishop Karol Wojtyla strongly defended the sovereignty of the church.

By the final session of Vatican II in September of 1965, Archbishop Wojtyla was one of the proponents of a new "Declaration on Religious

Freedom." He had elaborated on the relationship between freedom and truth. He thought it insufficient to simply say, "I am free," but rather thought it necessary to say, "I am responsible." Religious freedom becomes God's revealed will for the world and for human beings.

The council fathers would issue a final text titled *Dignitatis Humanae*. It begins as follows:

> The Vatican Council declares that the human person has a right to religious freedom. Freedom of this kind means that all men should be immune from coercion on the part of individuals, social groups, and every human power so that, within due limits, nobody is forced to act against his convictions in religious matters in private or in public, alone or in association with others. The Council further declares that the right to religious freedom is based on the very dignity of the human person as known through the revealed word of God and by reason itself. This right of the human person to religious freedom must be given such recognition in the constitutional order of society as will make it a civil right.

The final session of the Second Vatican Council ended in December 1965. A proposal of diplomatic relations from the Vatican under Paul VI's Ostpolitick was refused by Poland in 1967.

Pope Paul named Karol Wojtyla a cardinal on June 28, 1967. "The unity of the church with the nation always had, and still has, a fundamental meaning for both the Polish nation and the Church," said the new Cardinal. A pastoral letter was written in 1978 exemplifying the cardinal's thinking: "… the spirit of freedom is the proper climate for the full development of the person. Without freedom, a person is dwarfed, and all progress dies."

Among the many, many challenges presented to the Church during the Soviet occupation, in December 1970, army and security workers clashed with rioting workers in Gdansk, a port city on the Baltic. Once again, tanks fired on workers and scores were killed. Speaking in August of 1973, the cardinal expressed his concern about "the liberty of the Polish soul" as a result of a government education reform law that did "not say a single word about the contribution of Christ, Church and Christianity to Polish education."

Marxism was receiving poor grades in Poland. By June of 1976, food prices had spiked. Walkouts and strikes followed. Primate Wyszinski and Cardinal Wotjyla urged each side to scale down in-order to achieve a modicum of peace and normalcy, with workers returning to work and the government not prosecuting them.

On October 22, 1978, John Paul II assumed the pontificate as successor of St. Peter. As Cardinal Deskur commented, "Everything the Holy Father endured in his life, prepared him for what he had to be. Just as an arrow is readied for the shot from the bow, God prepares the proper people, He prepares his arrows …" The message from the new Bishop of Rome was "Be not afraid. Christ knows 'what is in man'."

John Paul would speak of the answer to humanity's fear of itself, saying that it lay in rediscovering that human nature is moral and spiritual and not simply material. He would say that religious freedom is the first of the human person's "objective and inalienable rights." With his immediate knowledge of the world behind the iron curtain, he could profess the following:

> [The] curtailment of the religious freedom of individuals and communities is not only a painful experience but is above all an attack on man's very dignity … [It is] a radical injustice with regard to what is particularly deep in man, what is authentically human … [A]theism as a human phenomenon is understood only in relation to the phenomenon of religion and faith. It is therefore difficult … … to accept a position that gives only atheism the right of citizenship in public and social life, while believers are … barely tolerated or are treated as second-class citizens or are even—and this has already happened—entirely deprived of the rights of citizenship.

GOOD LEADERS

John Paul II, on a papal pilgrimage, landed in Warsaw on the morning of June 2, 1979. Ten of the thirty-five million Polish citizens would celebrate his arrival in person. They would sing their song, "We want God!" Afterward, the Polish citizenry would speak of "our nine days of freedom," referring to the length of the pontiff's visit.

Moscow was less than pleased with the pontiff's reception and targeted top-secret studies and responses against this new Pope and the Vatican. The Pope would be undeterred in his life's efforts to bring forth freedom. He would rise above the ordinary in his patient diplomacy with the forces that be. His insight into the communist mind and the realities of life were distinctly helpful as he patiently addressed key and important issues between Poland and the Soviet Union. There would be many confidential missions between Warsaw, Moscow, and Rome in the years to follow.

August 14, 1980, began what would become known worldwide as the Lenin Shipyard strike. It was the beginning of a movement to become famously known as *Solidanosc*, meaning "solidarity". An unemployed electrician named Lech Walesa would jump the shipyard fence to become their leader. He would, indeed, later be elected as leader of a free Poland.

Although obsessed with the appearances of legality and judicial processes, the communist regimes essentially ran lawless states— some more effective than others, so to speak. The communist courts initially blocked recognition of Solidarnosc and always made life difficult for the Poles.

Lech Walesa, their revered leader, said, "If you choose the example of what we Poles have in our pockets and in our shops … communism has done very little for us. But if you choose the example of what is in our souls, I answer that communism has done very much for us. In fact, our souls contain exactly the opposite of what they wanted. They wanted us not to believe in God, and our churches are full."

For just a moment, let us take note of what a future president John F. Kennedy said was his view of communism as he spoke to an audience at Assumption College in June 1955. He told the audience that the communist had a "fear" of Christianity and allowed "no room for God."

JFK went on to say that communists sought "to make the worship of the State the ultimate objective in life" and that they could not "permit a higher loyalty, a faith in God, a belief in religion that elevates the individual, acknowledges his true value, and teaches him devotion and responsibility to something beyond the here and now." Later, as president, John Kennedy warned his fellow citizens of its "atheistic foe," of communism's "fanaticism and fury," and of a "communist conspiracy" that "represents a final enslavement" of peoples. He further warned that "the enemy is the communist system itself—implacable, insatiable, unceasing in its drive for world domination … This is a struggle for supremacy between two conflicting ideologies: freedom under God versus ruthless, godless tyranny."

On January 19, 1981, Lech Walesa visited and prayed with Pope John Paul II at the Vatican in Rome. Italian investigators detected a plot on Walesa's life near his hotel. Twenty-three-year-old Mehmet Ali Agca would be given another assassination opportunity on May 13, 1981, on the Feast Day of Our Lady of Fatima. On January 20, 1981, Ronald Wilson Reagan would take the oath of office to be the fortieth president of the United States of America.

On March 30, 1981, President Reagan felt the pain of an assassin's bullet. When he arrived at the hospital, he said to the doctors, "I hope you are all Republicans." "Today, Mr. President, we're all Republicans" was the reply. "My fear was growing," he wrote in his diary, "because no matter how hard I tried to breathe, it seemed I was getting less & less air." Reagan also prayed. He said later, "I focused on that tiled ceiling and prayed. But I realized I couldn't ask for God's help while at the same time I felt hatred for the mixed-up young man who had shot me. Isn't that the meaning of the lost sheep? We are all God's children and therefore equally beloved by him. I began to pray for his soul and that he would find his way back into the fold."

On May 13, 1981, a bullet fired by a Turk named Mehmet Ali Agca pierced the flesh of Pope John Paul. John Paul said later, "At the very moment I fell, I had this vivid presentiment that I should be saved." And yes, it would be later the pope himself would visit his would-be assassin in person. There he would forgive him.

President Reagan traveled to Notre Dame to give a commencement address on May 17, 1981. There he said, "The years ahead are great ones for this country, for the cause of freedom and the spread of civilization. The West won't contain communism, it will transcend communism …" He would invoke the words spoken by Winston Churchill during the most ominous days of the Battle of Britain: "When great causes are on the move in the world, we learn we are spirits, not animals, and that something is going on in space and time, and beyond space and time, which, whether we like it or not, spells duty."

Weeks later, on the fourth of June 1981, the president and first lady would sit down with a guest—a nun known as Mother Teresa. She said to the president, "Mr. President Reagan, do you know that we stayed up for two straight nights praying for you after you were shot? We prayed very hard for you to live." After a humble thank-you, she looked at the president and said, "You have suffered the passion of the cross and have received grace. There is purpose to this. Because of your suffering and pain, you will now understand the suffering and pain of the world. This happened to you at this time because your country and the world needs you." Nancy dissolved into tears, and Ronnie was speechless.

On the night of December 13, 1981, reporters stated that "all hell broke loose" in Poland. Tanks rolled in, gunshots rang out, sirens wailed, and police trucks raced down the streets. Solidarnosc members were arrested, and thousands of union leaders, dissidents, and intellectuals were shipped to internment camps. The long-threatened communist crackdown on the people of Poland had arrived. Under orders from the Kremlin, the Polish communist regime imposed martial law.

"Whatever time I have left is for Him" is how President Reagan put it after surviving his assassination attempt. In June of 1987, Ronald Reagan wrote and spoke at the Vatican, two days before another trip to Poland by Pope John Paul II:

> "As you embark on a pastoral visit to the land of your birth, Poland, be assured that the hearts of the American people are with you. Our prayers will go with you in profound hope that soon the hand of God will lighten

the terrible burden of brave people everywhere who yearn for freedom, even as all men and women yearn for the freedom that God gave us all when he gave us a free will. We see the power of the spiritual force in that troubled land, uniting a people in hope, just as we see the powerful stirrings to the East of a belief that will not die despite generations of oppression. Perhaps its' not too much to hope that true change will come to all countries that now deny or hinder the freedom to worship God. And perhaps, we'll see that change comes through the reemergence of faith, through the irresistible power of a religious renewal. For despite all the attempts to extinguish it, the people's faith burns with a passionate heat; once allowed to breathe free, that faith will burn so brightly it will light the world."

Later, Mikhail Gorbachev would simply and succinctly characterize the efforts of communism as a "war on religion".

On December 01, 1989, on his way to Malta for his first summit with the newly elected President George Herbert Walker Bush, the Soviet leader Mikhail Gorbachev visited the Vatican to meet with Pope John Paul II. The Pope listened and referenced fundamental human rights, freedom of conscience, religious freedom. John Paul also noted that "A person becomes a believer through free choice; it is impossible to make someone believe."

Even as Benjamin Franklin knew that He did, does God play a role in our history today? Two men suffering assassination attempts only weeks apart in the spring of 1981 believed so. John Paul II and Ronald Reagan shared not just this experience but also their belief that there was to be divine providence in their mutual efforts to defeat the "evil empire" of communism.

Thus, history is made. It is nurtured and developed. It is within the human dimension. It is made by each of us. It can be inspired by above if we allow it to be. It is all that we have. But it is always God's Creation.

Mikhail Gorbachev, leader of the Soviet Union, wrote in 1992, "Everything that happened in Eastern Europe in these last few years would have been impossible without the presence of this Pope and without the important role—including the political role—that he played on the world stage."

Pope John Paul II also said, "The gates of hell will not prevail, as the Lord has said. But that doesn't mean we are exempt from the trials from and battles against the Evil One," and, "Pope John XXIII, who was moved by God to summon the Council, used to say: 'what separates us as believers in Christ is much less than what unites us.' In this statement we find the heart of ecumenical thinking."

WILLIAM BOOTH

A Gentle War

On April 10, 1829, in Nottingham, England, the founder of the Salvation Army, William Booth was born. At thirteen, William was apprenticed to a pawnbroker. He despised the work. By the time he was fifteen, William had begun to preach to young people in the streets—after working hours. He would proudly lead a rabble of his ragged, rough-looking friends into the front pews of a Methodist church when he could. At twenty, he left for London to work, again unhappily, in a pawnshop. At night William preached in the streets.

On his twenty-third birthday, he became engaged to Catherine Munford. He became an evangelistic preacher. After nine years in the ministry, differences between William and the church became too much to ignore. At a meeting, William was ordered to give up his outdoor revival meetings. Catherine Booth leaned forward and called to him, "Never!"

After breaking with the Methodist New Connection, William held tent services in conjunction with another evangelist. In July of 1865, he formed the East London Revival Society, which soon became the Christian Mission. Most of those attending his meetings were the same unwanted, desperately poor people he would have in his congregations for the rest of his life. After a year, there were three hundred members of the Christian Mission. After four years, there were three thousand members. They began to refer to themselves as the "Hallelujah Army" and to William as their "general."

In 1878, William studied the title, *The Christian Mission—A Volunteer Army*. He wrote *The Salvation Army* and became the first general of the army. Uniforms, ranks, flags, a book of orders and regulations, and a rigid code of discipline were to follow.

The Salvation Army's battle lines extended outward to Canada, Australia, France, Switzerland, India, South Africa, Iceland, and elsewhere. The first American meeting was held in Philadelphia in October of 1879. The battle of and for men's souls was not always easy. For instance, in 1882 nearly seven hundred army people were knocked down, kicked, or otherwise hurt on the streets of Britain alone. Twenty-three were children. Despite abuse and barriers thrown in the way of the Salvation Army, General Booth always kept sight of his mission. Owing to the good work and mission of the Salvationists, as many as a quarter million souls had become Christian by 1885.

After a long and painful illness, Catherine Munford Boothe died in 1890. William then published his book *In Darkest England and the Way Out*, which he dedicated to Catherine.

His proposals for social reform, helping the poor, employment bureaus, vocational training, homes for young women, legal assistance, banking services, traveling hospitals, a missing persons' bureau, and other proposals were contained in this publication.

Much of Booth's dream was realized, and the scorn and ridicule he endured eventually gave way to sympathy and support. King Edward VII invited William Booth to his coronation in 1902. Before William Booth died, he had travelled five million miles and had given nearly sixty thousand sermons. At his last public meeting in London on his eighty-third birthday, he was as dauntless as ever, speaking the following words: "While women weep as they do now, I'll fight; while little children go hungry as they do now, I'll fight; while men go to prison, in and out, I'll fight. While there yet remains one dark soul without the light of God, I'll fight. I'll fight to the very end."

Four months later, on August 20, 1912, William Booth died. In tribute, more than sixty-five thousand people viewed his body. Seven thousand Salvationists marched in the funeral procession. Hundreds of thousands stood along the route.

And the Salvation Army would go on. The army would be sent into France in World War I. The women of the Salvation Army became famous for their efforts to make life a bit more bearable in that depressing war. They made apple pies and doughnuts for soldiers in the trenches. They mended uniforms. They played hymns and marches for the soldiers. They conducted Christian services for the soldiers in Salvation Army huts. The huts were also made available for Jewish services.

The Salvation Army's war was against human distress. That fight went on well after the armistice, bringing relief to the displaced, the homeless, refugees, the hungry, and families wrenched apart.

And the wars do not end. The Nazis came to power in Germany in 1933. The authorities informed the Salvation Army Commander, Commissioner William H. Howard, that the army's Life Saving Scouts of the World and Life Saving Guards were to be absorbed into Nazi youth organizations. Commissioner Howard simply disbanded both Salvation Army youth groups and sent the children home. Later the army would help many Jews to escape to Switzerland and Sweden.

When World War II ended, then again, there was enormous work to be done in caring for refugees, returning prisoners, and the thousands of stranded and orphaned children.

Once again, the Salvationists became the subjects of abuse and violence as one country after another fell to the communist allies of the Soviets in Eastern Europe. Communists considered the Salvation Army, with its Christian ethic and its international outlook, a threat to their doctrine, and it was abolished wherever communists took control. Salvationists and their families were jailed, exiled, or killed. Afterward, many continued to meet secretly for prayers, companionship, and remembrance.

When there is tragedy brought on by human beings—woes mankind inflicts on itself—one may find the Salvation Army alleviating the suffering. When there are natural tragedies, as from nature's erratic course, the Salvation Army can be found there to help. Per example, Hugh Redwood wrote "God in the Slums" and donated the royalties to the Salvation Army. "Is your religion your steering wheel or is it only your spare wheel?" he asked.

In the States, at a service, one will find a flag of the United States on one side of the altar; on the other side of the altar, the red Salvation Army flag, bearing the slogan "Blood and Fire." "Blood" refers to the sacrifice Jesus made for human souls, and "fire" refers to life, also represented by the Holy Spirit.

Mrs. Booth had designed the Salvation Army's flag. She was also persuasive with her husband. More than a century before most other churches began their uncertainty over the role of women in ministry, the Salvation Army was accepting women as preachers quite naturally. Mrs. Booth was among them. In 1859, Mrs. Booth wrote a pamphlet titled *Female Ministry, or Woman's Right to Preach the Gospel.*

The Salvation Army has been received worldwide in many circumstances: wars, famines, disasters, and the streets, where there is need. As was said by one Salvationist: "I don't care what it is that you do, you're doing it for somebody else. You're not doing it for yourself."

Today the Salvation Army serves in over one hundred countries worldwide, offering the message of God's healing and hope to all those in need. Every year, the army helps thirty million people— roughly one per second.

The Salvation Army helps disaster victims through
*emergency preparedness,
*immediate emergency response,
*long-term disaster recovery, and
*spiritual and emotional care.

The Salvation Army helps to overcome poverty through
*shelter,
*meal assistance,
*Pathway of Hope, and
*employment assistance.

The Salvation Army helps provide shelter through
*homeless shelters,
*transitional housing,
*permanent supportive housing, and
*re-entry resources.

The Salvation Army stops domestic abuse through
*the Cascade Women's and Children's Center,
*the Phoenix Elim House, and
*the Northwest Division Center.

The Salvation Army supplements and supports kids' educational opportunities through
*homework assistance and counseling,
*sports, clubs, and extracurricular activities,
*dance, art, and music programs, and
*parental involvement coaching.

The Salvation Army helps individuals secure gainful employment through
*skill-set evaluations,
*educational and skill supplementation,
*placement assistance, and
*continued support.

The Salvation Army is dedicated to serving seniors and the elderly through
*community,
*activities,
*residences, and
*adult day care centers.

The Salvation Army cures hunger by providing meals through
*food pantries,
*meal programs, and
*community gardens.

The Salvation Army is committed to serving the LGBTQ community through
*homeless shelters,
*job training,
*help with substance abuse,
*help with food insecurity, and
*teenage suicide prevention.

The Salvation Army fights the horror of human trafficking through
*awareness initiatives,
*comprehensive care management, and
*a legacy of justice.

The Salvation Army helps families thrive through
*the Kroc Community Center,
*after-school programs, and
*summer camps for kids.

The Salvation Army brings happy holidays to many through
*the Angel Tree Program,
*grocery and food assistance,
*bill-pay assistance, and
*holiday events.

The Salvation Army combats addiction through
*building work and social skills,
*fostering health and stability, and
*restoring families.

The Salvation Army serves veterans through
*shelters,
*adult rehabilitation centers, and
*community.

    The Salvation Army works to meet the greatest need in each person. As the army says, "Love has an army. We fight for good. Throughout the nation, The Salvation Army opens our arms and our hearts to serve those most desperate for physical, emotional, and spiritual assistance. Because human need differs from state to state, city to city, and even person to person, we seek to find solutions to each unique situation. By providing everything from feeding programs and emergency shelters to domestic abuse asylum and disaster relief services, we are able to do the most-good wherever and whenever it's needed."
    The Salvation Army is a worldwide church sharing God's love. Spread the word. Today's worldwide needs include the needs of refugees, the victims of modern human slavery, development needs, medical needs, and so many more. One tangible example in this hemisphere is the current need for food for the people of Venezuela. Four-fifths of those in Venezuela are now considered to be living in poverty. As many cross the border as refugees into Brazil, the element of human trafficking requires attention.
    As always, the Salvation Army dedicates its service to those in poverty and to the homeless. During the COVID-19 pandemic, this has been especially true.
    Many are familiar with the missions of their home communities. A local venue may have initiatives with names such as "Social Service," for those needing assistance with food, clothing, rent, utilities, etc.; "Prison Toy Lift Ministry," to assist prisoners in sending Christmas gifts and cards to their children; "Angel Tree," to partner and collect toys and gifts through an angel tree program. They may also offer Thanksgiving baskets, winter clothing, summer camps, family fun nights, and senior commodity food distribution, or a feeding program known as Sallie's Table.

As their mission statement says, "The Salvation Army, founded in 1865, is an international religious and charitable movement, which is an evangelical part of the universal Christian Church. Our message is based on the Bible. Our ministry is motivated by a love of God. Our mission is to preach the gospel of Jesus Christ and meet human needs in His name without discrimination."

Now the Lord is a Spirit. And where
the Spirit of the Lord is, there is liberty.

—2 Corinthians 3:17 RHE (Douay-Rheims)

ALEXANDER HAMILTON

A Brilliant Beam of Light

Can a penniless fourteen-year-old orphan with little formal education become the First secretary of the Treasury of the United States of America? Of course. It could be said that, in economic terms, Alexander Hamilton built the United States. Alexander Hamilton was born January 11, 1755, on the island of Nevis, near the island of St. Croix, where the Caribbean Sea meets the Atlantic Ocean. Speaking of his own birth in later years, Hamilton remarked, "My birth is the subject of the most humiliating criticism."

Needing to work, young Alexander began clerking in a mercantile house, buying, and selling, many necessary products in several languages, and by the age of sixteen, he was making decisions and giving instructions when the manager was away. A local minister, Hugh Knox, recognized the youthful Alexander's abilities. Young Alexander was determined to educate himself. Reverend Knox had a library of books and shared them. Reverend Knox also shared his moral beliefs, which included the immorality of slavery, as well as cautioning young Alexander on the dangers of drinking too much alcohol.

The economies of the "sugar islands" were based on the export of sugars, made possible by the labor of imported slaves. Alexander so looked forward to going forward in his life.

Also recognizing Alexander's abilities, in the fall of 1772, community leaders arranged for the seventeen-year-old to sail to the American

Colonies for his education. He studied day and night, in order, to apply to college. Alexander applied to King's College in New York entering as a private student in the fall of 1773. He helped form a debate club. According to his roommate, he prayed twice a day.

The Colonies were not united in their quest for liberty and independence. Many in New York favored the Crown and joined the Tory side. As a student in the Fall of 1774, Hamilton published essays defending the actions of the Continental Congress, signing them only "A Friend to America." He reiterated the colonialists' claims to liberty, including civil liberty, under their God-given rights. "The sacred rights of mankind are not to be rummaged for among old parchments or musty records. They are written, as with a sunbeam, in the volume of human nature, by the hand of the Divinity itself and can never be erased or obscured by mortal power."

"The shot heard round the world" was fired April 19, 1775, at Concord. That same year, Alexander joined a militia. His volunteer company wore leather hats with the words "liberty or death" across the front.

In March 1776, at the age of twenty-one, Hamilton was made artillery captain in the Continental Army. Amid the losses were two important wins: the Battle of Trenton on Christmas night 1776, and a week later, the Battle of Princeton, in 1777. Hamilton took part in each. After numerous retreats and defeats, the heartening surprise victory at Trenton was an imperative to maintain the revolution. On December 30, 1776, General Washington decided to recross the Delaware, but it would be only days before most of the Continental recruits were scheduled to leave for home. With every ounce of sincerity, Washington pleaded to his men to look inside themselves and stay for a final effort before the cause of liberty and independence was lost. Finally, one by one, each stepped forward to cross, by night, the icy Delaware.

At winter quarters in March of 1777, the young Hamilton was appointed to General Washington's Staff. From St. Croix, congratulations were sent from Hugh Knox. For four years, Hamilton served as aide-de-camp to General George Washington. Following the signing of the French Treaty of Alliance, Hamilton was helpful as he could both write and speak French and thereby communicated with the French commanders and soldiers. As the general had phrased it, Hamilton proved himself as a "principal and most confidential aide." At one time, Hamilton nearly died of illness, only to return to the dire conditions of Valley Forge.

Many free Blacks at the time, enrolled in the army and served during the War of Independence. In 1779, Hamilton recommended to John Jay, then president of Congress, a plan to enlist slaves with a provision for emancipation—further having "a good influence on those who remain, by opening a door to their emancipation."

Some of the events within the awakening tides and flourishing feelings of liberty were these: In 1781, a slave named Quock Walker sued for his freedom. He pointed out that the Massachusetts state constitution said that "all men are born free and equal." He won his case. Slavery ended in Massachusetts. A policy of gradual manumission began in Pennsylvania, where Quakers had opposed slavery for decades. All children born of slave parents were thereafter declared as free. In Virginia, the Methodist Church encouraged the legislature to begin a program of gradual emancipation. Virginia freed all who had fought in the Revolution. By the time of the Constitutional Convention, all, of the New England and Mid-Atlantic states, including Maryland and Virginia, had laws prohibiting the further importation of slaves. From 1775 to 1800, the number of free African Americans rose from fourteen thousand to one hundred thousand. With a lot of work yet to do, George Washington had written Robert Morris in 1786 that "there is not a man living, who wishes more sincerely than I do to see a plan adopted for the gradual abolition of [slavery]." As it was, within Washington's last will and testament, all were freed.

Elizabeth Schuyler and Alexander Hamilton married in 1780, during the last years of the Revolutionary War. Elizabeth was said to be of sterling character, strong willed, funny, and courageous. "A brunette with the most good-natured, lively dark eyes ... which threw a beam of good temper and benevolence over her whole countenance," wrote a family friend in his journal. Athletic, Elizabeth climbed up hills unassisted. She had also received the name "One-of-us" from the Six Nations at Saratoga. She was an active member of the Dutch Reformed

Church and became the ideal companion for Alexander. In later years, Eliza described Alexander and the "elasticity of his mind. Variety of his knowledge. Playfulness of his wit. Excellence of his heart. His immense forbearance [and] virtues."

Nathaniel Greene observed in 1781, "We fight, get beat, rise and fight again." Prospects for the Americans appeared to be dismal. Then came Yorktown. Having resigned as aide, Colonel Alexander Hamilton led one of the successful engagements within the battle. On October 19, 1781, the surrender of Yorktown was signed. After the ceremony, another American colonel wrote, "I noticed that the officers and soldiers could scarcely talk for laughing and they could scarcely walk for jumping and dancing and singing as they went about." Lafayette wrote in a letter to a friend in Paris, "The play, sir, is over."

In 1782, Hamilton was admitted to practice as an attorney before the New York Supreme Court and accepted a civilian post in government to receive taxes in New York State. That same year, Hamilton published a series of essays called the Continentalist, discussing currencies and funding. One result was passage of a resolution from New York to call for a convention of the states to revise and amend the confederation. Also, in 1782, Hamilton was elected as a delegate to the Continental Congress.

Shortly before the British evacuated New York City in November of 1783, Hamilton opened a law office on Wall Street. He drafted a bank constitution in 1784 and became director of the institution which is the present Bank of New York.

Alexander Hamilton, as a young lawyer, became a member of the Board of Regents of the University of the State of New York. He worked on a report recommending the establishment of public schools in the state. He later became a trustee of Columbia College. Alexander aided in organizing the New York State Society for Promoting the Manumission of Slaves in 1785 and was one of four appointed counselors. Their positions were presented to the Continental Congress.

January of 1787, Hamilton took a seat in the New York State Assembly. He joined a group of representatives from several states to discuss the Articles of Confederation. He wrote the report and submitted it to Congress. On June 17, 1787, at the Federal Assembly in Philadelphia, Hamilton made a speech presenting his views of government. These were critical moments for forming a strong, stable, republican government and one that would be respected abroad. Hamilton, declared: "It is a miracle that we were now here exercising our tranquil and free deliberations on the subject." He appraised the Constitution as a system that "without the finger of God, never could have been suggested and agreed upon by such a diversity of interests."

A first Publius paper written by Hamilton was published October 27, 1787. He outlined future topics to be covered including conformity of the Constitution to the principles of republican government. The project developed into a series of eighty-five essays published up to May 28, 1788. They had tremendous influence on ratification. Hamilton authored fifty-one along with James Madison and John Jay. Published later as The Federalist, it is studied and referenced today, including by the Supreme Court.

The Constitution was signed on September 17, 1787. Ratification by the states would be the next required step in order, to form a union. Hamilton's studied and well-thought-out arguments finally persuaded the assembly of New York to approve the Constitution by a 30–27 vote on July 26, 1788. On April 30, 1789, George Washington took the first oath of office as president. In September, the US Treasury Department was created. Washington selected Alexander Hamilton as the first secretary of the treasury. The bank would eventually grow into what is now called the Federal Reserve System.

In addition, Hamilton helped create the US Coast Guard and the US Navy. He proposed a naval academy. Alexander also promoted and drew plans for a training school for army officers, long wanted by George Washington. His proposals were influential in the establishment of the United States Military Academy at West Point.

In his reluctant acceptance of Alexander Hamilton's resignation from the Treasury, George Washington wrote, "In every relation which you have borne to me I have found that my confidence in your talents, exertions, and integrity, has been well placed."

The presidential election of 1800 landed in the House of Representatives in 1801. With some letters of influence, Hamilton helped swing the vote to Thomas Jefferson and not to Aaron Burr, who then became vice president for one term. Hamilton's political influence waned with that of the Federalist Party.

Aaron Burr would seek the governorship of New York State in the spring of 1804. Hamilton, it is said, told his friends that Burr could not be trusted with public office—that he was without principle but had insatiable ambition. Burr blamed Hamilton for his defeat and challenged Hamilton to a duel. As was the custom of the time, Hamilton had challenged other people to duels, but in every case the dispute was settled before the duel was fought. Burr challenged Hamilton to a duel, on the basis, of the latter's published disparagement of him.

In a rather prescient letter of advice to a friend, written beforehand on April 13, 1804, Hamilton had written the following:

> 'Tis by patience and perseverance that we can expect to vanquish difficulties, and better our unpleasant condition. Arraign not the dispensations of Providence – they must be founded in wisdom and goodness; and when they do not suit us, it must be because there is some fault in ourselves, which deserves chastisement, or because there is a kind intent to correct in us some vice or failing, of which, perhaps we may not be conscious; or because the general plan requires that we should suffer partial ill.
>
> In this situation it is our duty to cultivate resignation, and even humility, bearing in mind, in the language of the Poet, that it was "Pride which lost the blest abodes."

Days or weeks before this scheduled duel, Hamilton had written, "My religious and moral principles are strongly opposed to the practice of Duelling and it would ever give me pain to be obliged to shed the blood of a fellow in a private combat forbidden by the laws."

Knowing then there would be a duel between he and Burr, Alexander wrote a letter on July 4, 1804, to be given to his "very dear Eliza" only upon his death. Hamilton had determined to "expose himself" by reserving his first shot and perhaps a second so that Burr could have a "double opportunity to... pause and reflect."

On July 11, 1804, Hamilton was mortally wounded in the duel with Burr. Hamilton felt a deep-seated sense of "what men of the world denominate honor, imposed on me …. A peculiar necessity not to decline the call;" he had made up his mind not to shoot to kill Burr. Burr shot first. The bullet found its mark in Hamilton's left side. Hamilton shot in the air as he landed on the ground.

Later, the unscrupulous ambitions of Burr were even said to have led him to Napoleon Bonaparte himself, only to be turned down, albeit his object lay with the English and designs to detach territory from the Union. In 1807, Burr was arrested for treason and for trying to incite a war with Spain but was acquitted by Chief Justice John Marshall, who applied a strict definition of treason.

The final two paragraphs of the July 4 letter read,

> The consolations of Religion, my beloved, can alone support you; and these you have a right to enjoy. Fly to the bosom of your God and be comforted. With my last idea, I shall cherish the sweet hope of meeting you in a better world.
>
> Adieu best of wives and best of Women. Embrace all my darling Children for me. Ever yours AH

At 10:00 p.m. on the evening of July 10, Alexander wrote, "… rather I should die innocent than live guilty. Heaven can [preserve} me [and I humbly] hope will, but in the contrary event, I charge you to remember that you are a Christian. God's will be done! The will of a merciful God must be good. Once more Adieu My Darling darling Wife." AH

Elizabeth Hamilton lived another fifty years, dedicating herself to charitable causes, ever in endearing memory to her Alexander Hamilton.

THOMAS JEFFERSON

In His Own Words

Thomas Jefferson may have often been plainly dressed and plain in demeanor, but his words were not:

> It is error alone which needs the support of government. Truth can stand by itself ... The rights of conscience, we never submitted, we could not submit. We are answerable for them to our God.

> And can the liberties of a nation be thought secure when we have removed their only firm basis, a conviction in the minds of the people that these liberties are of the gift of God? That they are not to be violated but with his wrath? Indeed, I tremble for my country when I reflect that God is just: that his justice cannot sleep forever: that considering numbers, nature and natural means only, a revolution of the wheel of fortune, an exchange of situation, is among possible events: that it may become probable by supernatural interference! The Almighty has no attribute which can take side with us in such a contest. — But it is impossible to be temperate and to pursue this subject through the various considerations of policy, morals, of history natural and civil. We must

be contented to hope they will force their way into every one's mind. I think a change already perceptible since the origin of the present revolution. The spirit of the master is abating, that of the slave rising from the dust, his condition mollifying, the way I hope preparing, under the auspices of heaven, for a total emancipation, and that this is disposed, in the order of events, to be with the consent of the masters, rather than by their extirpation.

The ship of state has begun to sail; liftoff has been achieved in the experiment of republican democracy in human history. What, then, may be relied upon to guide? In whom may a pilot put his trust?

Let us pause for a moment, then, to listen to a magnificent mind and our third President, Thomas Jefferson, before we move on in the American journey. In addressing his fellow citizens in his first inaugural address, he stated,

> I shrink ... and humble myself before the magnitude of the undertaking ... But every difference of opinion is not a difference of principle. We have called by different names brethren of the same principle. We are all, Republicans, we are all Federalists. If there be any among us who would wish to dissolve this Union or to change its republican form, let them stand undisturbed as monuments of the safety with which error of opinion may be tolerated, where reason is left free to combat it.
>
> I know, indeed, that some honest men (women) fear that a republican government cannot be strong, that this Government is not strong enough; but would the honest patriot, in the full tide of successful experiment, abandon a government which has so far kept us free and firm on the theoretic and visionary fear that this Government, the world's best hope, may by possibility

want energy to preserve itself: I trust not. I believe this, on the contrary, the strongest Government on earth. I believe it the only one where every man, at the call of the law, would fly to the standard of the law, and would meet invasions of the public order as his own personal concern.

Sometimes it is said that man cannot be trusted with the government of himself. Can he, then, be trusted with the government of others? Or have we found angels in the forms of kings to govern him? Let history answer this question.

Let us, then, with courage and confidence pursue our own Federal and Republican principles, our attachment to union and representative government ... to honor and confidence from our fellow-citizens, resulting not from birth, but from our actions and their sense of them; enlightened by a benign religion, professed, indeed, and practiced in various forms, yet all of them inculcating honesty, truth, temperance, gratitude, and the love of man; acknowledging and adoring an overruling Providence, which by all its dispensations proves that it delights in the happiness of man here and his greater happiness hereafter—with all these blessings, what more is necessary to make us a happy and prosperous people? Still one thing more, fellow-citizens—a wise and frugal Government ...

And may the Infinite Power which rules the destinies of the universe lead our councils to what is best and give them a favorable issue for your peace and prosperity.

Let us tune an ear once more to listen to some of the second inaugural address of Thomas Jefferson:

In matters of religion, I have considered that its free exercise is placed by the constitution independent of the powers of the general government. I have therefore undertaken, on no occasion, to prescribe the religious exercises suited to it; but have left them, as the constitution found them, under the direction and discipline of state or church authorities acknowledged by the several religious societies.

...I shall now enter on the duties to which my fellow citizens have again called me and shall proceed in the spirit of those principles which they have approved. I fear not that any motives of interest may lead me astray; I am sensible of no passion which could seduce me knowingly from the path of justice; but the weakness of human nature, and the limits of my own understanding, will produce errors of judgement sometime injurious to your interests. I shall need, therefore, all the indulgence I have theretofore experienced—the want of it will certainly not lessen with increasing years. I shall need, too, the favor of the Being in whose hands we are, who led our forefathers, as Israel of old, from their native land, and planted them in a country flowing with all the necessaries and comforts of life; who has covered our infancy with his providence, and our riper years with his wisdom and power; and to whose goodness I ask you to join with me in supplications, that He will so enlighten the minds of your servants, guide their councils, and prosper their measures, that whatsoever they do, shall result in your good, and shall secure to you the peace, friendship, and approbations of all nations.

Preceding by eleven years his first inaugural address, Jefferson wrote on February 12, 1790, to the Citizens of Albemarle:

> The testimony of esteem with which you are pleased to honour my return to my native country fills me with gratitude and pleasure ... We have been fellow-labourers and fellow-sufferers, and heaven has rewarded us with a happy issue from our struggles. It rests now with ourselves alone to enjoy in peace and concord the blessings of self-government, so long denied to mankind: to shew by example the sufficiency of human reason for the care of human affairs and that the will of the majority, the Natural Law of every society, is the only sure guardian of the rights of man.
>
> ...Wherever I may be stationed, by the will of my country, it will be my delight to see, in the general tide of happiness, that yours too flows on in just place and measure. That it may flow thro' all times, gathering strength as it goes, and spreading the happy influence of reason and liberty over the face of the earth, is my fervent prayer to heaven.

Thomas Jefferson was also the principal author of the Declaration of Independence: "We hold these truths to be self-evident, that all men are created equal, that they are endowed by their Creator with certain unalienable Rights, that among these are Life, Liberty and the pursuit of Happiness."

Jefferson was a Continental Congressman; Virginia governor and legislator; ambassador to France; first secretary of state under George Washington; second vice president of the United States, serving under John Adams; and third president of the United States, serving two terms.

At age twenty-six, as a delegate to the Virginia House of Burgesses, Jefferson pursued reforms for slavery to make emancipation from slavery easier by allowing such to be a local decision. Also, as an attorney, he took cases for freedom-seeking slaves. "In 1769, I became a member of the legislature by the choice of the country in which I live & continued in that until it was closed by the revolution. I made one effort in that body for the permission of the emancipation of slaves, which was rejected: and indeed, during the regal government, nothing liberal could expect success."

Thomas Jefferson's Declaration of Independence was edited by Congress. Within his original enumeration of grievances against the king of England was the following:

> He has waged a cruel war against human nature itself, violating its most sacred rights of life and liberty in the persons of a distant people who never offended him, captivating & carrying them into slavery in another hemisphere, or to incur miserable death in their transportation thither. This piratical warfare, the opprobrium of INFIDEL powers, is the warfare of the CHRISTIAN (so-called—a capitalized sardonic reference by Mr. Jefferson) king of Great Britain. Determined to keep open a market where MEN should be bought and sold, he has prostituted his negative for suppressing every legislative attempt to prohibit or restrain this execrable commerce. And that this assemblage of horrors might want no fact of distinquished die, he is now exciting those very people to rise in arms among us, and to purchase that liberty of which he has deprived them, by murdering the people on whom he also obtruded them: thus paying off former crimes committed against the LIBERTIES of one people, with crimes which he urges them to commit against the LIVES of another.
>
> In every stage of these oppressions we have petitioned for redress, in the most-humble terms: our repeated petitions have been answered only by repeated injuries.

What further contributions could this self-cultivated, serene, civilized, and good-humored person contribute toward the building of this new country?

Jefferson's document written for the Constitutional Convention would divide the powers of government into three equal and independent departments—executive, legislative, and judicial. It gave all free male citizens the right to vote. It guaranteed religious freedom, trial by jury, and freedom of the press and made military clearly subordinate to civil power. Finally, it contained one more of Jefferson's timeless efforts to abolish slavery, forbidding further importation of slaves or the enslavement of any individuals born after December 31, 1800.

The first order of business at the Continental Convention would be to ratify the treaty of peace with Great Britain, which had been brilliantly negotiated by Benjamin Franklin, John Adams, and John Jay. The Articles of Confederation clearly stated that foreign treaties required the approval of nine states. The statement of ratification, prepared by Jefferson, was legally approved. And thus, the man whose resounding words had declared America's Independence fittingly wrote the words transforming that hope into reality.

Jefferson was then in charge of the committee working out the ceremony of the retirement of George Washington as commander-in-chief. At one point, Washington's voice broke, and he almost wept. Spectators and congressmen were already weeping.

Although Jefferson complained in numerous letters of bad health, it did not prevent him from working harder than anyone else in Congress. He was still deeply depressed by the death of his wife, Martha. In 1784, many thought Congress ought to keep any new territories in a kind of colonial dependency to the original thirteen. Jefferson, true as always to his instinct for freedom, went in the opposite direction, and his committee boldly set up the principle of new states being formed out of the western territories. Indeed, Jefferson's ordinance of 1787 envisioning an expanding Union incorporated the provision that "There shall be neither slavery nor involuntary servitude in said territory."

Then, once again, the most important of clauses to be ratified would be voted upon, changing the course of history. The Southern delegates had demanded it be sent back to committee.

As committee chairman, Thomas rephrased the motion, putting the question as follows: "Should the slavery clause be allowed to stand?"

The motion would confine slavery to the four original southern states. There, Jefferson was certain it would not thrive, and the country could live out the ideals of her founding.

As there were thirteen states, seven states would be needed to vote the motion forward. There were two delegates per state. For a state to vote yes, both delegates needed to vote yes. New Hampshire, Massachusetts, Rhode Island, Connecticut, New York, and Pennsylvania voted yes.

One more state was needed to push the motion forward. The one present New Jersey delegate voted yes. The other delegate was said to be sick and was not present to vote. Ten states had sent delegates. Maryland and South Carolina voted no. Virginia had sent two delegates. As Jefferson was the chair, he would be the third vote from Virginia. To Jefferson's dismay, the two Virginia delegates each voted no, thereby nullifying the yes vote cast by Jefferson.

The British General Cornwallis invaded Virginia in 1781. Lafayette and Jefferson would be helpless to stop him. On June 4, Virginia's Paul Revere, Jack Jouett, rode up Monticello's winding road on an exhausted horse, rousing Jefferson and several members of the Virginia Assembly. Tarleton—Cornwallis's commander of the cavalry—was coming! Another Virginian, Hudson, also came to the door with a warning. Jefferson left the house and disappeared into the woods. He began walking his horse up the neighboring mountain.

He paused, taking out his telescope to view Charlottesville and the surrounding area. He did not see any cavalry and decided to return to Monticello to gather some of his personal papers so the British would not destroy them.

A few steps down the mountainside, Jefferson noticed he had lost his dress sword. He retraced his steps. He then decided to take out his telescope to look once more toward Charlottesville. There, in the eye, were Tarleton's green dragoons swarming the main street. Jefferson hopped to his horse and galloped further into the woods on Carter's Mountain. The lost sword saved Jefferson's life.

"Sweetness of temper," "Spriteliness and Sensibility," as well as intelligence and so much more defined Martha. In an era when two of every three children failed to survive the so-called childhood diseases,

Thomas and Martha married in 1772 and would begin a family. Of Thomas and Martha's six children, only two lived beyond the age of three. Of these two, a daughter, aged twenty-six, passed away during Jefferson's first term as president. Only daughter Martha would outlive her father.

Thomas Jefferson held deep concern for the health and well-being of his dear wife, Martha. Congress had nominated Jefferson as one of three commissioners to go to France and negotiate a treaty of alliance. The other commissioners would be Benjamin Franklin and Sila Deane. President John Hancock wrote the letter announcing the nomination to Jefferson. Owing to Martha's condition, Jefferson mournfully declined. During the war, while Jefferson was a virtual refugee in Virginia, he was offered another diplomatic mission to France. Once again, for the same reasons, Jefferson declined.

In 1782, Jefferson, for four months, "was never out of calling" for his wife, who was ailing after childbirth. As she slipped away, he himself blacked out. His sensitivity, his devotion to Martha, his incredible grief, and his guilt that firsthand exposure to the revolution had caused her death, drove him to the brink. He would later write, "… a little emerging from that state of mind which had rendered me as dead to the world as she was whose loss occasioned it."

The pursuit of happiness by free men would only years later be lived by the author.

As Thomas Jefferson would write of his sentiments as he retired from the presidency:

> Never did a prisoner released from his chains, feel such relief as I shall on shaking off the shackles of power. Nature intended me for the tranquil pursuits of science, by rendering them my supreme delight. But the enormities of the times in which I have lived, have forced me to take a part in resisting them, and to commit myself on the boisterous ocean of political passions. I thank God for the opportunity of retiring

from them without censure and carrying with me the most consoling proofs of public approbation ... For I have sworn upon the altar of God eternal hostility against every form of tyranny over the mind of man.

On April 21, 1803, Thomas Jefferson wrote to Dr. Benjamin Rush (also a signer of the Declaration of Independence): "My views ... are the result of a life of inquiry and reflection, and very different from the anti-Christian system imputed to me by those who know nothing of my opinions. To the corruptions of Christianity, I am, indeed, opposed; but not to the genuine precepts of Jesus himself. I am a Christian in the only sense in which he wished any one to be, sincerely attached to his doctrines in preference to all others ..."

It has been written that in his later years Jefferson became more and more devoted to the doctrines and person of Jesus. "... told us only that God is good and perfect but has not defined Him. I am therefore of His Theology, believing that we have neither words nor ideas adequate to that definition. And if we could all, after this example, leave the subject as undefinable, we would all be of one sect, doers of good and eschewers of evil ..."

In referencing the Bible and his compilations thereof, Thomas Jefferson simply stated, "A more beautiful, precious morsel of ethics I have never seen; it is a document in proof that I am a real Christian, that is to say a disciple of the doctrines of Jesus ..."

On July 4, 1826, fifty years from the date of the signing of the Declaration of Independence, the life of Thomas Jefferson on this earth, would come, to a close. On that same day, the earthly life of John Adams—a cosigner of the Declaration of Independence, first vice president of the United States, and second president of the United States—would also end. The final words from John Adams were "Thomas Jefferson – still survives."

Yes. Jefferson lives. And the ideals of Jefferson still live within the heart of America.

Thomas Jefferson composed his own epitaph:

> Here was buried
> THOMAS JEFFERSON
> Author of the Declaration of American Independence
> of the Statute of Virginia for religious freedom
> & Father of the University of Virginia

With military confrontations with the British not only in sight but imminent and gathering, with fresh news of the Canadian disaster filtering into the Continental Congress, the serious and unresolved debates of reunion and professed loyalties to the Crown were pursued throughout June of 1776. With a lightning-crashing thunderstorm in the background, John Adams began his arguments for independence on July 1, 1776. After toiling through many drafts, Thomas Jefferson had presented his final draft of the Declaration of Independence on June 28.

After continental editing, the earth-shaking declaration was declared on July 4, 1776. John Hancock was first to sign the declaration, saying, "We must be unanimous; there must be no pulling different ways; we must all hang together."

"Yes, we must all hang together. Or most assuredly we shall all hang separately," replied Benjamin Franklin.

In Congress, July 4, 1776

A DECLARATION

BY THE REPRESENTATIVES OF THE UNITED STATES OF AMERICA, IN GENERAL CONGRESS ASSEMBLED.

When in the Course of human Events, it becomes necessary for one People to dissolve the Political Bands which have connected them with another, and to assume among the Powers of the Earth, the separate and equal Station to which the Laws of Nature and of Nature's God entitle them, a decent Respect to the Opinions of Mankind requires that they should declare the causes which impel them to the Separation.

We hold these Truths to be self-evident, that all Men are created equal, that they are endowed by their Creator with certain unalienable Rights, that among these are Life, Liberty, and the Pursuit of Happiness—That to secure these Rights, Governments are instituted among Men, deriving their just Powers from the Consent of the Governed, that whenever any Form of Government becomes destructive of these Ends, it is the Right of the People to alter or to abolish it, and to institute new Government, laying its Foundation on such Principles, and organizing its Powers in such Form, as to them shall deem most likely to effect their Safety and Happiness. Prudence, indeed, will dictate that Governments long established should not be changed for light and transient Causes; and accordingly, all Experience hath shewn, that Mankind are more disposed to suffer, while Evils are sufferable, than to right themselves by abolishing the Forms to which they are accustomed. But when a long Train of Abuses and Usurpations, proving invariably the same Object, evinces a Design to reduce them under absolute Despotism, it is their Right, it is their Duty, to throw off such Government, and to provide new Guards for their future Security. Such has been the patient Sufferance of these Colonies; and such is now the Necessity which constrains them to alter their former Systems of Government. The History of the present King of Great-Britain is a History of repeated Injuries and Usurpations, all having in direct

Object the Establishment of an absolute Tyranny over these States. To prove this let facts be submitted to a candid World. ... ...

* * * *

In every outrage of these Oppressions we have Petitioned for Redress in the most humble Terms: Our repeated Petitions have been answered only by repeated Injury. A Prince, whose Character is thus marked by every act which may define a Tyrant, is unfit to be the Ruler of a free People.

Nor have we been wanting in Attentions to our British Brethren. We have warned them from Time to Time of Attempts by their Legislature to extend an unwarrantable Justification over us. We have reminded them of the Circumstances of our Emigration and Settlement here. We have appealed to their native Justice and Magnanimity, and we have conjured them by the Ties of our common Kindred to disavow these Usurpations, which, would inevitably interrupt our Connections and Correspondence. They too have been deaf to the Voice of Justice and of Consanguinity. We must, therefore, acquiesce in the Necessity, which denounces our Separation, and hold them, as we hold the rest of Mankind, Enemies in War, in Peace, Friends.

We, therefore, the Representatives of the UNITED STATES OF AMERICA, in GENERAL CONGRESS, Assembled appealing to the Supreme Judge of the World for the Rectitude of our Intentions, do, in the Name, and by Authority of the good People of the Colonies, solemnly Publish and Declare, That these United Colonies are, and of Right ought to be, FREE AND

INDEPENDENT STATES; they have full Power to levy War, conclude Peace, contract Alliances, establish Commerce, and to do all other Acts and Things which INDEPENDENT STATES may of right do. And for the support of this Declaration, with a firm Reliance on the Protection of divine Providence, we mutually pledge to each other our Lives, our Fortunes, and our sacred Honor.

Thomas Jefferson had been invited to Washington, DC, to celebrate that golden fiftieth anniversary of the signing of the Declaration of Independence. Unable to attend, he wrote the committee expressing how much he wished he might join the "remnant of that host of worthies." In prophetic words, he wrote his final message: "May it be to the world, what I believe it will be...the signal of arousing men to...assume the blessings of self-government...All eyes are open, or, opening to the rights of man. .... For ourselves, let the annual return of this day, forever refresh our recollections of these rights and an undiminished devotion to them."

AN EARLY REFLECTION

As a simple matter of disclaimer, the author recognizes the differences between the Founders Hamilton and Jefferson, the complexities of human nature, and, of course, the historic complexities of the time. The formation of the United States was an experiment in responsible government and remains so. This republic was not a sure thing in its early years; nor is it today. There was not an immediate conversion to the principles and understandings of a democratic republic. Those, indeed, must be renewed and honored by each passing generation.

Not five years from the passing of Adams and Jefferson, Alexis de Tocqueville, a famous French statesman, historian, and social philosopher, began touring the country of America. His two-part work entitled *Democracy in America* was published in 1835 and 1840. It has been described as "the most comprehensive and penetrating analysis of the relationship between character and society in America."

But a handful of his many observations are as follows:

> Upon my arrival in the United States the religious aspect of the country was the first thing that struck my attention; and the longer I stayed there, the more I perceived the great political consequences resulting from this new state of things.
>
> Religion in America ... must be regarded as the foremost of the political institutions of that country; for if it does not impart a taste for freedom, it facilitates the use of it.

The safeguard of morality is religion, and morality is the best security of law as well as the surest pledge of freedom.

Christianity is the companion of liberty in all its conflicts – the cradle of its infancy, and the divine source of its claims.

I sought for the key to the greatness and genius of America in her harbors ... ; in her fertile fields and boundless forests; in her rich mines and vast world commerce; in her public-school system and institutions of learning. I sought for it in her democratic Congress and in her matchless Constitution.

Not until I went into the churches of America and heard her pulpits flame with righteousness, did I understand the secret of her genius and power.

America is great because America is good, and if America ever ceases to be good, America will cease to be great.

All thought that the main reason for the quiet sway of religion over the country was the complete separation of church and state.

Depotism may be able to do without faith, but freedom cannot.

Slavery, as we shall show later, dishonors labor; it introduces idleness into society and therewith ignorance and pride, poverty, and luxury. It enervates the powers of the mind and numbs human activity.

In these very times, it was a young man by the name of Lincoln observing that the founders had crafted a government more favorable to liberty "than any of which the history of former times tells us." It would be up to their children and their children's children to preserve and expand the great experiment.

De Tocqueville, again observing the explosion of liberty up close and personal, observed, "When both the privileges and the disqualifications of class have been abolished and men have shattered the bonds which once held them immobile, ... the idea of progress comes naturally into each man's mind; the desire to rise swells in every heart at once, and all men want to quit their former social position."

A PRELUDE TO A CIVIL WAR

Would this new experiment in liberty and self-governance survive? Would it fail, as many expected? Not but a generation from the Declaration of Independence would pass before another test of survival—a British invasion and the War of 1812. Independence would need to be fought for and won once more. It would be but fifty years hence that the new nation would succumb to a brutal civil war that would test its very soul. Would the belief in this new birth of freedom, the resolve, and principled beliefs of these new citizens, be sufficient to see the nation through? Would they have the stomach to weather an approaching unseen calamity? Those, among other questions, would be answered yet again by another generation. Could a future generation endure such testing of will and faith? But for resolve and faith and principle, can we survive the tests there will surely be? Perhaps we may learn from those many others who have been tested.

A SONG FROM JOHN NEWTON

Amazing grace! How sweet the sound
That saved a wretch like me!
I once was lost, but now am found
Was blind, but now I see.

'Twas grace that taught my heart to fear,
And grace my fears relieved;
How precious did that grace appear
The hour I first believed.

Through many dangers, toils, and snares,
I have already come;
'Tis grace hath brought me safe thus far,
And grace will lead me home.

The Lord has promised good to me,
His Word my hope secures;
He will my Shield and Portion be,
As long as life endures.

Yea, when this flesh and heart shall fail,
And mortal life shall cease,
I shall possess, within the veil,
A life of joy and peace.

The earth shall soon dissolve like snow,
The sun forbear to shine;
But God, who called me here below,
Will be forever mine.

> When we've been there ten thousand years,
> Bright shining as the sun,
> We've no less days to sing God's praise
> Than when we'd first begun.

John Newton grew up in a seafaring life. Captain Newton, his father, would be gone for long periods. His loving mother had died by the time he was seven. He, himself, sailed early and was also conscripted by the navy. Through circumstances, he became a slaver at the age of twenty in 1745. Newton had hardened himself and had taken the freethinkers' road and would not turn back until he "believed [his] own lie." Newton ridiculed faith and morals and took special delight in destroying any vestiges of religion which he detected in crew members. "My whole life when awake was a course of most horrid impiety and profaneness," he would later say, and he remarked of "the dreadful effects of the Slave Trade on the minds of those who engage in it."

John Newton would become a minister and a leading abolitionist. John Newton passed away in 1807, the year Parliament abolished the British slave trade.

A NOTE AND WARNING FROM THE LAST LIVING FRAMER OF THE CONSTITUTION, JAMES MADISON

James Madison was a member of the Anglican Church, which was established in Virginia. He offered an amendment to the state constitution draft proclaiming that all men (and women) were "equally entitled to the full and free exercise" of religion "according to the dictates of conscience." He was a member of the Continental Congress and the Virginia Congress. In the Virginia Assembly, Madison opposed a bill introduced by Patrick Henry. Madison declared that religion was not within the purview of civil power— that it was something separate, apart from and precedent to it.

Among Madison's contributions were his lengthy studies of ancient and modern confederacies, along with his criticisms of those governments. He was said to be the best informed of any point of debate. James Madison was appointed secretary of state by Thomas Jefferson. Madison, himself, became the fourth president of the United States in March 1809 and would serve two terms. He and Dolly Madison would each need to flee the White House in the War of 1812.

An Englishwoman who visited Montpelier in Madison's later years told of his "inexhaustible faith" in the future of his country. This faith shone brightly in all his conversation, except on, the subject of slavery— the "dreadful calamity which has so long afflicted our country." On June 27, 1836, at Montpelier, James Madison, the last of the framers of the Constitution, died. In his final message to his country, discovered among his papers, he concluded, "The advice nearest to my heart and deepest in my conviction is, That The Union Of The States Be Cherished And Perpetuated. Let The Open Enemy To It Be Regarded As A Pandora With Her Box Opened, And The Disguised One As The Serpent Creeping With His Deadly Wiles Into Paradise."

A DEBATE ALWAYS AND HENRY CLAY

Henry Clay was a central political and historical figure of the early 1800s who bridged the era between independence and civil war. Just as Hubert Horatio Humphrey became known by many as the greatest senator of the twentieth century, Henry Clay became known by many as the greatest senator of the nineteenth century. Henry is famously attributed with the saying, "… politics is the art of compromise."

Henry had listened in court to the great orator of the day, Patrick Henry. In the spring of 1813, he was sent to Ghent, Belgium, along with John Quincy Adams and others, to help make a peace treaty with England over the War of 1812. On December 24, 1814, a treaty was signed.

A mere half dozen years after a second war with Great Britain to preserve the independence of the new United States of America, the unity of this new nation would be tested once more. As early as 1819, in the House of Representatives, there was talk of civil war. Henry Clay is credited with the work that would save the Union of the States, preserving a constitution that would later be employed for an emancipation believed necessary by so many but not yet by all. Clay's greatest hopes and efforts in his political life were to maintain the Union, and his additional hope, as was the belief of so many, was to see an end to slavery as the nation grew. On March 3, 1820, the Missouri Compromise was passed. Henry returned to private life.

Henry Clay would run for president in 1824. He instead became secretary of state under John Quincy Adams. Daniel Webster urged him to run for the Senate in 1832. Again, he was pivotal in arriving at the Compromise Tariff Bill of 1833. Clay had referred to his own party as Whigs, referencing the Whigs in England, who had fought against the tyranny of King George. Henry often opposed President Andrew Jackson.

Henry was attending a Christmas Party in Washington in 1835 when a letter written by his son-in-law was delivered to him. His daughter was to be giving birth. A friend, John Clayton, picked up the letter beside a slumping Henry Clay. He told the others, "Anne died when the child was born. Now God give Henry Clay courage." Henry and his wife, Lucretia, had lost their last daughter. In a letter in 1832 he wrote, "I would rather be right than President."

1840, William Henry Harrison was elected the first Whig president. He was also the first president to die in office, doing so only weeks after assuming the office, from an illness. The vice president, John Tyler, assumed the presidency. Unsatisfied with Tyler, the Whigs then finally nominated Henry Clay in 1844. He was defeated by a margin of fifty-one hundred votes by James K. Polk.

In 1849, the Kentucky Legislature once again elected Henry to the Senate. Tensions were rising between North and South. No longer a young man, could Henry save the Union? Again, an old friend, Daniel Webster, was there in the Senate. Also there, were John C. Calhoun, William H. Seward, Sam Houston, Jefferson Davis, and other newer members. Slavery was the only topic discussed. Early in 1850, Henry read his compromise bill in the Senate. All through the spring and summer of 1850, the bill was debated. Day after day, Henry rose to defend the bill.

"I know no North – no South – no East – no West." Those are the words written on the four sides of the tomb of Henry Clay.

A WHISPER FROM BENJAMIN FRANKLIN TO YOU AND I

At the close of the Constitutional Convention, as Benjamin Franklin left Independence Hall on the last day of deliberation, he was asked, "Well, Doctor; what have we got?—a Republic or a Monarchy?"

He answered, "A Republic, Madam—if you can keep it!"

"If"—there is that two-letter word in history once again. Here there is an implied if–then statement: *If* you can keep it, *then* you have a republic. It is renewable with each generation. It is not a permanent figure chiseled into the landscape of history. You and I (me too?) will be tested. Will every generation pass this gift of freedom, this blessed experiment in liberty, to the following generation?

But before we turn a page of history, what prayerful advice or admonition may our great founder Benjamin Franklin whisper to our ears? What principles to keep? How do we keep the republic?

In July of 1776, Benjamin was appointed part of a committee to draft a seal for the new United States that would characterize the spirit of the nation. He proposed one depicting Moses lifting up his wand and dividing the red sea; Pharaoh in his chariot, being overwhelmed with the waters; and the motto, "Rebellion to tyrants is obedience to God."

In March 1778, Franklin wrote a letter to the French ministry, and he is attributed with writing, "Whosoever shall introduce into public affairs the principles of primitive Christianity will change the face of the world."

On June 28, 1787, Benjamin Franklin delivered a powerful speech to the Constitutional Convention addressing state representation. Within that speech were the following words:

> We indeed seem to feel our own want of political wisdom, since we have been running about in search of it. We have examined the different forms of those Republics which, having been formed with the seeds of their own dissolution, now no longer exist. And we have

viewed Modern States all round Europe; but find none of their Constitutions suitable to our circumstances.

In this situation of this Assembly, groping as it were in the dark to find political truth, and scarce able to distinguish it when presented to us, how has it happened, Sir, that we have not hitherto once thought of humbly applying to the Father of lights to illuminate our understanding?

In the beginning of the Contest with G. Britain, when we were sensible of danger, we had daily prayer in this room for Divine protections.—Our prayers, Sir, were heard, & they were graciously answered. All of us who were engaged in the struggle must have observed frequent instances of a superintending Providence in our favor.

To that kind Providence we owe this happy opportunity of consulting in peace on the means of establishing our future national felicity. And have we now forgotten that powerful Friend? or do we imagine we no longer need His assistance?

I have lived, Sir, a long time, and the longer I live, the more convincing proofs I see of this truth—that God Governs in the affairs of men ...

We have been assured, Sir, in the Sacred Writings, that "except the Lord build the House, they labor in vain that build it." I firmly believe this; and I also believe that without his concurring aid we shall succeed in this political building no better than the Builders of Babel: We shall be divided by our partial local interests; our projects will be confounded, and we ourselves shall become a reproach and bye word down to future ages.

And what is worse, mankind may hereafter from this unfortunate instance, despair of establishing Governments by Human wisdom and leave it to chance, war, and conquest.

I therefore beg leave to move—that henceforth prayers imploring the assistance of Heaven, and its blessing on our deliberations, be held in this Assembly every morning before we proceed to business, and that one or more of the clergy, of this city, be requested to officiate in that service.

An interesting historical note is that in earlier years, Franklin was a close friend of George Whitefield, the famous preacher of the Great Awakening revivals in the colonies prior to the Revolutionary War. Franklin wrote of over thirty thousand being in attendance, at just one such gathering. Franklin also built a grand auditorium for the purpose of having his friend preach in it.

Franklin observed, "It was wonderful to see the change soon made in the manners of our inhabitants. From being thoughtless or indifferent about religion, it seemed as if all the world were growing religious, so that one could not walk thro' the town in an evening without hearing psalms sung in different families of every street."

Also, within his autobiography, Benjamin Franklin wrote the prayer he prayed each day: "O powerful goodness! Bountiful! Father! Merciful Guide! Increase in me that wisdom which discovers my truest interest. Strengthen my resolution to perform what that wisdom dictates. Accept my kind offices to thy other children as the only return in my power for thy continual favours to me."

Benjamin Franklin also founded the American Philosophical Society in 1743. It was reorganized in 1769. History records that it was "The First Learned Society in the British Plantations in America." At the age of twenty-one, Franklin had begun his work in a printing house in Philadelphia beside indentured servants. As a young man, Benjamin wrote, "I grew convinc'd that truth, sincerity and integrity in dealings between man and man were of the utmost importance to the felicity of life; and I form'd written resolutions, which still remain in my journal book, to practice them ever while I lived." Franklin recorded his birth as January 6, 1705, under the older Julian calendar. He lived through the revolution and died April 17, 1790. Most men in that century did not surpass the age of fifty.

During one perilous monthlong voyage to England, avoiding capture by French ships, Franklin had apparently contracted malaria. Benjamin avoided death but was sick for a year. With assistance, he persisted in conducting the business of his newly forming country. Political viruses antithetical to liberty, freedom, and the individual have sickened the environments of peoples since the inception of civilizations. America may not be immune but, like Franklin, shall persist and overcome, thereby providing inspirations to the generations to follow.

The Treaty of Alliance with France, as well as amity and commerce, during the course, of the War of Independence, so integral to the successful outcome of the Revolution, had been negotiated with brilliant wisdom at many levels by Benjamin Franklin. The Treaty of Paris, signed in September of 1783, ended the war between the future United States and England. Again, Franklin took the lead to finalize the treaty, to the benefit of a new United States. At the Constitutional Convention of 1787, as the delegates adjourned to celebrate the Fourth of July, they found the convention deadlocked. Roger Sherman observed that it had come to a "full stop". Luther Martin, from Maryland, declared that the convention was "on the verge of dissolution, scarce held together by the strength of a hair." A grand committee was called for to discuss a way out. Franklin had thus far said very little at the convention. He arrived, however, at what was to be known as the "great compromise."" The compromise passed by only one vote, saving the convention—and the United States of America—from collapse.

Now in the offing would be that epic contest to be fought on the American continent between truth and justice and the principles of freedom from our founding and those vestiges of the past that no longer live up to the light of freedom so nobly expressed in our founding documents.

ABRAHAM LINCOLN

A Recollection

On February 11, 1861, the new president-elect Abraham Lincoln would leave his home in Springfield, Illinois. He would turn his own personal page of history. He would shake hands with friends and hear their heartfelt well-wishes. A reporter wrote that "his face was pale and quivered with emotion so deep as to render him almost unable to utter a single word." Another observed, "As Mr. Lincoln mounted the platform car, many in the crowd seemed deeply affected, and he himself scarcely able to check the emotions of the hour."

Abraham proceeded to seat himself in the rail car. He then rose and returned to the platform to say a few words. A friend of Lincoln, James C. Conkling wrote to his son: "It was quite affecting. Many eyes were filled to overflowing as Mr. Lincoln uttered those few and simple words which you will see in the papers. His own breast heaved with emotion, and he could scarcely command his feelings sufficiently to commence."

Abraham Lincoln removed his hat to say the following:

> My friends—No one, not in my situation, can appreciate my feeling of sadness at this parting. To this place, and the kindness of these people, I owe everything. Here I have lived a quarter of a century and have passed from a young to an old man. Here my children have been born, and one is buried. I now leave, not knowing when, or

whether ever, I may return, with a task before me greater than that which rested upon Washington. Without the assistance of that Divine Being, who ever attended him, I cannot succeed. With that assistance I cannot fail. Trusting in Him, who can go with me, and remain with you and be every-where for good, let us confidently hope that all will yet be well. To His care commending you, as I hope in your prayers you will commend me, I bid you an affectionate farewell.

Later, on the train, Mr. Lincoln wrote the text of his thoughts delivered to his friends. And thus, began perhaps the greatest journey of all, in the course, of this great nation.

An impending Civil War, or War between the States, would soon arrive. Surely the depth of this conflict could not have been foreseen. The total loss of life would exceed that of all US wars and conflicts until the cost of Vietnam was added: an estimated over six hundred twenty thousand deaths, with another five hundred thousand wounded. The total population at the time was just over thirty million.

Described as a gawky country boy by some, Lincoln's secretary remembered him saying that his troubles "were so great that could I have anticipated them, I would not have believed it possible to survive them." And that was said before the fall of Fort Sumter.

Let us go back in time for a moment to recall some of those early recollections of Lincoln.

As we all know, Abraham Lincoln was born in a log cabin. The year was 1809. The State was Kentucky. He had one older sister and a brother who died in infancy. As a young boy, Lincoln's father had watched his own father murdered by a raiding party. To Lincoln, it left him "a wandering laboring boy" and "he never did more in the way of writing than to bunglingly sign his own name."

While campaigning in 1860, Lincoln was asked about his early life. Lincoln told the gentleman, "Why Scripps, it is a great piece of folly to attempt to make anything out of my life. It can all be condensed into a single sentence you will find in Gray's Elegy: 'The short and simple annals of the poor.'"

Nancy Hanks, now well-known, was the mother of Abraham Lincoln. (In fact, as a child, this author would have a Miss Hanks for a librarian and a distant relative.) A neighbor would say of Nancy that "she was a woman known for the extraordinary strength of her mind among the family and all who knew her: she was superior to her husband in every way. She was a brilliant woman."

A cousin recalled that Mrs. Lincoln "read the good Bible to [Abe]—taught him to read and to spell—taught him sweetness and benevolence as well." When Abraham was nine years old, his mother became ill with what was called "milk sickness." It would not be long before she would tell her dear son, "I am going away from you, Abraham, and I shall not return."

Lincoln and his sister, Sarah, were now alone as their father ventured to find a wife. Lincoln would later recall those days when "the panther's scream, filled the night with fear and bears preyed on the swine."

Sarah was said to be much like her brother: "a quick minded woman" with a "good-humored laugh." Within months, their new stepmom returned with their father. She found them "wild—ragged and dirty," but after some scrubbing, "more human."

A few years later, Sarah would die giving birth. A relative recalled that Lincoln "sat down on a log and hid his face in his hands while the tears rolled down through his long bony fingers. Those present turned away in pity and left him to his grief. From then on, he was alone in the world you might say."

As a boy, a childhood friend recalled that Abe's mind and ambition "soared above us. He naturally assumed the leadership of the boys. He read and thoroughly reread his books whilst we played. Hence, he was above us and became our guide and leader." If Abe's initial self-confidence was fostered by his mother, then his stepmother assumed the baton and recognized that Abe was "a Boy of uncommon natural Talents." She encouraged him. She said, "Abe never gave me a cross word or look and never refused in fact, or Even in appearance, to do any-thing I requested him. I never gave him a cross word in all my life.

He was Kind to Everybody and Everything and always accommodated others if he could—" A friend related, "He was a strong athletic boy, good natured, and ready to out-run, out-jump and out-wrestle or out-lift anybody in the neighborhood."

As with every family in these early times, evenings would be full of visiting and storytelling. This was also true in the Lincoln household as Abe's father, Thomas, had learned the craft well. As every young lad would do, the young Abe sat listening intently to all, of the stories told. Abe related that he would spend "no small part of the night walking up and down and trying to make out what was the exact meaning of some of their, to me, dark sayings." Finally, "I had put it in language plain enough, as I thought, for any boy I knew to comprehend." Next day he would stand on a stump, talking to the other boys. Little did he know how valuable this gift would become.

Lincoln earned the nickname "Honest Abe" as a young man working as a store clerk. It is recorded that if he realized he had accidentally short-changed a customer a few pennies, he thought nothing of closing-up the shop and walking several miles to deliver the correct change. Recognizing Lincoln's honesty, people were soon asking him to act as judge or referee at various events. He became a popular arbiter of wrestling matches, horse races, and petty squabbles.

Young Abe attended school, but not frequently, and usually it was in second place to working on the farm and other places. He later noted there was no qualification for the teachers "beyond 'readin, writin, and cipherin'." Lincoln admitted "the aggregate of all his schooling did not amount to one year." He had never even set foot "inside of a college or academy building" until he acquired his license to practice law. The young Lincoln, however, would scour the countryside looking for books to read and could not contain his excitement when finding treasures, such as *The Pilgrim's Progress*, that some of his neighbors kept in their cabins. Lincoln could recite whole passages of the Bible.

It would be said, by more than a few, that Abe Lincoln learned more of human nature and right and wrong around the cracker barrel and in real-life experiences while clerking in a store or performing manual jobs outdoors, such as splitting rails, than many of his contemporaries learned from years of formal, expensive education. Some might call it common sense. Lincoln would one day become one of the shrewdest politicians of all time, as well.

Judge David Douglas, in whose court Lincoln practiced law for fourteen years, said of Lincoln, "The framework for [Lincoln's] mental and moral being was honesty, and a wrong cause was poorly defended by him."

Lincoln moved to New Salem, Illinois, in 1832, at the age of twenty-three. After just six months, he decided to run for the state legislature from the county. He would run on a Whig platform, calling for internal improvements. He wrote,

> Every man is said to have his peculiar ambition. I have no other so great as that of being truly esteemed of my fellow men, by rendering myself worthy of their esteem. How far I shall succeed in gratifying this ambition, is yet to be developed. I am young, and unknown to many of you. I was born, and have ever remained, in the most-humble walks of life. I have no wealthy or popular relations or friends to recommend me. My case is thrown exclusively upon the independent voters of the country; and, if elected, they will have conferred a favor upon me for which I shall be unremitting in my labors to compensate. But, if the good people in their wisdom shall see fit to keep me in the background, I have been too familiar with disappointments to be very much chagrined.

Lincoln's campaign was interrupted for three months when serving in the state militia during the Black Hawk war. Not surprisingly, he lost the election.

Two years later, Lincoln ran again, and this time he easily won. He would serve four successive terms in the state legislature. A political colleague wrote, "His Stories were fresh and sparkling; never tinctured with malevolence ... His face revealed nothing and then, when animated, ... his eyes would sparkle ... all, terminating in an unrestrained Laugh in which everyone, present, willing, or unwilling were compelled to take part." Once he was challenged by the words "See here Lincoln, if you can throw this Cannon ball further than we Can - We'll vote for you." His reply was "Well boys, if that's all I have to do I'll get your votes." And so, he would. Lincoln moved to Springfield in 1837.

Lincoln would build his law practice during the day and would often gather round a fire at Joshua Speed's general store in the evening, reading newspapers and entertaining with stories. Remarkably, often gathered around the fire, discussing the politics of the day, would be a future US senator, Stephen A. Douglas, as well as other future officeholders. It was a kind of "social club."

His 1840 campaign would upgrade so that every Whig could be brought to the polls. Improving waterways was one issue Lincoln ran on. Lincoln had worked on flatboats going down the Mississippi to New Orleans. Similar, to the Erie Canal improvement, Lincoln wished to leave his mark with a program of internal improvements. In the legislature, Lincoln straightforwardly proclaimed that "the institution of slavery is founded on both injustice and bad policy." His parents, too, had not favored slavery and had moved to the free state of Indiana "partly on account of slavery."

Young Abraham had not yet married while in his twenties. In fact, he thought that he may not. As proficient in writing skills as he was, he also considered writing to women a "business which I do not understand." Well, as half the population at the time were women—and as he was surely fond of them—something may change.

At one social gathering in the flows of Springfield society, according to mutual friends and relatives, he would find the very creature of excitement and one said to be capable of "making a Bishop forget his prayers." Friends also considered Mary Todd to be "the exact reverse" of Abe, "physically, temperamentally, [and] emotionally." She was intelligent, having attained the highest marks in school. She had also grown up in Kentucky as a daughter of a State Senator. In fact, she had met and gotten to know Henry Clay, who Lincoln admired enormously.

Beyond this, her sisters recalled her as being a "violent little Whig" and "destined to be the wife of some future President."

Beyond each having a love for poetry and politics, it would seem the die was cast for the future of Mary and Abraham. But as a casual observer may say, not so fast.

Each also shared the deaths of their mothers at early ages. Mary, though, was less fortunate than Abe with her stepmother, in that the relationship was more difficult. Mary was said to have "an emotional temperament much like an April day, sunning all over with laughter one moment, the next crying as though her heart would break." Nonetheless, both were very discerning people, maybe too much so. Lincoln, perhaps a little unsure of his career, but also uncertain of "his ability and capacity to please and support a wife," called off the engagement. After eighteen months, mutual friends would finally bring the two together once again.

Abraham Lincoln had a tremendous sense of inborn, as well as learned, sympathy and empathy toward others. There is an oft repeated story describing Lincoln riding his horse when he heard the screams of a trapped pig in a bog. Down the road, he turned the horse around to rescue the pig "just to take a pain out of his own mind," said a friend. It was said that Lincoln did not hunt deer. "The never-absent idea" he had apparently discussed with Mary also bothered him in their absence, as he may have felt some guilt.

"With his wealth of sympathy, his conscience, and his unflinching sense of justice, he was predestined to sorrow," observed the daughter of Lincoln's press secretary. She further said, "His crowning gift of political diagnosis, was due to his sympathy ... which gave him the power to forecast with uncanny accuracy what his opponents were likely to do." A caucus attendee described Lincoln's approach, "Lincoln said: 'From your talk, I gather the Democrats will do so and so ... I should do so and so to checkmate them.'" The attendee added that Lincoln then outlined "the moves for days ahead; making them all so plain that his listeners wondered why they had not seen it that way themselves."

After Lincoln was elected to Congress, he would serve one term. Walking the halls of Congress, he would find John Quincy Adams;

listen to the orations of Daniel Webster; weigh the southern views of John Calhoun; and take measure of the likes of Jefferson Davis and Stephen Douglas, who would become his future opponents.

Mary and Abraham returned to Springfield to practice law. Lincoln felt he was losing interest in politics. Their second son, three-year-old Eddie, died from pulmonary tuberculosis on February 1, 1850. Mary joined the First Presbyterian Church. Lincoln rented a family pew. From afar, the Lincolns kept up with the politics of the day, Henry Clay, and the debate over the Compromise of 1850. To Lincoln, Clay was "regarded by all as the man for a crisis."

At home with gatherings of fellow members of the bar, Lincoln's law partner Herndon recalled Lincoln's ability to keep an audience. With his back to a fire, he would juggle one tale after another, keeping his audience "in full laugh till near daylight." His "eyes would sparkle with fun," one old-time friend remembered, "and when he had reached the point in his narrative which invariably evoked the laughter of the crowd, nobody's enjoyment was greater than his."

A wheel of history would turn in 1854 with the introduction of the Kansas-Nebraska Act, which in turn would result in the formation of the Republican Party. The notable Senator Salmon P. Chase accused Senator Stephen A. Douglas of introducing the bill in his bid for the presidency. The idea of the bill to allow a "popular sovereignty" to the new states to determine their own stances on the issue of slavery was challenged. The bill could be considered to negate the old Missouri compact or compromise and fly headlong against the principles, hopes, and beliefs that slavery "ought, atrophy" and become extinct in the ever expanding and growing country. As to the outcome, "They celebrate a present victory but the echoes they awake will never rest until slavery itself shall die"—so said Senator Salmon P. Chase.

Lincoln was riding the countryside, doing law work with another attorney, when he read the news. That night, T. Lyle Dickey said that Abe "sat on the edge of his bed and discussed the political situation far into the night." When Dickey woke in the morning, Abe "was sitting up in bed, deeply absorbed in thought." He said, "I tell you, Dickey, this nation cannot exist half-slave and half-free."

Abraham Lincoln would deliver his first masterful speech against slavery in Springfield, Illinois, at the annual state fair, on October 4, 1854. "The inspiration that possessed him took possession of his hearers also. His speaking went to the heart because it came from the heart. I have heard celebrated orators who could start thunders of applause without changing any man's opinion. Mr. Lincoln's eloquence was of the higher type, which produced conviction in others because of the conviction of the speaker himself." So said a young reporter, Horace White, on that day. In 1914, he would say the initial impression was "overwhelming and it has lost nothing by the lapse of time."

Lincoln emphasized, "the plain unmistakable spirit of that age, towards slavery, was hostility to the principle, and toleration, only by necessity." He pointed out that neither the word *slave* nor the word *slavery* was in the Constitution. The words could not be reconciled into the spirit of the document, but hidden "just as an afflicted man hides away a wen or a cancer, which he dares not cut out all at once, lest he bleed to death; with the promise, nevertheless, that the cutting may begin at the end of a given time."

Lincoln viewed the Nebraska Act in legal methods, advancing the continuation and expansion of slavery. Abraham frequently invoked the Declaration of Independence: "The doctrine of self-government is right—absolutely and eternally right." "No man is good enough to govern another man, 'without that other's consent'. I say this is the leading principle—the sheet anchor of American republicanism." He asserted that by not following those first principles and ideals expressed within the Declaration of Independence, it would lead to an open war on that very declaration, thus "depriving our republican example of its just influence in the world."

Days later, Lincoln reminded his audience that the South had "joined the North, almost unanimously, in declaring the African slave trade (as) piracy, and in annexing to it the punishment of death. In so doing they must have understood that selling slaves was wrong, for they never thought of hanging men for selling horses, buffaloes, or bears. Likewise, though forced to do business with the domestic slave dealer, they did not 'recognize him as a friend or even as an honest man' Now why is this?" He further observed that over four hundred thousand blacks had been freed "at vast pecuniary sacrifices" by those who understood all this. "In all these cases it is your sense of justice, and human sympathy, continually telling you", that the slave is not to be considered as "mere merchandise." Finally, Lincoln implored his audience to readopt the Declaration of Independence and "return [slavery] to the position our fathers gave it; and there let it rest in peace." This accomplishment would save the Union, and "succeeding millions of free happy people, the world over, [would] rise up, and call us blessed, to the latest generations."

With new purpose, Lincoln won a seat in the Illinois State Assembly and promptly declared as a candidate for the US Senate. The antislavery Whigs and independent Democrats won a slim majority over what were known as the Douglas Democrats. The House Chamber met early in 1856 to vote for a new US Senator. Lincoln received forty-five votes on the first ballot to forty-one for a Douglas Democrat and five for a Congressman Trumbull. After nine ballots and nigh to the next morning, Lincoln swung his votes to support Trumbull to avoid a Douglas–Nebraska win. Lincoln shook hands with Trumbull.

The Whigs' influences at that time were gradually disappearing. The Democrats assumed a Southern dominance, and Stephen Douglas, an according prominence. A conglomeration of sorts, to include Conscience Whigs, independent Democrats, and antislavery Know-Nothings opposed to extending slavery, formed various coalitions in state after state, becoming known in their respective states as the Fusion Party, the People's Party, the Anti-Nebraska Party, and so on. Eventually they would find common ground and form the new Republican Party.

The general election for the presidency of 1856 comprised three competing parties: the American Party had nominated Millard Fillmore, the first-time Republican Party ran John C. Fremont, and the winner was the Southern-leaning Democrat James Buchanan. On March 4, 1857, James Buchanan was inaugurated as president, and on March 6 would come the dreadful Dred Scott decision. The court ruled that blacks "are not included, and were not intended to be included, under the word 'citizens' in the Constitution." The court justice further concluded that neither the Declaration of Independence nor the Constitution was meant to apply to blacks. He further stated that Congress had exceeded its authority in its passage of the Missouri Compromise. The Nebraska Act, in effect, had repealed the Compromise of 1820. For lack of better terms to be spoken from any quarter, then, "the stage had been set" for no less than an impending civil war.

Lincoln attacked the decision and the logic of the court. He restated his deeply held belief: "We hold these Truths to be self-evident, that all Men are created equal, that they are endowed by their Creator with certain unalienable Rights, that among these are Life, Liberty, and the Pursuit of Happiness." The document did not "declare all men equal in all respects." "They meant simply to declare the 'right', so the 'enforcement' of it might follow as fast as circumstances should permit."

As Abraham Lincoln, chief architect of the Republican Party of Illinois, prepared to challenge Steven A. Douglas for the Senate in 1858, another lesser group of proslavery forces met in Lecompton, Nebraska to draft a proslavery state constitution. They then applied for statehood. Regardless, of the fact that the overwhelming number of settlers opposed slavery, the Buchanan Administration endorsed the Lecompton Constitution. Steven Douglas broke with his fellow Democrats, as the act would not embody his idea of "popular sovereignty." This divide would set the stage for the famous Lincoln– Douglas debates.

A statewide Republican convention was called to be held in Springfield in June of 1858. On June 16, an enthusiastic convention endorsed Abraham Lincoln "for the United States Senate, as the successor of Stephen A. Douglas." "A house divided against itself cannot stand," declared Lincoln.

> I believe this government cannot endure, permanently, half slave and half free. I do not expect the Union to be dissolved—I do not expect the house to fall—but I do expect it will cease to be divided. It will become all one thing or all the other. Either the opponents of slavery will arrest the further spread of it, and place it where the public mind shall rest in the belief that it is in the

course of ultimate extinction; or its advocates will push it forward, till it shall become lawful in all the States, old as well as new—North as well as South.

Would the Constitution itself—the same document guaranteeing freedom—be overthrown? William H. Seward thought so. Lincoln, too, was beginning to discern the timbers of the house being joined to build another house, unlike the intentions of the Founders. "And when we see these timbers joined together, and see they exactly make a frame of a house … all the lengths and proportions of the different pieces exactly adapted to their respective places … we find it impossible to not believe that Stephen and Franklin and Roger and James, all understood one another from the beginning, and all worked upon a common plan or draft up before the first lick was struck." Lincoln warned that with those timbers in place, then only one other "nice little niche" needed to be filled to declare a constitutional protection of private property, thereby preventing states and territories from excluding slavery; thus, all laws outlawing slavery, even in the Northern states, could be invalidated.

The stage would now be set for what would become famously known as "The Lincoln Douglas Debates." There were seven debates in all. The first candidate spoke for an hour, followed by an hour and a half reply. Then the first speaker was given another half an hour to speak. Douglas initially declined. Senator Stephen A. Douglas said of Lincoln, "I shall have my hands full. He is the strong man of his party—full of wit, facts, dates—and the best stump speaker, with his droll ways and dry jokes, in the West. He is as honest as he is shrewd, and if I beat him my victory will be hardly won."

Each of the candidates, in the course, of their campaigns, would deliver hundreds of speeches and travel several thousands of miles. Partisan papers often gave partisan descriptions of the crowds' responses and outcomes.

Lincoln was said to have said in many forums that slavery was a violation of the Declaration' of Independence's "majestic interpretation of the economy of the Universe." He would, with frequency, repeat the Declaration of Independence's proclamation that "all men are created equal, that they are endowed by their Creator with certain unalienable Rights, that among these are Life, Liberty and the pursuit of Happiness." To Lincoln, to say that blacks were not included in the Declaration of Independence was to mold public opinion in the wrong direction. Borrowing a phrase from Henry Clay, Lincoln stated, "He is blowing out the moral lights around us, eradicating the light of reason and the love of liberty in this American people."

Lincoln made the influencing of public opinion a primary issue. "If the public had been led to believe by the actions of the founders and subsequent developments that slavery had been placed on a course of ultimate extinction, then Douglas and his Democratic cohorts," Lincoln argued, "had been deliberately trying to undermine that sentiment." Later, in a fifth debate, Lincoln stressed again that Douglas was "in every possible way preparing the public mind, by his vast influence, for making the institution of slavery perpetual and national."

Just as Lincoln had told a gathering of Illinois Republicans in the new Republican Party, "Our government rests in public opinion. Whoever can change public opinion, can change the government, practically just as much. If public opinion was thus malleable, then politicians with the power of office and the gift of persuasion could potentially do as much harm as good, especially if they could effect a change in basic American ideals and values."

Honest Abe Lincoln would implore, "Think nothing of me—take no thought for the political fate of any man whomsoever, but come back to the truths that are in the Declaration of Independence ... I charge you to drop every paltry and insignificant thought for any man's success. It is nothing; I am nothing; Judge Douglas [that is, Stephen A. Douglas] is nothing. But do not destroy that immortal emblem of Humanity—the Declaration of American Independence."

Because of Douglas's departure from the Democrat view that Nebraska should arrive as a slave state but that, the majority, of Nebraskans should determine for themselves to be either a free or a slave state, there were some influential Whig leaders who publicly supported Douglas; among them was the influential Senator John Crittenden of Kentucky. Lincoln's law partner and aide William Herndon complained that "thousands of Whigs dropped [them] just on the eve of the election, through the influence of Crittenden."

Lincoln wrote to Crittenden, "The emotions of defeat, at the close of a struggle in which I felt more than a merely selfish interest, and to which defeat the use of your name contributed largely, are fresh upon me, but, even in this mood, I cannot for a moment suspect you of anything dishonorable."

Abraham Lincoln was a clear dark horse to any aspiration of presidential ambition in 1859, well behind the likes of New York Senator William H. Seward, Ohio governor Salmon P. Chase, and Missouri's stateman Edward Bates. Even by the time of the approaching Republican National Committee meeting of December 21, 1859, Lincoln had not committed publicly to run for the nomination. The committee would narrowly choose Chicago as their convention site for the following May. Lincoln would make himself better known during the preceding months.

William Seward was the presumed candidate. Even by midnight before the day of the nomination, the presumption was that the presumed candidate, William Seward, would, receive, the nomination. The voices heard in late-night meetings stated that this nominee could not win the general election. Lincoln and his team had resolved not to disparage or to antagonize anyone. Lincoln hoped to be the second choice of many delegates. On the fourth ballot, Lincoln supporters "rose to their feet applauding rapturously, the ladies waving their handkerchiefs, the men waving and throwing up their hats by thousands, cheering again and again." For the Stewardites, one New Yorker observed, "Great men wept like boys." William Seward would become Lincoln's trusted secretary of state. The convention had chosen a man "notably free of pettiness, malice, and overindulgence" for the supreme challenges looming over the nation. From the outside, upon hearing that the Republican Convention had nominated Lincoln for the presidency, Stephen Douglas remarked, "You have nominated a very able and very honorable man."

Abraham Lincoln was what Ralph Waldo Emerson called a "causationist." According to Emerson, all successful men fit this description, by which he meant "they believed that things went not by luck, but by law." Herndon testified repeatedly that his law partner was, indeed, such a man. Lincoln's settled view, according to Herndon, was something like this: "God starts causes, & effects follow those causes; & those Effects are at once, in the ages, causes as well as Effects—Hence the universal chain of causation."

Mrs. Lincoln told Lincoln's law partner William Herndon that Mr. Lincoln had never joined a church, but, yet, she believed, as did Herndon, that "He was a religious man always, as I think," and that "he felt religious More than Ever about the time he went to Gettysburg."

During campaign trips, Lincoln would write letters to his dear wife, Mary Todd, inquiring of her and how their children were. In one letter, he wrote, "This is Sunday morning; and according to [son] Bob's orders, I am to go to church once today."

Some were blind to Lincoln's writing ability, but others admired it in his first inaugural address and his July 4 message to Congress. But even with discerning supporters, the national crisis was too grave, the focus on preconceived issues and antagonisms too intense, for serious attention to the president's literary skill. His purpose, of course, was not literary but political—to find a way to reach a large and diverse American audience.

Thomas Jefferson wrote of his efforts to shape public opinion. In a letter to a friend, he wrote with insight, "the wisdom of Salon's remark, that no more-good must be attempted than the nation can bear." Lincoln may or may not have read books written by Salon, Aristotle, and so forth, but he had read Jefferson's works.

So, what then, could be done? As early as 1842, in what is known as his Temperance Address, he stated that to attempt to bully others into submission under pretense—that to "assume to dictate to [someone's] judgement or to command his action …"— is counterproductive. "If you would win a man to your cause, first convince him you are his sincere friend." An account of an early Lincoln speech given in 1841 reports, "As a speaker, he is characterized by a sincerity, frankness and evident honesty …" He understood that he would be better served by simply giving the listener reason to believe, that, whatever his faults, he was essentially honest and trustworthy. Horace Greeley wrote, "The power of Mr. Lincoln is not in his presence or in his speech, but in his honesty and gloriously refreshing sincerity of the man."

Before Lincoln would even be inaugurated as president, a convention of seven seceded states organized a provisional government called the Confederate States of America on February 4, 1861. On March 4, Abraham Lincoln became the sixteenth president of the United States. Fort Sumter surrendered on April 14. On April 15, President Lincoln called for seventy-five thousand volunteers to put down the insurrection. Later that month, Virginia joined the new Confederacy; Arkansas and North Carolina in May; and in June, Tennessee threw its lot in with the Confederacy proclaimed by Mississippi, Florida, Alabama, Georgia, Louisiana, Texas, and South Carolina.

"Honest Old Abe" reflected, "I don't know but that God has created some one man great enough to comprehend the whole of this stupendous crisis and transaction from beginning to end and endowed him with sufficient wisdom to manage and direct it. I confess I do not fully understand and foresee it all. But I am placed here where I am obliged to the best of my poor ability to deal with it." Lincoln also wrote, "I am naturally anti-slavery. If slavery is not wrong, nothing is wrong. I cannot remember when I did not so think, and feel …"

Before we advance the story further, let us look at a few of those thoughts that the new president, Lincoln, may have pondered and considered as he looked out at a most uncertain landscape:

> I have never had a feeling, politically, that did not spring from the sentiments embodied in the Declaration of Independence.
>
> Most governments have been based, practically, on the denial of the equal rights of men … Ours began by affirming those rights.
>
> If we have patience, if we restrain ourselves, if we allow ourselves not to run off in a passion, I still

have confidence that the Almighty, the Maker of the universe, will, through the instrumentality of this great and intelligent people, bring us through this as he has through all the other difficulties of our country.

I am exceedingly anxious that this Union, the Constitution, and the liberties of the people shall be perpetuated in accordance with the original idea for which that struggle was made, and I shall be most happy indeed if I shall be an humble instrument in the hands of the Almighty, and of this, his almost chosen people, for perpetuating the object of that great struggle.

I have never done an official act with a view to promote my personal aggrandizement, and I don't like to begin now.

As I would not be a slave, so I would not be a master. This expresses my idea of democracy. Whatever differs from this, to the extent of the difference, is no democracy.

What is it that we hold most dear amongst us? Our own liberty and prosperity. What has ever threatened our liberty and prosperity, save and except this institution of slavery?

A man has no time to spend half his life in quarrels.

I shall do nothing in malice. What I deal with is too vast for malicious dealing.

And this issue embraces more than the fate of these United States. It presents to the whole family of man the question whether a constitutional republic or democracy—a government of the people, by the same people—can or cannot maintain its territorial integrity against its own domestic foes. It presents the question whether discontented individuals, too few in numbers to control administration according to organic law, in any case, can always, upon the pretenses made in this case, or on any other pretenses, or arbitrarily without any pretense, break up their government and thus practically put an end to free government upon the earth. It forces us to ask: "Is there, in all republics, this inherent and fatal weakness?" "Must a government, of necessity, be too strong for the liberties of its own people, or too weak to maintain its own existence?"

Fellow-citizens, we cannot escape history. We of this Congress and this administration will be remembered, in-spite of, ourselves ... in giving freedom to the slave, we assure freedom to the free—honorable alike in what we give and what we preserve. We shall nobly save or meanly lose the last, best hope of earth. Other means may succeed; this could not fail. The way is plain, peaceful, generous, just—a way which, if followed, the world will forever applaud, and God must forever bless.

I am not at all concerned about that [that is, God's being on the Northern side in the war], for I know the Lord is always on the side of the right. But it is my constant anxiety and prayer that I and this nation should be on the Lord's side.

I have not permitted myself, gentlemen, to conclude that I am the best man in the country; but I am reminded, in this connection, of a story of an old Dutch farmer, who remarked to a companion once that "It was not best to swap horses when crossing streams."

Many free countries have lost their liberty; and ours may lose hers; but if she shall, be it my proudest plume, not that I was the last to desert, but that I never deserted her.

The point of this writing is not to outline the course of the Civil War. In August of 1862, Robert E. Lee and Stonewall Jackson conducted successful offenses in their eastern campaigns against the North. Union armies scurried to assume their defensive positions protecting the Capitol.

During that same month, a different unsettling turn of events occurred in the new state of Minnesota. The 1862 Minnesota Sioux Uprising, or the Dakota War of 1862, cannot be explained in a paragraph; nor the Civil War in a sentence. Additional greenbacks were now being printed to cover the cost of war. A treaty had been signed with annual payments to be made in gold. The 1862 payment was late in arriving.

The Sioux and the settlers lived near one another in southern Minnesota. One of the pioneer children later remarked, "It was a little lonely, for our nearest neighbors were some distance away." She also recalled, "The country was wild, though it was very beautiful. We had no schools or churches, and did not see many white people, and we children were often lonesome and longed for companions."

The individuals and characters were many and diverse. Among them were Chief Little Crow, who lived then in a house; Red Middle Voice and his band of "troublemakers"; Cut-Nose; and Chief Shakopee, among others. Some settlers were killed. A treaty was broken. A spark was lit. A prairie fire of battle began. As "things got out of hand," a request for support was sent to Washington.

A Mrs. Margaret King Hern described some of the action from inside nearby Fort Ridgely: "Friday was a terrific battle … It was the soldiers who saved Minneapolis and St. Paul and the towns between, when the Indians failed to capture the fort … These hundreds of Indian warriors had fought bravely, courageously, but they were facing with their few muskets and their bows and arrows the brutal, powerful weapons that would cause such carnage at Antietam and Gettysburg."

Major General John Pope, who had led the second battle of Bull Run just two weeks earlier, was relieved of command by President Lincoln and dispatched to Minnesota. Pope saw it as "banishment to a distant and unimportant department." Some eight hundred settlers were soon killed. Late in the year, when "all this" was over, the State of Minnesota would sentence some three hundred to be hanged.

A Bishop Whipple made a point to write the president and go to Washington to talk in person with President Lincoln. Lincoln could hear and understand the bishop. Lincoln commented, "He [Bishop Whipple] came here the other day and talked with me about the rascality of this Indian business until I felt it down to my boots."

Lincoln had malice toward none. General Pope supported the number of over three hundred to be hanged. Lincoln reduced the number by nearly 90 percent. The Indians, or Natives, referred to Bishop Whipple as "Straight Tongue," which was a straightforward sign of respect. (Still, yet today, every year, the Dakota 38 Riders ride a memorial ride from the Lower Brule of South Dakota to Mankato, a journey of about 325 miles, on horseback. It is a "prayer ride." The purpose of the ride is reconciliation and healing, and it is a good reminder for those of us who wish to call ourselves American.

Tocqueville wrote of the languages of America, commenting that the idioms were "the product of a very complicated system of ideas and of very expert combinations."

The author is not so gifted as to have learned one of the languages, but as a lad, he learned a "war whoop" from Sam Heritage.

Judge Owen T. Reeves, soldier, and legal scholar, commented,

> Lincoln was the apostle of the common people. Their rights, their conditions, their hardships, their opportunities, their aspirations, their hopes, their joys and their sorrows—all these were subjects upon which his mind brooded and sought to work out plans for their betterment and happiness. No man ever knew the common people better than he or was closer in sympathy with them. Having sprung from the innumerable

common throng, his heart never ceased to beat in sympathy with them. Besides, he was endowed with that best sense—common sense. This, with his broad, clear grasp of every subject that touched the interest of the masses, made him preeminently the advocate of the rights of the common people.

In February of 1862, Abraham Lincoln lost his dear young son Willie at age eleven from typhoid fever. So many more than imagined or conceived were being lost in that great and heartfelt Civil War. In September of 1862, he would issue a preliminary Emancipation Proclamation, with the final Emancipation Proclamation issued January 1, 1863. "I made a solemn vow before God, that if General [Robert E.] Lee was driven back from Pennsylvania I would crown the results by the declaration of freedom to the slaves," Lincoln stated.

Abraham Lincoln would live this Civil War within himself, and he would visit the generals and soldiers in the front lines of that war. One such story is told about our Uncle Abe: Abe Lincoln came upon some Pennsylvania volunteers assigned to guard him who were "grumbling around the campfire that their talents were being wasted on this unnecessary duty." "With a twinkle in his eye," he said, "You boys remind me of a farmer friend of mine in Illinois, who said he could never understand why the Lord put a curl in a pig's tail. It never seemed to him to be either useful or ornamental, but he reckoned the Almighty knew what he was doing when he put it there."

For himself, Abe Lincoln would humbly observe: "I should be the most presumptuous blockhead upon this footstool if I for one day thought that I should discharge the duties which have come upon me, since I came to this place, without the aid and enlightenment of One who is stronger and wiser than all others."

Lincoln, it is written, went to great lengths to understand what may, be the will of the Almighty; but he would never position himself as a consummate judge of the determination or of what that may be. He resolved not to cast blame and judgement upon either the North or the South, yet somehow, he effected an outcome. Emancipation, he would say, "was the central act of my administration." "Let us be quite sober. Let us diligently apply the means, never doubting that a just God, in his own good time, will give us the rightful result."

> As a pilot I have used by best exertions to keep afloat our Ship of State and shall be glad to resign my trust at the appointed time to another pilot more skillful and successful than I may prove. In every case and at all hazards the government must be perpetuated. Relying, as I do, upon the Almighty Power, and encouraged as I am by these resolutions which you have just read, with the support which I receive from Christian men, I shall not hesitate to use all the means at my control to secure the termination of this rebellion, and will hope for success.

While Lincoln believed he was not the captain of the ship that "carried him on life's rough waters," neither did he regard himself as an "idle passenger but a sailor on a deck with a job to do."

The final Emancipation Proclamation was proclaimed by the president of the United States of America:

> That on the first day of January, in the year of our Lord one thousand eight hundred and sixty-three, all persons held as slaves within any State or designated part of a State, the people whereof shall then be in rebellion against the United States, shall be then, thenceforward, and forever free; and the Executive Government of the United States, including the military and naval authority thereof, will recognize and maintain the freedom of such persons, and will do no act or acts to repress such persons, or any of them, in any efforts they may make for their actual freedom ...

Charles A. Dana, assistant secretary of war, observed, "Even in [Lincoln's] freest moments one always felt the presence of a will and an intellectual power which maintained the ascendancy of the president. He never posed or put on airs or attempted to make any particular impression; but he was always conscious of his own ideas and purposes, even in his most unreserved moments."

President Abraham Lincoln wrote a proclamation appointing a National Fast Day for March 30, 1863. The honest oratory and written words of Abraham Lincoln may not have themselves turned the tide and changed history, but some of those honest sentiments can be forgotten lest we remind ourselves; some of those thoughts of Abraham Lincoln can resonate loudly in our own ears in our present day. He said,

> It is the duty of nations as well as of men to own their dependence upon the overruling power of God; to confess their sins and transgressions, in humble sorrow, yet with assured hope that genuine repentance will lead to mercy and pardon; and to recognize the sublime truth, announced in the Holy Scriptures and proven by all history, that those nations only are blessed whose God is the Lord ...
>
> We have been preserved, these many years, in peace and prosperity. We have grown in numbers, wealth, and power as no other nation has ever grown; but we have forgotten God. We have forgotten the gracious hand which has preserved us in peace and multiplied and enriched and strengthened us; and we have vainly imagined, in the deceitfulness of our hearts, that all these blessings were produced by some superior wisdom and virtue of our own. Intoxicated with unbroken success, we have become too self-sufficient to feel the necessity of redeeming and preserving grace, too proud to pray to the God that made us ... It behooves us, then, to humble ourselves before the offended Power,

to confess our national sins, and to pray for clemency and forgiveness.

While General Robert E. Lee began his retreat from Gettysburg on July 4, Independence Day, 1863, General Ulysses S. Grant accepted the surrender of Vicksburg, Mississippi, after a lengthy siege.

Upon the battlefield of Gettysburg, Abraham Lincoln would deliver his never-to-be-forgotten Gettysburg Address on November 19, 1863. Spoken after lengthy orations, it was met with near silence after spoken. Let us, too, never forget:

> Four score and seven years ago our fathers brought forth on this continent a new nation, conceived in liberty and dedicated to the proposition that all men are created equal.
>
> Now we are engaged in a great civil war, testing whether that nation or any nation so conceived and so dedicated can long endure. We are met on a great battlefield of that war. We have come to dedicate a portion of that field as a final resting-place for those who here gave their lives that that nation might live. It is altogether fitting and proper that we cannot consecrate, we cannot hallow this ground. The brave men, living and dead who struggled here have consecrated it far above our poor power to add or detract. The world will little note nor long remember what we say here, but it can never forget what they did here. It is for us the living rather to be dedicated here to the unfinished work which they who fought here have thus far so nobly advanced. It is rather for us to be here dedicated to the great task remaining before us – that from these honored dead we take increased devotion to that cause for which they gave the last full measure of devotion – that we here highly resolve that these dead shall not have died in

vain, that this nation under God shall have a new birth of freedom, and that government of the people, by the people, for the people shall not perish from the earth.

Following is one small story recorded, but it is indeed the story of America:

It was dawn on June 22, 1861, at Fort Snelling in St. Paul. The First Regiment of Minnesota Volunteers was addressed by the chaplain: "Your errand is not to overturn, but to uphold the most tolerant and forbearing government on earth. You go to war with misguided brethren, not with wrathful, but with mourning hearts . . . To fight for a great principle is a noble work. We are all erring and fallible men; but the civilized world feel that you are engaged in a just cause, which God will defend."

As the First Regiment Volunteers arrived at Gettysburg, Anderson's Confederate Division was advancing with great rapidity and confidence. It was but a short half mile that they had to come. A few minutes more and they would be on the crest. Hancock of the Union Army was riding furiously up and down to meet the reinforcements he had ordered. They were coming on the run, but they did not arrive, and the precious minutes were passing.

He galloped to the center of the supporting regiment on its left. "What regiment is this?" he asked of Colonel Colvill.

"First Minnesota" was the reply.

"Charge those lines," Hancock firmly said, pointing to the front of Wilcox's Confederate brigade, now not more than four hundred yards away. Colvill and his men knew what that meant—a sacrifice to save five minutes of time.

The usual orders put the little battalion in movement at right shoulder shift on double time. The line was less than one hundred yards long. The ground to be traversed was an old pasture field. At the foot of the considerable slope of three hundred yards there was a dried-up ditch, or "run". From the start, the enemy's fire began to thin the ranks, but not a man flinched. When near the foot of the slope, Colvill ordered, "Charge!" and, on full run with bayonets fixed, the Minnesotans rushed upon the Confederate line, which was momentarily disordered while climbing up the hither bank of the run. The mass was small, but velocity gave momentum to the onset. The men of the South scrambled back across the run and gathered.

Many brave officers and men had fallen by the way on the slope; some of them were smitten by fire from the right of their little front, thrown in by one of Wilcox's regiments which had not been so suddenly halted in its advance. At dusk the battle ceased, the enemy drew back to the pike, and there was leisure to reckon the living and the dead. Of the 262 officers and men of the First Minnesota who began that fatal charge, 47 answered roll call and 215 lay dead, dying, or wounded in the pasture, on the slope, or in the swale below. Colvill was crippled for life.

Hancock said later, "There is no more gallant deed recorded in history. I ordered these men in there because I saw I must gain five minutes' time. I would have ordered that regiment in if I had known that every man would be killed. It had to be done." The sacrifice was necessary; those Minnesota troops knew it and marched proudly into the jaws of death. "When shall their glory fade?"

A close friend of Lincoln, Leonard Swett, said of the man,

> As [Lincoln] became involved in matters of the greatest importance, full of great responsibility and great doubt, a feeling of religious reverence, a belief in God and his justice and overruling power increased with him … He believed in the great laws of truth, and the rigid discharge of duty, his accountability to God, the ultimate triumph of the right and the overthrow of wrong. If his religion were to be judged by the lines and rules of Church creeds, he would fall far short of the standard; but if by the higher rule of purity of conduct, of honesty of motive, of unyielding fidelity to the right, and acknowledging God as the supreme ruler, then he filled all the requirements of true devotion, and his whole life was a life of love to God, and love of his neighbor as of himself.

Sojourner Truth, a former slave and Underground Railroad "conductor" who visited Lincoln at the White House in October 1864, said, "I must say, and I am proud to say, that I never was treated by anyone with more kindness and cordiality than was shown me by the great and good man, Abraham Lincoln, by the grace of God president of the United States."

Another friend of Abraham Lincoln, whom Lincoln once personally came to the door of the White House to let in, was Frederick Douglas. Douglas said of Lincoln,

> In all my interviews with Mr. Lincoln I was impressed with his entire freedom from popular prejudice against the colored race. He was the first great man that I talked with in the United States freely, who in no single instance reminded me of the difference between himself and myself, of the difference of color ... Then, too, there was another feeling that I had with reference to him, and that was that while I felt in his presence I was in the presence of a very great man, as great as the greatest, I felt as though I could go and put my hand on him if I wanted to, to put my hand on his shoulder. Of course, I did not do it, but I felt that I could. I felt as though I was in the presence of a big brother, and that there was safety in his atmosphere.

The night before his speech at Gettysburg, he told a crowd, "In my position, it is somewhat important that I should not say any foolish things." A voice inserted, "If you can help it," to which the president replied, "It very often happens that the only way to help it is to say nothing at all." His secretaries would write in their joint biography, "Modest as he was, he knew the value of his own work," referencing his letters and writings.

One on one, might Mr. Lincoln speak a tart word here and there? Two ladies asked for the release of their husbands from prison. One of these ladies urged that her husband was a religious man. The president ordered the release of the prisoners and then said to this lady, "You say your husband is a religious man; tell him when you meet him, that I say I am not much of a judge of religion, but that, in my opinion, the religion that sets men to rebel and fight against their government because, as they think, that government does not sufficiently help some men to eat their bread on the sweat of other men's faces, is not the sort of religion upon which people can get to heaven!" This seems harsh, perhaps, but within his second inaugural address, Lincoln stated, "Both read the same Bible and pray to the same God; and each invokes His aid against the other. It may seem strange that any men should dare to ask a just God's assistance in wringing their bread from the sweat of other men's faces; but let us judge not that we be not judged."

Also within Lincoln's Second Inaugural address were the following words: "If we shall suppose that American slavery is one of those offences which, in the providence of God, must needs come, but which, having continued through His appointed time, He now wills to remove; and that He gives to both north and south this terrible war as the woe due to those by whom the offense came, shall we discern therein any departure from those divine attributes which the believers in a living God always ascribe to Him?"

And his address would end as follows: "With malice toward none; with charity for all; with firmness in the right, as God gives us to see the right, let us strive on to finish the work we are in; to bind up the nation's wounds; to care for him who shall have borne the battle, and for his widow, and his orphan— to do all which may achieve and cherish a just, and a lasting peace, among ourselves, and with all nations."

A petition signed by 195 schoolchildren asking the president to free "all the little slave children in the country" was received by the president. He replied to Mary Mann, the author of the petition, "Please tell these little people I am very glad their young hearts are so full of just and generous sympathy, and that, while I have not all the power to grant all they ask, I trust they will remember that God has, and that, as it seems, He wills to do it … Amid the greatest difficulties of my Administration, when I could not see any other resort, I would place my whole reliance in God, knowing that all would go well, and that He would decide for the right."

Abraham Lincoln issued on October 20, 1864, a proclamation of thanksgiving. Then, on October 24, 1864, he gave a speech to the 189th New York Volunteers: "SOLDIERS: I am exceedingly obliged to you for this mark of respect. It is said that we have the best Government the world ever knew, and I am glad to meet you, the supporters of that Government. To you who render the hardest work in its support should be given the greatest credit …"

And in conclusion, and in honor and profound respect to the greatest president of the United States, let us honor and defend that cause for which he lived and for which he died. In this we have come full circle in honor of this man and in honor of those brave Founders who declared independence, giving the hope of liberty to the world for all future time. Abraham Lincoln would speak at Independence Hall in Philadelphia, Pennsylvania, on February 22, 1861, on his way to history:

> Mr. CUYLER: — I am filled with deep emotion at finding myself standing here in the place where were collected together the wisdom, the patriotism, the devotion to principle, which sprang the institutions under which we live. You have kindly suggested to me that in my hands is the task of restoring peace to our distracted country. I can say in return, sir, that all the political sentiments I entertain have been drawn, so far as I have been able to draw them, from the sentiments which originated, and were given to the world from this hall in which we stand. I have never had a feeling politically that did not spring from the sentiments embodied in the Declaration of Independence. (Great cheering.)
>
> I have often pondered over the dangers which were incurred by the men who assembled here and adopted that Declaration of Independence—I have pondered

over the toils that were endured by the officers and soldiers of the army, who achieved that Independence. (Applause.) I have often inquired of myself, what great principle or idea it was that kept this Confederacy so long together. It was not the mere matter of the separation of the colonies from the mother land; but something in that Declaration giving liberty, not alone to the people of this country, but hope to the world for all future time. (Great applause.) It was that which gave promise that in due time the weights should be lifted from the shoulders of all men, and that All should have an equal chance. (Cheers.) This is the sentiment embodied in the Declaration of Independence.

Now, my friends, can this country be saved upon that basis? If it can, I will consider myself one of the happiest men in the world if I can help to save it. If it can't be saved upon that principle, it will be truly awful. But if this country cannot be saved without giving up that principle—I was about to say I would rather be assassinated on this spot than to surrender it. (Applause.)

Now, in my view of the present aspect of affairs, there is no need of bloodshed and war. There is no necessity for it. I am not in favor of such a course, and I may say in advance, there will be no blood shed unless it be forced upon the Government. The Government will not use force unless force is used against it. (Prolonged applause and cries of "That's the proper sentiment.")

My friends, this is a wholly unprepared speech. I did not expect to be called upon to say a word when I came here—I supposed I was merely to do something towards raising a flag. I may, therefore, have said something indiscreet, (cries of "no, no"), but I have said nothing but what I am willing to live by, and, in the pleasure of Almighty God, die by.

The Reverend Noyes W. Miner, a Baptist minister, read the book of Job at the president's funeral.

As Lincoln was laid to rest, let us, going forward, rest in these few final words spoken by Abraham Lincoln:

Take all, of this Book [that is, the Bible] upon reason that you can and the balance on faith, and you will live and die a happier and better man.

In regard, to this Great Book, I have but to say, it is the best gift God has given to man. All the good the Savior gave to the world was communicated through this book. But for it, we could not know right from wrong. All things most desirable for man's welfare, here and hereafter, are to be found portrayed in it.

It is difficult to make a man miserable when he feels worthy of himself and claims kindred to the great God who made him.

Our reliance is in the love of liberty which God has planted in our bosoms. Our defense is in the preservation of the spirit which prized liberty as the heritage of all men, in all lands, everywhere. Destroy this spirit and you have planted the seeds of despotism around your own doors. Familiarize yourselves with the chains of bondage, and you are preparing your own limbs to wear them.

REVEREND MARTIN LUTHER KING JR.

A Weight of History

Blessed are those who are persecuted because of righteousness, for theirs is the kingdom of heaven.

—Matthew 5:10 NIV

When a history is written without God, without belief, without sacrifice, and without forgiveness – one may see the results of the slave trade on a new experiment in democracy in the new world.

After a civil war never to be forgotten, came the unbridled optimism of the Western Frontier. There came to be new states and new lands. Old states were not forgotten but left behind. The Industrial Revolution was impacting so many in so many ways: transitioning lifestyles from horses and wagons and logs on the fire to the horseless carriage and a phenomenon known as electricity to the telephone and more.

There became a brimming optimism, tempered then with a reluctant participation in a War to End All Wars – World War I. After a Great Depression was a Second World War to save civilization itself. Millions were lost and millions more in the aftermath.

Yet the loss of life from that internal confl ict—the Civil War, or the war between the states—would not be surpassed till the losses of Vietnam were added.

Albert Woolson, the last surviving Union soldier of the Civil War died August 2, 1956, in Duluth, Minnesota. In an August 1954 newspaper interview, he said, "One day father and I went to the Capitol building at Albany, N.Y. There was a meeting there and one man was tall, had large bony hands. It was old Uncle Abe, and he talked about human slavery." Albert's father, Willard, would receive a leg wound at the Battle of Shiloh and later would die from the effects of that wound. Albert said, "We were fighting our brothers. In that there is no glory."

No less a person than the Reverend Doctor Martin Luther King Jr. would begin his pastorate and pastoral mission in May 1954. He and Coretta Scott King took up residence in Montgomery, Alabama in September of that year in the heart of Dixie. That same year, the Supreme Court would rule on "separate but equal" and on school integration in May.

The following year would be the year Mrs. Rosa Parks would maintain her seat on a bus. The Reverend King addressed a gathering of the bus boycott at the Holt Street Church, with four thousand gathered outside. Normally Pastor King would take maybe fifteen hours to prepare a sermon. That evening he had but five minutes to pray and minutes to think. Following is some of what he said:

> One of the great glories of democracy, is the right to protest for right. ... We will be guided by the highest principles of law and order ... Our method will be that of persuasion, not coercion. We will only say to the people, 'Let your conscience be your guide.' Our actions must be guided by the deepest principles of our Christian faith. Love must be our regulating ideal. Once again, we must hear the words of Jesus echoing across the centuries: 'Love your enemies, bless them that curse you, and pray for them that despitefully use you'.

If we fail to do this our protest will end up as a meaningless drama on the stage of history, and its memory will be shrouded with the ugly garments of shame. In spite, of mistreatment, that we have confronted, we must not become bitter and end up by hating our white brothers. As Booker T. Washington said, 'Let no man pull you down so low as to make you hate him' …

If you will protest courageously and yet with dignity and Christian love, when the history books are written in future generations, the historians will have to pause and say, 'There lived a great people—a black people—who injected new meaning and dignity into the veins of civilization.' This is our challenge and our overwhelming responsibility!

Martin Luther King would head the Montgomery Improvement Association in negotiations with officials of the city. It proved a frustrating business. Months later, after a barrage of threatening phone calls, a white friend confided to him that the threats were in earnest. Martin felt a chill of fear. Soon thereafter, he told a mass meeting, "If one day you find me sprawled out dead, I do not want you to retaliate with a single act of violence. I urge you to continue protesting without a single act of violence. I urge you to continue protesting with the same dignity and discipline you have shown so far."

The night after his arrest for going thirty miles per hour in a twenty-five-mile-per-hour zone, Martin and Coretta were lying in bed. Coretta was already asleep, and Martin dozing, when the telephone aroused him. Nerves on edge and unable to sleep, Martin sat for a long time in the kitchen, exhausted and brooding over a cup of coffee as it grew cold. *How can I beat a graceful retreat?* he asked himself. *How can I get out of this without looking like a coward?* Exhausted and afraid, he prayed aloud: "I am here taking a stand for what I believe is right. But now I am afraid. The people are looking to me for leadership, and if I stand before them without strength and courage, they too will falter.

I am at the end of my powers. I have nothing left. I've come to the point where I can't face it alone." As if in answer, he felt a resurgence of energy and inner peace. A voice from the depths of his being seemed to be saying to him, "Stand up for righteousness, stand up for truth, and God will be at your side forever."

On a Monday night, January 30, 1956, the regular mass meeting at the Reverend Abernathy's church was, coming, to a close. King noticed Ralph and another looking worriedly around and conferring. King called to them. "What is it? What's wrong?" Ralph turned. "Your house has been bombed." "Oh, my God!" exclaimed Martin. "What about Coretta and Yoki—are they all right?" Coretta had been sitting in the living room with a visitor. She'd heard something land on the porch. *Probably a brick*, she thought, but she suggested that she and her guest go to the bedroom "just in case." When they were halfway down the hall, they heard the explosion and a hail of broken glass.

Word spread quickly. By nine thirty, a thousand black men and women thronged South Jackson Street, armed with knives, guns, sticks, rocks, and bottles. Firemen and police filled the house. Mayor Gayle and the fire chief were there, along with the police commissioner and other officials. Martin King arrived and hurried through the crowd. "Thank God you're all right!" he said breathlessly, hugging Coretta. He looked in on Yoki, who was unharmed. Then he hastened to the front porch and, flanked by Montgomery officials, who had visibly paled, he raised his arms for silence. The crowd seethed with threats and curses. He heard one man talking of "shooting it out" with the police.

Dr. King's deep baritone voice rang out over the crowd: "Don't get panicky! Don't do anything panicky at all! If you have weapons, take them home; if you do not have them, please do not seek to get them. We cannot solve this problem through retaliatory violence ... We must love our white brothers no matter what they do to us. We must make them know that we love them. Jesus still cries out in words that echo across the centuries: 'Love your enemies; bless them that curse you; pray for them that despitefully use you.' This is what we must live by. We must meet hate with love."

The crowd had fallen silent. "I did not start this boycott," he continued. "I was asked by you to serve as your spokesman. I want it to be known the length and breadth of the land that if I am stopped, this movement will not stop. What we are doing is just, and God is with us." "God bless you, son!" a woman shouted. Cries of "amen" could be heard as the crowd drifted away.

Martin would further pray and say,

> We have before us the glorious opportunity to inject a new dimension of love into the veins of our civilization. There is still a voice crying out in terms that echo across generations, saying: Love your enemies, bless them that curse you, pray for them that despitefully use you, that you may be the children of your Father which is in Heaven ...
>
> I have also become more and more convinced of the reality of a personal God. True, I have always believed in the personality of God. But in past years the idea of a personal God was little more than a metaphysical category which I found theologically and philosophically satisfying. Now it is a living reality that has been validated in the experiences of everyday life. Perhaps the suffering, frustration, and agonizing moments which I have had to undergo occasionally, as a result, of my involvement in a difficult struggle have drawn me closer to God. Whatever the cause, God has been profoundly real to me in recent months. In the-midst of outer dangers, I have felt an inner calm and known resources of strength that only God could give. In many instances I have felt the power of God transforming the fatigue of despair into the buoyancy of hope. I am convinced that the universe is under the control of a loving purpose and that in the struggle for righteousness man has cosmic companionship. Behind the harsh appearances of the

world there is a benign power. To say God is personal is not to make him an object among other objects or attribute to him the finiteness and limitations of human personality; it is to take what is finest and noblest in our consciousness and affirm its perfect existence in him. It is certainly true that human personality is limited, but personality as such involves no necessary limitations. It simply means self-consciousness and self-direction. So, in the truest sense of the work, God is a living God. In him there is feeling and will, responsive to the deepest yearnings of the human heart: thus, God both evokes and answers prayers.

Some months later, the Rev. Martin Luther King would conclude an oration with these words:

> Then we will be able to sing the great tradition of our nation: 'My country, 'tis of thee, sweet land of liberty, of thee I sing! Land where my fathers died, land of the Pilgrim's pride, from every mountainside, let freedom ring!' This must become literally true. Freedom must ring from every mountainside. Yes, let it ring from the snow-capped Rockies of Colorado, from the prodigious hilltops of New Hampshire, from the mighty Alleghenies of Pennsylvania, from the curvaceous slopes of California. But not only that. Let freedom ring from every mountainside—from every molehill in Mississippi, from Stone Mountain in Georgia, from Lookout Mountain in Tennessee, yes, and from every hill and mountain in Alabama. From every mountainside—let freedom ring. When this day finally comes, 'the morning stars will sing together, and the suns of God will shout for joy.'

In 1947 Martin was ordained and accepted his father's invitation to become assistant pastor at Ebenezer Baptist Church. The following June, at the age of nineteen, the Reverend Martin Luther King Jr. graduated from Morehouse College with a Bachelor of Arts degree. Martin then pursued a theological education at Crozer Theological Seminary in Upland, Pennsylvania, some six hundred miles from home. Martin made friends easily. But one of a half dozen African Americans of a class of one hundred, he also was an A student and would graduate as class valedictorian.

There, at Crozer, he furthered his biblical studies. Some of his studies were extracurricular. The Cold War had begun, and he read about Karl Marx and communism. He also listened to lectures about Mahatma Gandhi of India.

He found in Marx a challenge to the social conscience of the churches, but he found even more to disagree with. In so doing, he began to sharpen his own sense of values. Marx's historical materialism had no place for God; it involved an ethical relativism that countenanced all kinds of evil to attain its goals, and it led to a political order in which, as King wrote, "man becomes hardly more … than a depersonalized cog in the turning wheel of the state." In contrast, the young seminarian felt that there must be God—not just any God, but "a creative personal power in this universe who is the ground and essence of all reality … History, is ultimately guided by spirit, not matter." Moreover, he thought, the universe, because this divine power is at its center, must have a moral order to it; it must involve certain principles that are themselves right and good. Among these is the principle that man is "a child of God"—not a means to some impersonal end but "an end within himself." To be adequate, to be Christian, any attempt to change society and overcome its evils must embody these tenets. As never before, Martin came to think that social change must occur and that it could occur. It remained to find a way, and already, however dimly, that way was beginning to come into focus. It would have to be, for Martin, a way acceptable to God—a way of spiritual and moral force such as that which Jesus and Paul had experienced.

Martin set his heart on attaining a doctorate. He decided on Boston University. It was in Boston that he would meet Coretta. Talented and charming and more than a pretty girl with a lovely singing voice was Coretta Scott. She, too, studied in the North, at a conservatory in Boston. She was encouraged by her friends to follow her singing talent. With so much in common in ideals and aspirations and mind, the two became inseparably in love.

With such an excellent record, there were plenty of offerings for King to choose from. If he wished, he could be dean of a college, a teacher, or an administrator. He would have openings from churches in the North and South. They decided he would first serve in a pastorate—but which pastorate? Coretta thought a pastorate in the North would be best. Martin felt his duty and mission would be best fulfilled at the Dexter Avenue Baptist Church in Montgomery, Alabama. It was near Alabama State College and less than a two-hour drive to Coretta's parents.

We may see Martin through the eyes of Coretta and the words echoing still today, to bring our own hearts closer to truth. As a most simple introduction to the writings and speeches that changed the world, Coretta Scott King stated, "Dr. King was not merely a great speaker but a passionately committed American patriot who repeatedly put his life on the line to make real the promise of democracy."

Martin would observe,

> The Greek language uses three words for love. It talks about eros. Eros is a sort of aesthetic love. It has come to us to be a sort of romantic love and it stands with all of its beauty. But when we speak of loving those who oppose us, we're not talking about eros. The Greek language talks about philia and this is a sort of reciprocal love between personal friends. This is a vital, valuable love. But when we talk of loving those who oppose you and those who seek to defeat you, we are not talking about eros or philia. The Greek language comes out with another word, and it is agape. Agape is

understanding, creative, redemptive good will for men. Biblical theologians would say it is the love of God working in the minds of men. It is an overflowing love which seeks nothing in return. And when you come to love on this level you begin to love men not because they are likable, not because they do things that attract us, but because God loves them, and here we love the person who does the evil deed while hating the deed that the person does. It is the type of love that stands at the center of the movement that we are trying to carry on in the Southland—agape ... We must continue to move on. Our self-respect is at stake; the prestige of our nation is at stake. Civil rights - is an eternal moral issue which may well determine the destiny of our civilization in the ideological struggle with communism. We must keep moving with wise restraint and love and with proper discipline and dignity.

And then he wrote a letter from a Birmingham jail to his fellow clergymen: "I am in Birmingham because injustice is here. Just as the eighth-century prophets left their little villages and carried their 'thus saith the Lord' far beyond the boundaries of their hometowns; and just as the Apostle Paul left his little village of Tarsus and carried the gospel of Jesus Christ to practically every hamlet and city of the Graeco-Roman world, I too am compelled to carry the gospel of freedom beyond my particular hometown. Like Paul, I must constantly respond to the Macedonian call for aid." And so, Martin was. And so, he did.

He further wrote,

> We must come to see that human progress never rolls in on wheels of inevitability. It comes through the tireless efforts and persistent work of men willing to be co-workers with God, and without his hard work, time itself becomes an ally of the forces of social stagnation. We must use time creatively, and forever realize that

the time is always ripe to do right. Now is the time to make real the promise of democracy and transform our pending national elegy into a creative psalm of brotherhood. Now is the time to lift our national policy from the quicksand of racial injustice to the solid rock of human dignity ...

I started thinking about the fact that I stand in the middle of two opposing forces in the Negro community. One is a force of complacency made up of Negroes who, as a result of long years of oppression, have been so completely drained of self-respect and a sense of "somebodiness" that they have adjusted to segregation, and of a few Negroes in the middle class who, because at points they profit by segregation, have unconsciously become insensitive to the problems of the masses. The other force is one of bitterness and hatred and comes perilously close to advocating violence. It is expressed in the various black nationalist groups that are springing up over the nation, the largest and best-known being Elijah Muhammad's Muslim movement. This movement is nourished by the contemporary frustration over the continued existence of racial discrimination. It is made up of people who have lost faith in America, who have, absolutely, repudiated Christianity, and who have concluded that the white man is an incurable "devil." I have tried to stand between these two forces, saying that we need not follow the "do-nothingism" of the complacent or the hatred and despair of the black nationalist. There is the more excellent way of love and nonviolent protest. I'm grateful to God that, through the Negro church, the dimension of nonviolence entered our struggle. If this philosophy had not emerged ... And I am further convinced that if our white brothers dismiss as "rabble-rousers" and "outside agitators" those of us who are working through the channels of nonviolent direct action and refuse to support our nonviolent efforts, millions of Negroes, out of frustration and despair, will seek solace and security in black nationalist ideologies, a development that will lead inevitably to a frightening racial nightmare ... But I have tried to say that this normal and healthy discontent can be channelized through the creative outlet of nonviolent direct action. ... as I continued to think about the matter, I gradually gained a bit of satisfaction from being considered an extremist. Was not Jesus an extremist in love— "Love your enemies, bless them that curse you, pray for them that despitefully use you." Was not Amos an extremist for justice— "let justice roll down like waters and righteousness like a mighty stream." Was not Paul an extremist for the gospel of Jesus Christ— "I bear in my body the marks of the Lord Jesus." Was not Martin Luther an extremist— "Here I stand; I can do none other so help me God." Was not John Bunyan an extremist— "I will stay in jail to the end of my days before I make a butchery of my conscience." Was not Abraham Lincoln an extremist— "This nation cannot survive half slave and half free." Was not Thomas Jefferson an extremist— "We hold these truths to be self-evident, that all men are created equal." So, the question is not whether we will be extremist but what kind of extremist will we be. Will we be extremists for hate, or will we be extremists for love? Will we be extremists for the preservation of injustice— or will we be extremists for the cause of justice? In that dramatic scene on Calvary's hill, three men were crucified. We must not forget that all three were crucified for the same crime—the crime of extremism. Two were extremists for immorality, and thusly fell below their environment. So, after all, maybe the South, the nation and the world are in dire need of creative extremists.

Martin said, "Indeed, these students are not struggling for themselves alone. They are seeking to save the soul of America. They are taking our whole nation back to those great wells of democracy which were dug deep by the Founding Fathers in the formulation of the Constitution and the Declaration of Independence. In sitting down at the lunch counters, they are, in reality, standing up for the best in the American dream."

He would continue to pray and to preach, and the nation would listen. He would also say, "I must continue by faith, or it is too great a burden to bear and violence, even in self-defense, creates more problems than it solves. Only a refusal to hate or kill can put an end to the chain of violence in the world and lead us toward a community where men can live together without fear. Our goal is to create a beloved community, and this will require a qualitative change in our souls as well as a quantitative change in our lives."

Martin Luther King Jr. would be awarded the Nobel Peace Prize on December 10, 1964, in Oslo, Norway. He said, "I think Alfred Nobel would know what I mean when I say that I accept this award in the spirit of the curator of some precious heirloom which he holds in trust for its true owners—all those to whom beauty is truth and truth beauty—and in whose eyes the beauty of genuine brotherhood and peace is more precious than diamonds or silver or gold."

1963 was the centennial of the signing of the Emancipation Proclamation. Before the Lincoln Memorial on August 28, 1963, Martin Luther King Jr. would deliver his keynote address to the March on Washington DC for Civil Rights.

Mrs. Coretta King would comment, "At that moment it seemed as if the Kingdom of God appeared."

Dr. King's address is as follows:

> I AM HAPPY TO JOIN WITH YOU TODAY IN WHAT WILL GO DOWN IN HISTORY as the greatest demonstration for freedom in the history of our nation.

Five score years ago, a great American, in whose symbolic shadow we stand today, signed the Emancipation Proclamation. This momentous decree came as a great beacon light of hope to millions of Negro slaves who had been seared in the flames of withering injustice. It came as a joyous daybreak to end the long night of their captivity.

But one hundred years later, the Negro still is not free; one hundred years later, the life of the Negro is still sadly crippled by the manacles of segregation and the chains of discrimination; one hundred years later, the Negro lives on a lonely island of poverty in the midst of a vast ocean of material prosperity; one hundred years later the Negro is still languished in the corners of American society and finds himself in exile in his own land.

So, we've come here today, to dramatize a shameful condition. In a sense we've come to our nation's capital to cash a check. When the architects of our republic wrote the magnificent words of the Constitution and the Declaration of Independence, they were signing a promissory note to which every American was to fall heir. This note was the promise that all men, yes, black men as well as white men would be guaranteed the unalienable rights of life, liberty, and the pursuit of happiness.

It is obvious today that America has defaulted on this promissory note in so far as her citizens of color are concerned. Instead of honoring this sacred obligation, America has given the Negro people a bad check; a check which has come back marked "insufficient funds." We refuse to believe that there are insufficient funds in the great vaults of opportunity of this nation. And so, we've come to cash this check, a check that will give us upon demand the riches of freedom and the security of justice.

We have also come to this hallowed spot to remind America of the fierce urgency of now. This is no time to engage in the luxury of cooling off or to take the tranquilizing drug of gradualism. Now is the time to make real the promises of democracy; now is the time to rise from the dark and desolate valley of segregation to the sunlit path of racial justice; now is the time to make justice a reality for all God's children. It would be fatal for the nation to overlook the urgency of the moment. This sweltering summer of the Negro's legitimate discontent will not pass until there is an invigorating autumn of freedom and equality.

Nineteen sixty-three is not an end, but a beginning. And those who hope that the Negro needed to blow off steam and will now be content, will have a rude awakening if the nation returns to business as usual.

There will be neither rest nor tranquility in America until the Negro is granted his citizenship rights. The whirlwinds of revolt will continue to shake the foundations of our nation until the bright day of justice emerges.

But there is something that I must say to my people who stand on the warm threshold which leads into the palace of justice. In the process of gaining our rightful place we must not be guilty of wrongful deeds.

Let us not seek to satisfy our thirst for freedom by drinking from the cup of bitterness and hatred. We must forever conduct our struggle on the high plane of dignity and discipline. We must not allow our creative protest to degenerate into physical violence. Again, and again we must rise to the majestic heights of meeting physical force with soul force.

The marvelous new militancy which has engulfed the Negro community must not lead us to a distrust of all white people, for many of our white brothers, as evidenced by their presence here today, have come to realize that their destiny is tied up with our destiny and they have come to realize that their freedom is inextricably bound to our freedom. This offense we share mounted to storm the battlements of injustice must be carried forth by a biracial army. We cannot walk alone.

And as we walk, we must make the pledge that we shall always march ahead. We cannot turn back. There are those who are asking the devotees of civil rights, "When will you be satisfied?" We can never be satisfied as long as the Negro is the victim of the unspeakable horrors of police brutality.

We can never be satisfied as long as our bodies, heavy with fatigue of travel, cannot gain lodging in the motels of the highways and the hotels of the cities. We cannot be satisfied as long as the Negro's basic mobility is from a smaller ghetto to a larger one.

We can never be satisfied as long as our children are stripped of their selfhood and robbed of their dignity by signs stating: "for whites only." We cannot be satisfied, as long as a Negro in Mississippi cannot vote, and a Negro in New York believes he has nothing for which to vote. No, we are not satisfied, and we will not be satisfied until justice rolls down like waters, and righteousness like a mighty stream.

I am not unmindful that some of you come here out of excessive trials and tribulation. Some of you have come fresh from narrow jail cells. Some of you have come from areas where your quest for freedom left you battered by the storms of persecution and staggered by the winds of police brutality. You have been the veterans of creative suffering. Continue to work with the faith that unearned suffering is redemptive.

Go back to Mississippi; go back to Alabama; go back to South Carolina; go back to Georgia; go back to Louisiana; go back to the slums and ghettos of the northern cities, knowing that somehow this situation can, and will be changed. Let us not wallow in the valley of despair.

So, I say to you, my friends, that even though we must face the difficulties of today and tomorrow, I still have a dream. It is a dream deeply rooted in the American dream that one day this nation will rise-up and live out the true meaning of its creed— we hold these truths to be self-evident, that all men are created equal.

I have a dream that one day on the red hills of Georgia, sons of former slaves and sons of former slave-owners will be able to sit down together at the table of brotherhood.

I have a dream that one day, even the state of Mississippi, a state sweltering with the heat of injustice, sweltering with the heat of oppression, will be transformed into an oasis of freedom and justice.

I have a dream my four little children will one day live in a nation where they will not be judged by the color of their skin but by the content of their character. I have a dream today!

I have a dream that one day, down in Alabama, with its vicious racists, with its governor having his lips dripping with the words of interposition and nullification, that one day, right there in Alabama, little black boys and black girls will be able to join hands with little white boys and white girls as sister and brothers. I have a dream today!

I have a dream that one day every valley shall be exalted, every hill and mountain shall be made low, the rough places shall be made plain, and crooked places shall be made straight and the glory of the Lord will be revealed, and all flesh shall see it together.

This is our hope. This is the faith that I go back to the south with.

With this faith we will be able to hew out of the mountain of despair a stone of hope. With this faith we will be able to transform the jangling discords of our nation into a beautiful symphony of brotherhood.

With this faith we will be able to work together, to pray together, to struggle together, to go to jail together, to stand up for freedom together, knowing that we will be free one day. This will be the day when all of God's children will be able to sing with new meaning— "my country 'tis of thee; sweet land of liberty; of thee I sing; land where my fathers died, land of the pilgrim's pride;

from every mountain side, let freedom ring"—and if America is to be a great nation this must become true.

So, let freedom ring from the prodigious hilltops of New Hampshire. Let freedom ring from the mighty mountains of New York Let freedom ring from the heightening Alleghenies of Pennsylvania.

Let freedom ring from the snow-capped Rockies of Colorado.

Let freedom ring from the curvaceous slopes of California.

But not only that.

Let freedom ring form Stone Mountain Georgia.

Let freedom ring from Lookout Mountain of Tennessee.

Let freedom ring from every hill and molehill of Mississippi, from every Mountainside, let freedom ring.

And when we allow freedom to ring, when we let it ring from every village and hamlet, from every state and city, we will be able to speed up that day when all of God's children—black men and white men, Jews and Gentiles, Catholics and Protestants—will be able to join hands and to sing in the words of the old Negro spiritual, "Free at last, free at last; thank god Almighty, we are free at last."

Amid a deep sense of religious vocation, the Reverend Martin Luther King would preach his final sermon—say his final words. He would conclude his final public oration as follows:

And so, the first question that the Levite asked was, "If I stop to help this man, what will happen to me?" But then the Good Samaritan came by. And he reversed the question: "If I do not stop to help this man, what will happen to him?"

That's the question before you tonight. Not, "If I stop to help the sanitation workers, what will happen to all of the hours that I usually spend in my office every day and every week as a pastor?" The question is not, "If I stop to help this man in need, what will happen to me?" "If I do not stop to help the sanitation workers, what will happen to them?" That's the question.

Let us rise-up tonight with a greater readiness. Let us stand with a greater determination. And let us move on in these powerful days, these days of challenge to make America what it ought to be. We have an opportunity to make America a better nation. And I want to thank God, once more, for allowing me to be here with you.

You know, several years ago, I was in New York City autographing the first book that I had written. And while sitting there, autographing books, a demented black woman came up. The only question I heard from her was, "Are you Martin Luther King?"

And I was looking down writing, and I said yes. And the next minute I felt something beating on my chest. Before I knew it, I had been stabbed by this demented woman. I was rushed to Harlem Hospital. It was a dark Saturday afternoon. And that blade had gone through, and the X-rays revealed that the tip of the blade was on the edge of my aorta, the main artery. And once that's punctured, you drown in your own blood—that's the end of you.

It came out in the New York Times the next morning, that if I had sneezed, I would have died. Well, about four days later, they allowed me, after the operation, after my chest had been opened, and the blade had been taken out, to move around in the wheelchair in the hospital. They allowed me to read some of the mail that came in, and from all over the states, and the world, kind letters came in. I read a few, but one of them I will never forget. I had received one from the President and the Vice-President. I've forgotten what those telegrams said. I'd received a visit and a letter from the Governor of New York, but I've forgotten what the letter said. But there was another letter that came from a little girl, a young girl who was a student at the White Plains High School.

And I looked at that letter, and I'll never forget it. It said simply, "Dear Dr. King: I am a ninth-grade student at the White Plains High School." She said, "While it should not matter, I would like to mention that I am a white girl. I read in the paper of your misfortune, and of your suffering. And I read that if you had sneezed, you would have died. And I'm simply writing you to say that I'm so happy that you didn't sneeze."

And I want to say tonight, I want to say that I am happy that I didn't sneeze. Because if I had sneezed, I wouldn't have been around here in 1960, when students all over the South started sitting-in at lunch counters. And I knew that as they were sitting in, they were really standing up for the best in the American dream. And taking the whole nation back to those great wells of democracy which were dug deep by the Founding Fathers in the Declaration of Independence and the Constitution. If I had sneezed, I wouldn't have been around in 1962, when Negroes in Albany, Georgia, decided to straighten their backs up. And whenever men and women straighten their backs up, they are going somewhere, because a man can't ride your back unless it is bent. If I had sneezed, I wouldn't have been here in 1963, when the black people of Birmingham, Alabama, aroused the conscience of this nation, and brought into being the Civil Rights Bill. If I had sneezed, I wouldn't have had a chance later that year, in August, to try to tell America about a dream that I had had. If I had sneezed, I wouldn't have been in Memphis to see the community rally around those brothers and sisters who are suffering. I'm so happy that I didn't sneeze.

And they were telling me, now it doesn't matter now. It really doesn't matter what happens now. I left Atlanta this morning, and as we got started on the plane, there were six of us, the pilot said over the public address system, "We are sorry for the delay, but we have Dr. Martin Luther King on the plane. And to be sure that all-of the bags were checked, and to be sure that nothing would be wrong with the plane, we had to check out everything carefully. And we've had the plane protected and guarded all night."

And then I got into Memphis. And some began to say the threats, or talk about the threats that were out; What would happen to me from some of our sick white brothers?

Well, I don't know what will happen now. Because I've been to the mountaintop. And I don't mind. Like anybody, I would like to live a long life. Longevity has its place. But I'm not concerned about that now. I just want to do God's will. And He's allowed me to go up to the mountain. And I've looked over. And I've seen the promised land. I may not get there with you. But I want you to know tonight, that we, as a people, will get to the promised land. And I'm happy, tonight. I'm not worried about anything. I'm not fearing any man. Mine eyes have seen the glory of the coming of the Lord.

JOHN QUINCY ADAMS

A Son

There is neither Jew nor Gentile, neither slave nor free, nor is there male and female, for you are all one in Christ Jesus.

—Galatians 3:28 NIV

John Quincy Adams was the son of John Adams, the second president of the United States. His guiding star was the principle of Puritan statesmanship his father had laid down many years before: "The magistrate is the servant not of his own desires, not even of the people, but of his God."

His father, John, was clearly one of the leading Founders of our country. In an essay, he declared: "… that we should be thrown into existence at a period when the greatest philosophers and law-givers of antiquity would have wished to live … a period when a coincidence of circumstances without example has afforded to thirteen colonies at once an opportunity of beginning government anew from the foundation and building as they choose. How few of the human-race have ever had an opportunity of choosing a system of government for themselves and their children? How few have ever had anything more of choice in government than in climate?"

John Adams looked beyond independence, beyond the outcome of the war, to see what could be established once independence and victory were achieved. Much as he anticipated the hard truth about the war to be waged, Adams had, it is said, the clearest idea of anyone in Congress of what independence would entail: the great difficulties and risks, no less than the opportunities. When arguing cases in court, he liked to state, "… in every-thing one must consider the end."

This could be said to be an example of Prudence, one of the four "pivotal" "cardinal" virtues which all civilized people recognize. Prudence means practical common sense, taking the trouble to think out what you are doing and what is likely to come of it. Altogether, Temperance, Justice, and Fortitude compliment, one another.

"The happiness of the people was the purpose of government," Adams wrote. And since all "sober inquirers after truth" agreed that happiness derived from virtue, that form of government with virtue as its foundation was more likely than any other to promote the general happiness.

In his later writings, Adams recalled stressing certain points repeatedly. Among his words spoken to the Continental Congress in 1776 were these: "We shall be driven to the necessity of declaring ourselves independent and we ought now to be employed in preparing a plan for confederation of the colonies, and treaties to be proposed to foreign power … together with a declaration of independence … Foreign powers cannot be expected to acknowledge us, till we have acknowledged ourselves and taken our station among them as a sovereign power, and independent nation." His words, at times, were interposed with a tap of a cane.

In his writings, John Adams would add to his thoughts on the simplicity of government. "Government is a plain, simple, intelligent thing, founded in nature and reason, quite comprehensible by common sense … The true source of our suffering has been our timidity. We have been afraid to think … Let us dare to read, think, speak, and write … Let it be known that British liberties are not the grants of princes or parliaments … that many of our rights are the inherent and essential, agreed on as maxims and established as preliminaries, even before

Parliament existed ... Let us read and recollect and impress upon our souls the views and ends of our more immediate forefathers ... Let us recollect it was liberty, the hope of liberty, for themselves and us and ours, which conquered all discouragements, dangers, and trials."

John Adams called on his readers to exercise independence of thought—to use their own minds. "And liberty cannot be preserved without a general knowledge among the people who have a right from the frame of their nature to knowledge, as their great Creator who does nothing in vain, has given them understandings and a desire to know. But besides this they have a right, an indisputable, unalienable, indefeasible divine right to the most dreaded and envied kind of knowledge, I mean of the characters and conduct of their rulers"

John Adams, when considering his calling as a young man, said, "The point is now determined, and I shall have the liberty to think for myself."

And for John Adams, a father of our country, what of Adams's father? John said that his father was "the honestest man" he ever knew. "In wisdom, piety, benevolence and charity in proportion to his education and sphere of life, I have never known his superior." John Adams said his father's honesty, independent spirit, and love of country were his lifelong inspiration.

And what of Abigail, wife of John and mother to John Quincy? Intelligence and wit shone in her. She was consistently cheerful. She loved conversation quite as much as did John. She was in all respects his equal, and the part she would play in American history and as a mother of our country was unforeseen. It is said that John Adams's marriage to Abigail Smith was the most important decision of his life. During the Adams administration, Abigail was sometimes referred to as "Mrs. President." Some years before his marriage to Abigail, John had thoughtfully written, "Ballast is what I want. I totter, with every breeze. My motions are unsteady." Abigail would become that ballast.

Abigail wrote long letters from home in 1776. She wrote lucidly of her own feelings about all that was transpiring in Philadelphia and all that it would mean for "our country". Among her thoughts to John in that First Congress—and John understood well her thinking on the subject—were these: "I wish sincerely there was not a slave in the province. It always seemed a most iniquitous scheme to me—[to] fight ourselves for what we are daily robbing and plundering from those who have as good a right to freedom as we have."

As she saw the British fleet sail out from Boston harbor, the buoyancy of spring was transforming. She experienced an uncommon *"gaiety de Coeur,"* she wrote. "I think the sun shines brighter; the birds sing more melodiously." She longed to hear word of independence declared. Her spirit took flight at the thought.

Both John and Abigail regarded the upbringing of children as a sacred and solemn obligation. John wrote Abigail in 1775, stating, "It should be your care, therefore, and mine, to elevate the minds of our children and exalt their courage; to accelerate and animate their industry and activity; to excite in them a habitual contempt of meanness, abhorrence of injustice and inhumanity, and an ambition to excel in every capacity, faculty and virtue."

For a child—for John and Abigail—the building blocks to the intellect began with the building blocks of morality. Goodness, usefulness, and happiness then became attainable.

In one of her letters to her husband, Abigail explained why she had decided not to send Johnny to Braintree's primary school. "I have always thought it of very great importance that children should in the early part of life be unaccustomed to such examples as would tend to corrupt the purity of their words and actions that they may chill with horror at the sound of an oath, and blush with indignation at an obscene expression." Although often apart, John and Abigail were always together. Their correspondence was frequent. John wrote to her. "If I could write as well as you, my sorrows would be as eloquent as yours, but upon my Word I cannot."

Abigail, well read, spent long hours reading to her son. She also enlisted one of Adam's law clerks to work as John Quincy's tutor. Abigail made clear her preferences when she described education as "rearing the tender thought."

As the poet observes:

> Each Boistrous passion to control
> And early Humanize the Soul
> The noblest Notions to inspire,
> Her offspring conscious of her care
> Transported hang around her chair

Abigail also wrote, "Great events are most certainly in the womb of futurity."

On the morning of June 17, 1775, John Quincy Adams walked with his mother, Abigail, to an orchard atop Penn's Hill. There, at dawn, the British forces had begun their cannonade of Bunker Hill. John Adams was three hundred miles away at the Continental Congress. So much depended on this long-awaited battle that Abigail wished to see it for herself.

John Quincy, not quite eight years old, would see for himself the mortal consequences of the fight his father and his fellow colonists had undertaken. Even from ten miles distant they could see the flash of cannon fire from the British ships in the harbor. The noise was deafening. Bunker Hill was the opening of a war. Every night during these months, his mother instructed him to repeat, along with the Lord's Prayer, an ode to martyred soldiers written by the British poet William Collins: "How sleep the brave who sink to rest / By all their country's wishes blest!"

In late November 1777, John Adams finally came home. He was prepared to resume the legal career he had left four years earlier. General Washington won a smashing victory over Burgoyne at Saratoga. American prospects had begun to look less dim than the year before, but the British had vast advantages over the Americans. Victory seemed impossible without foreign—that is, French—help. The Continental Congress asked John Adams to go to France to replace Silas Deane, who had been negotiating for assistance and recognition of American sovereignty, along with Benjamin Franklin and Arthur Lee Jr. John

Quincy implored his father to let him come with. Amid the dangers, John would relent.

John Quincy Adams would become minister to the Netherlands at the age of twenty-seven under President George Washington; minister to Prussia under President John Adams; a Massachusetts legislator; a United States senator from Massachusetts; minister to Russia under President James Madison; a member of the delegation that signed the Treaty of Ghent, ending the War of 1812; minister to the United Kingdom, also in the Madison administration; and US secretary of state under President James Monroe.

John Quincy Adams was elected as the sixth president of the United States, serving from March 4, 1825, to March 4, 1829.

John Quincy Adams would be the first and only former president to be elected to the United States House of Representatives, serving from March 4, 1831, till February 23, 1848. John Quincy was imbued with the belief that the United States is the greatest experiment in government the world has ever known.

As John Fitzgerald Kennedy would write, "The story of the son is not wholly separable from the story of the father." John Quincy Adams was, as Samuel Eliot Morison described him, "above all an Adams." The Adams' regard for a truth higher than themselves exemplified an example of steadfast loyalty to principles. It was also said of John Quincy that, although he would be one of the most talented men to ever serve his nation, he had few of the personal characteristics which ordinarily gave color and charm to personality.

The Adams' displayed undeviating devotion to the public interest. One example of this: After returning home from diplomatic service abroad, John Quincy was elected to the Massachusetts Legislature as a Federalist. Within two days of his election, without consulting his senior colleagues, he proposed that the Republican (Jeffersonian, or Democratic) Party be allowed proportional representation on the governor's council. John Quincy later noted that this act of nonpartisan independence "marked the principle by which [his] whole public life [had] been governed from that day to this."

This same state legislature would later select the young John Quincy Adams for the US Senate. In his diary, he noted that "the qualities of mind most peculiarly called for are firmness, perseverance, patience, coolness and forbearance."

Loyalty to party and the more customary freshman reticence would not be the approach of John Quincy Adams. He became the only Federalist to support President Jefferson's treaty for the purchase of the Louisiana Territory, voting for the unprecedented $11 million appropriation. The remarkable treaty excluded Napoleon and France from the continent and stretched America's continental limits. He considered this to be more important than the disapproval of his Federalist colleagues.

In his diary, the young Adams summed up his first months in the Senate in this way:

> I have already had occasion to experience, which I had before the fullest reason to expect, the danger of adhering to my own principles. The country is so totally given up to the spirit of party that not to follow blindfolded the one or the other is an expiable offence ... Between both, I see the impossibility of pursuing the dictates of my own conscience without sacrificing every prospect, not merely of advancement, but even of retaining that character and reputation I have enjoyed. Yet my choice is made, and, if I cannot hope to give satisfaction to my country, I am at least determined to have the approbation of my own reflections.

(Writer's note: Hear, Hear John Quincy—thou hast spoken well. May ye keep your courage and convictions to the blessings of our land. Ah, but that we today should have but one or two John Quincy Adams, then how much better the conscience and direction of the country today!)

History goes forward, and relations with Great Britain would get worse and not better. Ships were seized at sea, and their cargoes were confiscated. Our seamen, by the hundreds—and by some estimates, the thousands—were "imprisoned" and compelled to serve on British cruising vessels. American merchant ships simply drifted and were lost at sea after their crews were forced to abandon them. The Federalist merchants, however, felt their only recourse was to appease the British as they didn't have the means to defend their ships.

John Quincy Adams, on the other hand, introduced resolutions condemning the British for their unlawful actions. The resolutions requested that President Jefferson demand the British indemnify and restore the harmed merchants. The administration, in turn, put forward a bill that would limit British imports, and Adams supported the measures. Tensions between America and Britain, continued, on their escalating path. The President called on Congress to enact an embargo of British goods. John Quincy threw his support in favor of the embargo. By so doing, he had stepped off the plank of Federalist support and was thereby replaced as a senator before the expiration of his term. John SR supported John Quincy in his actions, irrespective of the fact that it was Jefferson who had defeated SR in his bid for a second term as President.

As secretary of state under President James Monroe, John Quincy Adams was rather astute in his views of foreign policy and America's interests, differentiating the two. His knowledge and understanding were deftly applied to the Monroe formulation of the Monroe Doctrine. Adams wisely considered the powers as England, France, Spain, and Russia and their interests in the Americas. He, like the initial Founders, was wary of "entangling alliances" and cautious of the perceived European drift to Despotism. For example, Adams interpreted Russian support for King Ferdinand and the Spanish Throne over any expressions of republicanism as an "Io Triomphe' over the fallen cause of revolution, with sturdy promises to keep it down." The doctrines gave expression to an "American sphere of influence."

Now Adams was not an elected official. Like his mother Abigail, he despised slavery and the hypocrisy surrounding it. Listening to the orations of the day, he wrote, "If but one man could arise with a Genius capable of comprehending, a heart capable of supporting and an utterance capable of communicating those eternal truths that belong to this question, to lay bare in all its nakedness that outrage upon the goodness of God, human slavery, now is the time, and this is the occasion which such a man would perform the duties of an Angel upon Earth." Not charismatic and somewhat stiff in demeanor, he dreamed of someone to champion the efforts. He would eventually become a champion.

Within his orations given on July 4, John Quincy Adams always read the Declaration of Independence. He would rise to the occasion, commending Jefferson's great work as "a beacon on the summit of the mountain, to which all the inhabitants of the earth may turn their eyes for a genial and saving light, till time shall be lost in eternity, and this globe itself dissolve, nor leave a wreck behind." The British press of the time had been running articles on the theme "What has America done for mankind?" Adams provided the answer to this impertinent question: It had "proclaimed to mankind the inextinguishable rights of human nature, and the only lawful foundations of government." The Declaration "had demolished at a stroke the lawfulness of all governments founded upon conquest."

Abolitionist sentiment had been growing. Early in 1823, the House of Representatives had overwhelmingly passed a resolution calling upon the president to negotiate a treaty "for the effectual abolition of the African slave trade, and its ultimate denunciation, as piracy, under the law of nations, by the consent of the civilized world." As secretary of state, Adams wrote out a draft of the treaty that was signed. However, provisions of it were exempted, causing the better part of two years of work by Adams to come to naught.

John Quincy Adams was elected to the presidency by a vote from the House of Representatives. He received votes over the likes of Henry Clay and Andrew Jackson. His father, John Adams, said of his son's election, "Never did I feel so much solemnity as upon this occasion." John Quincy later wrote that he knew his time in office would not be "a bed of roses." Adams's nervousness showed as he was sworn into office. Justice Joseph Story wrote to his wife that the president-elect "trembled so as barely to hold his papers" but, at the same time, "he spoke with prodigious force, and his sensibility had an electrical effect."

President Adams would stake out his course in the ideal of nonpartisanship. In his view of the office of the presidency, it would not be one of party-building, but rather of building unified public policy. The Constitution had not provided for political parties. He would consider it his moral imperative to make nonpartisan appointments within his administration.

Some of Adams's objectives were national union, tariff protections, internal improvements, encouraging manufacturing, and improving the navy. The Erie Canal was completed at the end of 1825, and the citizenry showed a strong interest in the designs of additional internal improvements. John Quincy also had conversation about the topic of what, years later, would become the Panama Canal.

In his first State of the Union address, Adams submitted goals for a Pacific exploratory expedition, an astronomical observatory, and a naval academy. In his closing, he would remind the representatives of the people that human beings are here on this earth to improve themselves, society, and the earth on which they live. He added that the point of government was "the improvement of the condition of those who are parties to the social compact." This was to be seen as not only a physical, but a "moral, political, and intellectual improvement." It would be America's turn to lead, to cultivate and enlighten the homeland, to make progress toward improvements and union, and to build a better future by building on the achievements of the past.

His Administration was invited to send delegates to the congress of South American countries to be held in Panama. Amid opposition, Adams's nominees were narrowly confirmed in 1826. The participation would bolster the idea of the Monroe Doctrine as well as defend South American independence. Besides fostering a friendly spirit between North and South America, it could also promote trade, encourage religious liberty, and look for cooperation in suppressing the slave trade.

Such were the times that John Quincy Adams had no staff. His son John acted as his secretary. There was no one to screen visitors. Adams believed he was obliged to meet with any citizen who took the trouble to reach his doorstep. His reading load was backbreaking. It was often midnight before he extinguished his candle. Henry Clay, clearly a man of the politics of the day (and who had run against Adams), became a part of the administration. The extroverted Henry Clay wrote to a friend that he had begun to rise early, "but not so early as the president." Clay determined that he rather enjoyed working with the man he had so long considered an ill-tempered puritan. Unlike the discord dividing Monroe's cabinet in his second term, cabinet members openly discussed their disagreements. Eventually the workload took a toll on Clay's health, and he asked the president to let him step down.

John Quincy Adams would rise as early as four o'clock in the morning and go for his daily walks "between the peep of dawn and sunrise." "I rise from bed, dress myself, and sally forth from my door in darkness and solitude."

John Quincy Adams was a distinguished servant of the nation from a most distinguished family. By the measures of the republican politics of the day, he would be the last of those early servants of the nation to rise to the presidency. Perhaps feeling misunderstood, he would not and could not compete with the rising democratic politics of the day and Andrew Jackson.

Not long after Adams's presidency ended, he and Louisa found themselves in prayer once again over the loss of a second child. For all the public recognition we may have of public personages, their private lives and concerns can nearly overwhelm them, as indeed may our own.

After leaving the White House in 1829, Adams hoped to write a biography of his father. He was approached by the citizens of the District of Plymouth. Would he consider representing the District in the House of Representatives? With John Quincy's absolute love of country, he agreed to run if he could remain independent, if he were not expected to campaign, and if the positions and courses he would pursue within Congress would be reserved for his best judgement. John Quincy Adams was overwhelmingly elected to Congress. He also became known as "old man eloquent" and as "the astutest, the archest enemy of Southern Slavery that ever existed." "Territory was inanimate. It was matter. Man had an immortal soul—man had rights peculiar to himself, and they could not, without his consent, transfer man from one country to another," said John Quincy Adams.

In his diary Adams wrote, "I am a member-elect of the Twenty-Second Congress. No election or appointment conferred upon me ever gave me so much pleasure. My election as President of the United States was not half so gratifying to my inmost soul."

As early as his first term in Congress, there was talk of nullification of law and of secession. The result of this would be no less than the end of the founding fathers' vision, and the ideals of the Declaration of Independence would be betrayed. It would be, in Adams's words, a "calamity to all." Adams referred to the words Daniel Webster spoke, "Were the breath which now gives utterance to my feelings the last vital air I should draw, my expiring words to you and your children should be, independence and union forever!"

John Quincy, in his readings of history, would comparatively mention the political tools of violence in the twelfth century as "not exactly congenial with the manners of our own age and country." A twenty-five-year-old Alexis de Tocqueville interviewed Adams in 1832. Adams was plain and direct in his responses. "There are two facts which have had a great influence on our character. In the North, the political and religious doctrines of the founders of New England; in the South, slavery." Tocqueville asked, "Do you look on slavery as a great plague for the United States?" Adams answered, "Yes, certainly. That is the root of almost all the troubles of the present and fears for the future." De Tocqueville went on to ask John Quincy about "the immediate dangers to the Union and the causes which might lead to its dissolution." Alexis de Tocqueville did not receive a verbal answer but summed up the response in this manner: "Mr. Adams did not answer at all, but it was easy to see that in this matter he felt no more confidence in the future than I did."

In 1834, the Marquis de Lafayette, integral to the birth of America's independence, passed-away. A tribute was given in Congress. Adams spoke to the truth rather than to the French diplomatic delegation at the ceremony. He noted that no two people more unfit to occupy the thrones of Great Britain and France could have been found than the

German George II, who was ignorant of the customs and language of the English, and the infant Louis XV. Adams went on to say, "Yet, strange as it may sound to the ear of unsophisticated reason, the British nation were wedded to the belief that ... fixing their Crown upon the heads of this succession of total strangers, was the brightest and most glorious exemplification of their national freedom." He explained that Lafayette's principles "were in advance of the age and hemisphere in which he lived ... The principle of hereditary power was, in his opinion, the bane of all republican liberty in Europe." Adams went on to say that the genius of Lafayette was his love of liberty and where it came from and that it could only be understood as the inalienable right to life, liberty, and the pursuit of happiness that was the birthright of every human being. Adams concluded that when France was once again a republic and the people themselves the repository of national authority, then it would be "the time for contemplating the character of Lafayette, not merely in the events of his life, but in the full development of his intellectual conceptions, of his fervent aspirations, of the labors and perils and sacrifices of his long and eventful career upon earth."

Adams submitted and forwarded numerous petitions from his District for the abolition of slavery. In 1835 and 1836, he urged the House to maintain the right of petition. "The right of petition is well known and understood; it is a sacred right." There came into effect a gag rule whereby slave petitions would not be allowed. In one instance, when Adams was cut off from debate, he exploded and said, "Am I being gagged or am I not?" The argument for Adams was, that even the consideration of admitting new states into the union as slave states, was a violation of the constitution.

To dig into the rules, he also presented papers said to be signed by slaves, themselves. Up for the controversy, Adams continued to defend the rights of the individual slave.

On February 9, 1837, John Quincy Adams held the floor of Congress for the entire day. "Let that gentleman, let every member of this house, ask his own heart, with what confidence, with what boldness, with what freedom, with what firmness, he would give utterance to his opinions on this floor, if, for every word, for a mere question asked of the speaker, involving a question belonging to human need, to the rights of man, he was liable to be tried as a felon or an incendiary, and sent to the penitentiary!" The next day, the House resolved, that slaves did not have the right of petition.

On February 25, 1839, Adams proposed a constitutional amendment "abolishing hereditary slavery in the United States, prohibiting admission of new slave states, and abolishing slavery and the slave trade in the District of Columbia."

John Quincy composed a letter to his constituents. It was a "Petition of Prayer." "It was the cry of the suffering for relief, of the oppressed for mercy. It was what God did not disdain to receive from man, whom he had created; and to listen to prayer—to hearken to the groan of wretchedness—was not merely a duty; it was a privilege; it was enjoyment; it was the exercise of a godlike attribute, indulged to the kindly sympathies of man. I would therefore not deny the right of petition to slaves—I would not deny it to a horse or a dog, if they could articulate their sufferings, and I could relieve them."

Adams expressed to his fellows that "we are told that the national government has no right to interfere with the institution of domestic slavery in the state, in any manner. What right, then, has domestic slavery to interfere in any manner with the national government? What right has slavery to interfere in the free states with the dearest institutions of their freedom? With the right of habeas corpus? With the right of trial by jury? With the freedom of the press? With the freedom of speech? With the sacred privacy of correspondence by the mail? Would the freemen of Massachusetts, the descendants of the Pilgrims allow themselves to be manacled? Children of Carver, and Bradford, and Winslow and Alden! The pen drops from my hand!"

In another speech, speaking of the message of Protestant Christianity—of which he was familiar and from which he learned—he said, "He came to teach, and not to compel. His Law was a Law of Liberty. He left the human mind and human action free." Adams spoke of the Founders and said that they "spoke of the laws of Nature, and in the name of Nature's God; and by that sacred adjuration, they pledged us, their children, to labor with united and concerted energy from the cradle to the grave, to rid the earth of all slavery."

On February 21, 1848, John Quincy Adams collapsed in Congress. Just before his collapse, another vote in agreement with Adams was cast by Abraham Lincoln.

At the behest of the Massachusetts delegation, Daniel Webster inscribed the following words: "John Quincy Adams / born an inhabitant of Massachusetts July 11, 1767 / Died a citizen of the United States, in the Capitol, at Washington, February 23, 1848 / Having served his country for half a century; And enjoyed its highest honors."

The House appointed a committee of arrangements to prepare for the funeral. Of the thirty members on this committee was a freshman congressman from Illinois, Abraham Lincoln.

Perhaps we may listen, ever so briefly, to a small segment of a speech given by our John Quincy Adams. What has the United States as a nation contributed to civilization?

In the words of John Quincy, "It demolished at a stroke the lawfulness of all governments founded upon conquest. It swept away all the rubbish of accumulated centuries of servitude. It announced in practical form to the world the transcendent truth of the unalienable sovereignty of the people. It proved that the social compact was no figment of the imagination but a real, solid, and sacred bond of the social union."

Further, "Her glory is not dominion, but liberty. Her march is the march of mind. She has a spear and a shield; but the motto upon her shield, Freedom, Independence, Peace."

BOOKER T. WASHINGTON

An Example

One of the questions that come to mind when thinking of the life of Booker T. Washington would be; How did he do it?

Washington was either born in the year 1858 or 1859. His earliest memories were of the plantation and the slave quarters. "My life had its beginning in the midst of the most miserable, desolate, and discouraging surroundings. This was so, however, not because my owners were especially cruel, for they were not, as compared with many others. I was born in a typical log cabin, about fourteen by sixteen feet square. In this cabin I lived with my mother and a brother and sister till after the Civil War, when we were all declared free." Booker T. Washington wrote this description of his early childhood in his book *Up From Slavery*.

Booker recalled being asked a question. "I was asked not long ago to tell something about the sports and pastimes that I engaged in during my youth. Until that question was asked it had never occurred to me that there was no period of my life that was devoted to play. From the time that I can remember anything, almost every day of my life had been occupied in some kind of labour; though I think I would now be a more useful man if I had time for sports. During the period that I spent in slavery I was not large enough to be of much service, still I was occupied most of the time in cleaning the yards, carrying water to the men in the fields, or going to the mill to which I used to take the corn, once a week, to be ground."

"So far as I can now recall, the first knowledge that I got of the fact that we were slaves, and that freedom of the slaves was being discussed, was early one morning before day, when I was awakened by my mother kneeling over her children and fervently praying that Lincoln and his armies might be successful, and that one day she and her children might be free." One day, rumors from the grapevine began flying through the cabins of the slaves and on the Burroughs's plantation. One morning, it happened, a stranger who represented the Union stood among them and read the Emancipation. This would be an unforgettable moment seared into Booker T. Washington's memory. His mother slowly began crying in near utter disbelief. With tears and hugs, "she explained to us what it all meant," remembered Washington.

There was wild rejoicing before a more somber tone emerged. "In a few hours, the great questions with which the Anglo-Saxon race had been grappling for centuries had been thrown upon these people to be solved. These were questions of a home, a living, the rearing of children, education, citizenship, and the establishment and support of churches," wrote Booker.

It was thereafter that the family moved to Malden, West Virginia, to join their stepfather working at the salt works. Booker and his older brother John often began their workdays as early as four o'clock in the morning. After they packed salt into barrels for the day, a foreman identified the barrels with the number 18. Booker wrote that number for practice, and this was the first writing experience of his life. His mother purchased Webster's blue book speller for him, but as literacy had not been legal to learn, it was to no avail.

Booker wished, more than anything, to learn to read. "From the time that I can remember having any thoughts about anything, I recall that I had an intense longing to learn to read." His mother surely helped him. "Though she was totally ignorant, she had high ambitions for her children, and a large fund of good, hard, common sense, which seemed to enable her to meet and master every situation. If I have done anything in life worth attention, I feel sure that I inherited the disposition from my mother."

A young black man from Ohio, where educating blacks was not illegal, became a popular newcomer in Malden. He would audibly read the newspapers at the end of the workday. Booker became a regular listener. Soon afterward, Lewis Davis, another black Ohioan, arrived in town and agreed to set up a school. Families raised money and took turns boarding him.

Reverend Lewis Rice volunteered to turn his home into a schoolhouse. One Sabbath, Booker and some friends were playing marbles on the street. Along happened Reverend Lewis. He knelt down to talk with them. After that, Booker began attending Sunday Service. His family decided to join him.

As much as Booker longed to attend the new school, his stepfather needed him at the salt furnaces. He was later overjoyed to hear that Davis planned to open a night school. As long, as the workday was, Booker was animated to begin the evening school class. Later his stepfather allowed him to attend day classes if he worked from four o'clock to nine o'clock in the morning and after school. "There was never a time in my youth, no matter how dark and discouraging the days might be, when one resolve did not continually remain with me, and that was a determination to secure an education at any cost."

Finally, the salt industry declined. Booker was reassigned to a coal mine at the ripe old age of ten. He took his blue-backed speller into the mine with him and read by lamplight whenever he could.

One day at work, he overheard that the mine owner's wife was looking for a new houseboy. A northerner, she was known to be rather meticulous and fastidious. Booker overcame his initial fear of Mrs. Ruffner and came to like the sense of order she maintained within the house. Mrs. Ruffner also maintained a small library, and she provided young Booker with some books for his own.

Eventually Booker would move into the well-ordered house. The Ruffners' trust in Booker grew, and he would manage a big vegetable garden, selling the surplus vegetables in town. Booker began to experience his first feelings of success.

Viola Ruffner noticed a "particular determination to emerge from obscurity" in young Booker. He had heard about Hampton Normal and

Agricultural Institute while working in the coal mines. It was a school for poor but worthy students. Should he consider leaving some day for Hampton, which was some distance away, he feared that he may not see his mother again. Booker later wrote that she feared he might be wasting his time and money on a wild goose chase.

The kindness shown to young Booker by his fellow townspeople overwhelmed him. They would drop by the Ferguson family cabin with their coins and other gifts that might help him on his way to a brighter future.

In the fall of 1872, young Booker boarded the Chesapeake & Ohio Railroad in Charleston. He had no idea the distance to the Hampton Institute, near Newport News on the James River, was upward of five hundred miles. He ran out of money. His travel on foot was occasionally relieved by kindhearted conductors. At the end of the line, a stagecoach met passengers for their journeys east.

After the long ride on the stagecoach, the coach finally reached the Appalachians. All, of the passengers then lined up for a room at the hotel. However, to his modest surprise, Booker was not allowed a room and spent a chilly night walking just to keep warm. He said, "This was my first experience in finding out what the colour of my skin meant. My whole soul was so bent upon reaching Hampton that I did not have time to cherish any bitterness toward the hotel-keeper."

Eventually Booker made it to Richmond, once the capital of the Confederacy and about eighty miles or so from Hampton. After weeks of traveling hundreds of miles over terrain he had never seen, Booker now stood at the gates of Hampton. He thought to himself, "It seemed to me to be the largest and most beautiful building I had ever seen. The sight of it seemed to give me new life. I felt that a new kind of existence had now begun—that life would now have a new meaning. I felt that I had reached the promised land, and I resolved to let no obstacle prevent me from putting forth the highest effort to fit myself to accomplish the most-good in the world." He later thought, "If the people who gave the money to provide that building could appreciate the influence the sight of it had upon me, as well as upon thousands of other youths, they would feel all the more encouraged to make such gifts."

Finally, Booker had arrived—but he had not been admitted to Hampton. Mary Mackie, a stern New Yorker in charge of assigning students to classes was unimpressed with his appearance. Looking up from processing other applicants' admissions, she said to Booker that the adjoining room needed sweeping and to "take the broom and sweep it." Owing to his cleaning experience with Mrs. Ruffner, this assignment was right in his wheelhouse. Miss Mackie was impressed with his cleaning and respectfully said, "I guess you will do to enter this institution." This is said to be the most joyful moment of Booker's life. He was one of the youngest students enrolled. He was also offered a job as a janitor.

General Samuel Chapman Armstrong was the founder and president of Hampton Institute. Born to missionary parents in the Hawaiian Islands, Armstrong moved to the United States in 1860. He stated that to "build up character is the true objective point in education."

Armstrong had enlisted in the Union Army and had assumed command of the 9th US Colored Troops. With the war over, so much suddenly fell on the shoulders of these newly freed citizens: voting, owning property, serving on juries, swearing depositions, and more. Naturally, with his military training, order, discipline, responsibility, and a busy schedule were top learning priorities at Hampton. Coeducation was also a part of the mix, with separate dormitories. Of the general and older, dedicated students Booker encountered, he later said, "The older I grow, the more I am convinced that there is no education which one can get from books and costly apparatus that

is equal to that which can be gotten from contact with great men and women. Instead of studying books so constantly, how I wish that our schools and colleges might learn to study men and things!"

Booker T. Washington further added, "The education that I received at Hampton out of the text-books was but a small part of what I learned there. One of the things that impressed itself upon me deeply, the second year, was the unselfishness of the teachers. It was hard for me to understand how any individuals could bring themselves to the point where they could be so happy in working for others. Before the end of the year, I think I began learning that those who are happiest are those who do the most for others. This lesson I have tried to carry with me ever since."

Booker struggled over what he should do with his life. One of his teachers remembered that "to help his people was uppermost in his thoughts." Booker at one point wanted to be a lawyer, and he also explored the idea of becoming a minister. Miss Nathalie Lord suggested that Booker set aside fifteen minutes each day to read the Bible. They and a couple of classmates met daily in a classroom to read to each other. "Perhaps the most valuable thing that I got out of my second year was an understanding of the use and value of the Bible," reflected Booker.

Booker participated in the Hampton debate societies and became one of the outstanding speechwriters. Modest in nature, his speech was both natural and personable. His gift of observation produced inside jokes and wry remarks. "The debating societies at Hampton were a constant source of delight to me."

At first, Booker had not thought much of manual training education, but as the years passed, he changed his mind. "I not only learned that it was not a disgrace to labour, but learned to love labour, not alone for its financial value, but for labour's own sake and for the independence and self-reliance which the ability to do something which the world wants done brings." He also observed that "the happiest individuals are those who do the most to make others useful and happy." In sum, "Amid Christian influences I was surrounded by an atmosphere of business, and a spirit of self-help that seemed to awaken every faculty in me and cause me for the first time to realize what it means to be a man instead of a piece of property."

Booker Washington returned to Malden to find a teaching position at the black school in Tinkersville waiting for him. Booker would carry forward all the discipline learned at Hampton. Beginning early each morning, his days would normally extend until late in the evenings. Good manners, personal cleanliness, punctuality—all, of the appearances and disciplines he had learned at Hampton, he would pass on to his students. To Booker, more than "mere book education" was required in-order to succeed. Without an assistant, Booker would teach up to two hundred students every day. He also opened a night school. He introduced a debate society and taught Sunday school. The two years Booker taught at Malden were said to be some of the happiest of his life.

Booker would enter Wayland Seminary in Washington, DC. He would later leave DC and reconsider the prospect of a career in politics or law. General Armstrong invited him to speak at the Hampton commencement. There, at Hampton, Booker continued teaching. The chairman of a board of commissioners charged with starting a school for blacks wrote the general looking for a qualified white man to serve as principal. General Armstrong had been impressed with Booker Washington on many levels. In the general's reply, he wrote that the only man he could suggest was "one Booker T. Washington ..." The reply telegram from Tuskegee read, "Booker Washington will do. Send him."

When Booker Taliaferro Washington stepped off the train on a June day in 1881, he would need to assess the entire situation for himself. The conditions were generally poor in the rural countryside, but he wrote that "there were many encouraging exceptions to the conditions which I have described." Booker being Booker, he drew a sense of optimism from the promising students he encountered and from the church congregations he visited. He also noted some history of local interracial cooperation to be found in Tuskegee, so work would begin. A location was found at the Zion Church to begin a school.

In a later reflection of this time, Booker reflected the following:

> In the midst of all the difficulties which I encountered in getting the little school started, and since then through a period of nineteen years, there are two men among the many friends of the school in Tuskegee upon whom I have depended constantly for advice and guidance; and the success of the undertaking is largely due to these men, from whom I have never sought anything in vain. I mention them simply as types. One is a white man and an ex-slaveholder, Mr. George W. Campbell; the other is a black man and an ex-slave, Mr. Lewis Adams.

These were the men who wrote to General Armstrong for a teacher.

Mr. Campbell is a merchant, and banker, and had little experience in dealing with matters pertaining to education. Mr. Adams was a mechanic, and had learned the trades of shoemaking, harness-making, and tinsmithing during the days of slavery. He had never been to school a day in his life, but in some way, he had learned to read and write while a slave. From the first, these two men saw clearly what my plan of education was, sympathized with me, and supported me in every effort. In the days which were darkest financially for the school, Mr. Campbell was never appealed to when he was not willing to extend all the aid in his power. I do not know two men, one an ex-slaveholder, one an ex-slave, whose advice and judgment I would feel more like following in everything which concerns the life and development of the school at Tuskegee than those of these two men.

The church would only be temporary. Traveling the countryside, Washington found an ideal location. When arriving in Tuskegee, he did not anticipate building a school, but Booker T. Washington always led by example. He located an old hundred-acre plantation called the Burnt Farm, because the house had been burned to the ground years before and never rebuilt. It had been owned by a Confederate veteran. The first order of business was repairing buildings. A great deal of work needed to be done in clearing land and in building and constructing. He and some initially reticent students all pitched in with the building and constructing.

Booker said, "Nearly all the work of getting the new location ready for school purposes was done by the students after school was over in the afternoon." In further reflecting on the school's progress, "The first animal that the school came into possession of was an old blind horse … Perhaps, I may add here that at the present time the school owns over two hundred horses, colts, mules, cows, calves, and oxen, and about seven hundred hogs and pigs, as well as a large number of sheep and goats." In sum, "In all our difficulties and anxieties, however, I never went to a white or a black person in the town of Tuskegee for any assistance that was in their power to render, without being helped according to their means."

A legislative act appropriating money for teachers for a free school for blacks in Tuskegee was approved and then signed by the governor on Abraham Lincoln's birthday, February 12, 1881. Booker was invited to return to Hampton by General Armstrong to deliver a Commencement "post-graduate address." His faith as a Christian had carried him through many crises and disappointments in life. Strongly nondenominational, he read his Bible every day and held prayer in his classroom twice a day.

In 1882, Booker T. Washington raised funds for permanent buildings on the new campus. The cornerstone was laid on the last day of class. The ceremony was well attended by the local, residents, both black and white. Reverend C. C. Petty spoke, "I thank God for what I have witnessed today, something I never saw before, nor did I ever expect to see it. I have seen one who but yesterday was one of our owners, today lay the cornerstone of a building dedicated to the education of my race. For such a change let us all thank God."

Concluding his efforts, Washington, too, spoke to the supporting crowd, saying that only a few years before, "no Negro could be taught from books without the teacher receiving the condemnation of the law or of public sentiment ... About the corner stone were gathered the teachers, the students, their parents, and friends, the county officials—who were white—and all the leading white men in that vicinity, together with many of the black men and women whom these same white people but a few years before had held a title to as property."

All present then joined in singing the following:

> Praise God from whom all blessings flow,
> Praise Him all creatures here below,
> Praise Him above ye heavenly host,
> Praise Father, Son and Holy Ghost.

Later, reflecting on the growth and accomplishments realized, Booker wrote,

> During the now nineteen years' existence of the Tuskegee school, the plan of having the buildings erected by student labour has been adhered to. In this time forty buildings, counting small and large, have been built, and all except four are almost wholly the product of student labour. As an additional result, hundreds of men are now scattered throughout the South who received their knowledge of mechanics while being taught how to erect these buildings. Skill and knowledge are now handed down from one set of students to another in this way, until at the present time a building of any description or size can be constructed wholly by our instructors and students, from the drawing of the plans to the putting in of the electric fixtures, without going off the grounds for a single workman.

After much trial and error, "brickmaking has now become such an important industry at the school that last season our students manufactured twelve hundred thousand of first-class bricks … The same principal of industrial education has been carried out in the building of our own wagons, carts, and buggies … we help supply the local market with these vehicles."

Booker T. Washington addressed the National Education Association in 1884. He was roundly applauded after giving an impressive speech on the topic of black education. Unfortunately, a tide of confusing segregation was starting to form. By 1890, some of the southern white members looked to form a separate association. Booker discreetly began consulting with legal advisors, editors, and others to see what might be done to diffuse the rising tide.

The 1894 Cotton States and International Exposition, a major event, was held in Atlanta. Booker T. Washington was invited as a guest speaker. He went to Washington to speak to and lobby the US

Appropriations Committee for funding of the event. He assisted in successfully persuading an appropriation of $200,000.

> Booker T. Washington was then scheduled to be a keynote speaker for the opening ceremonies. He would be the first black speaker ever scheduled to speak at the prestigious event. No guidelines were given for the speech by the exposition. He would need to swing a safe hit. He said, I was also painfully conscious of the fact that, while I must be true to my own race in my utterances, I had it in my power to make such an ill-timed address as would result in preventing any similar invitation being extended to a black man again for years to come. I was equally determined to be true to the North, as well as to the best element of the white South, in what I had to say.

On the morning of September 17, Booker and his third wife, Maggie, and his three children boarded a train to go to the exposition. He had already experienced two heartbreaking losses with the deaths of his first two wives. The big question he heard people discussing was how he might address the northern white, southern white, and black audiences all at the same time.

In his book *Up from Slavery* he wrote,

> Atlanta was literally packed, at the time, with people from all parts of the country, and with representatives of foreign governments, as well as with military and civic organizations. The afternoon papers had forecasts of the next day's proceedings in glaring headlines. All this tended to add to my burden. I did not sleep much that night. The next morning, before day, I went carefully over what I planned to say. I also kneeled down and asked God's blessing upon my effort. Right here, perhaps, I ought to add that I make it a rule never to go

before an audience, on any occasion, without asking the blessing of God upon what I want to say.

Washington began speaking of "a new era of industrial progress" without the political posturing and misdirected interests of reconstruction, but in the skills and industries transforming the black people into financially responsible, morally upright, self-made citizens. To his fellows, he then spoke a metaphor:

> A ship lost at sea for many days suddenly sighted a friendly vessel. From the mast of the unfortunate vessel was seen a signal, "Water, water: we die of thirst!" The answer from the friendly vessel at once came back, "Cast down your bucket where you are." The distressed ship sent its frantic cry again and got the same response, and again a third time. In desperation the captain lowered buckets to the sea and drew up sparkling clear water flowing from the unseen mouth of the Amazon River nearby.
>
> To my race I would say ... "Cast down your bucket where you are"—cast it down in agriculture, mechanics, in commerce, in domestic service, and in professions ... Our greatest danger is that in the great leap from slavery to freedom we may overlook the fact that the masses of us are to live by the production of our hands, and fail to keep in mind that we shall prosper in proportion as we learn to dignify and glorify common labour and put brains and skill into the common occupations of life; shall prosper in proportion as we learn to draw the line between the superficial and the substantial ... No race can prosper till it learns that there is as much dignity in tilling a field as in writing a poem."

Washington turned to the whites in the audience and said:

> "Cast down your buckets where you are" ... among the eight millions of Negroes whose habits you know, whose fidelity and love you have tested in days when to have proved treacherous meant the ruin of your firesides ... among these people who have tilled your fields, cleared your forests, builded your railroads and cities, and brought forth treasures from the bowels of the earth ... in our humble way, we shall stand by you with a devotion that no foreigner can approach, ready to lay down our lives, if need be, in defense of yours, interlacing our industrial, commercial, civil, and religious life with yours in a way that shall make the interest of both races one.

At the speech's end, Booker T. Washington ended with a prayer in the hope of a new heaven and a new earth in the beloved south. The speech had received intermittent and even a "delirium of applause."

What did Booker have to say about it?

> The first thing that I remember, after I had finished speaking, was that Governor Bullock rushed across the platform and took me by the hand, and that others did the same. I received so many and such hearty congratulations that I found it difficult to get out of the building. I did not appreciate to any degree, however, the impression which my address seemed to have made, until the next morning, when I went into the business part of the city. As soon as I was recognized, I was surprised to find myself pointed out and surrounded by a crowd of men who wished to shake hands with me. This was kept up on every street onto which I went, to an extent which embarrassed me so much that I went back to my boarding-place. The next morning, I returned to Tuskegee.

The speech was a home run. It made Booker T. Washington a national figure. The *Boston Evening Transcript* declared that the speech "[seemed] to have dwarfed all the other proceedings and the Exposition itself." Washington sent a copy to President Grover Cleveland. The president telegrammed, stating that Washington's words "[could not] fail to delight and encourage all who [wished] well for [Washington's] race."

Tuskegee continued its growth in the 1890s. The name was changed to Tuskegee Normal and Industrial Institute. Washington also founded the Phelps Bible Training School at Tuskegee.

In 1893, General Armstrong from Hampton was a guest of honor at one of many conferences held at Tuskegee. A few weeks before the old soldier passed away, he spoke once more at Hampton. He told his audience, "If you find something not right in the world, act as Mr. Washington has. He couldn't work a miracle, but he got the people together to see what is, the matter and not spend their time in blaming others but see what they can do to improve themselves."

Booker observed the following:

> Another thing at Tuskegee out of which I get a great deal of pleasure and satisfaction is in the meeting with our students, and teachers, and their families, in the chapel for devotional exercises every evening at half-past eight, the last thing before retiring for the night. It is an inspiring sight when one stands on the platform there and sees before him eleven or twelve hundred earnest young men and women; and one cannot but feel that it is a privilege to help to guide them to a higher and more useful life.

On December 16, 1898, Tuskegee Institute was visited by President and Mrs. McKinley and the entire cabinet minus one.

In preparation for the visit, Washington remarked, "the thing that touched me almost as deeply as the visit of the President itself was the deep pride which all classes of citizens in Alabama seemed to take in our work."

Among the speakers, the secretary of the navy, John D. Long, spoke the following remarks in a grand fashion:

> I cannot make a speech to-day. My heart is too full—full of hope, admiration, and pride for my countrymen of both sections and both colours. I am filled with gratitude and admiration for your work, and from this time forward I shall have absolute confidence in your progress and in the solution of the problem in which you are engaged. The problem, I say, has been solved. A picture has been presented to-day which should be put upon canvas with the pictures of Washington and Lincoln, and transmitted to future time and generations—a picture which the press of the country should spread broadcast over the land, a most dramatic picture, and that picture is this: The President of the United States standing on this platform; on one side the governor of Alabama, on the other, completing the trinity, a representative of a race only a few years ago in bondage, the coloured President of the Tuskegee Normal and Industrial Institute.
>
> God bless the President under whose majesty such a scene as that is presented to the American people. God bless the state of Alabama, which is showing that it can deal with this problem for itself. God bless the orator, philanthropist, and disciple of the Great Master—who, if he were on earth, would be doing the same work—Booker T. Washington.

In a follow-up letter, President Booker T. Washington wrote,

> Twenty years have now passed since I made the first humble effort at Tuskegee, in a broken-down shanty and an old henhouse, without owning a dollar's worth of

property, and with but one teacher and thirty students. At the present time the institution owns twenty-three hundred acres of land, one thousand of which are under cultivation each year, entirely by student labour. There are now upon the grounds, counting large and small, sixty-six buildings; and all except four of these have been almost wholly erected by the labour of our students. While the students are at work upon the land and in erecting buildings, they are taught, by competent instructors, the latest methods of agriculture and the trades connected with building.

There are in constant operation at the school, in connection with thorough academic and religious training, thirty industrial departments. All of these teach industries at which our men and women can find immediate employment as soon as they leave the institution.

The 1899–1900 academic year at Tuskegee began with an all-time high of more than twelve hundred students. The generation born after Reconstruction had grown up under a confusing combination of legally guaranteed freedom and legally mandated discrimination. Still, a notice at the head of a chapel flyer titled *Things to Remember and Practice in 1900* stated, "Do not stand still and complain but go forward—mere fault-finders accomplish little."

In 1900, Washington founded the National Business League. It would grow to include over six hundred chapters. The business league helped to establish fifty black-owned banks across the country, as well as insurance companies.

After McKinley's assassination, then vice-president Theodore Roosevelt would assume the presidency on September 01, 1901, and serve till March 04, 1909. Roosevelt sought Washington's advice and invited Booker T. Washington to dinner at the White House. They had also spoken together at a celebration honoring Frederick Douglass two years before, then weeks later, marched together to receive their honorary degrees at the Yale bicentennial.

Roosevelt was eligible for another term, but he declined the Republicans' invitation to run for a second term. William Howard Taft succeeded him in 1908. Taft and Washington had several meetings before Taft's inauguration in March 1909. On April 1, 1910, Booker T. warned Taft's advisors, "Unless one is perfectly frank with the President, he may go on feeling that the Negroes are satisfied, when they are not and when the time comes to expect their support, he will be disappointed, hence it is disloyalty for any person to deal in a manner that is not frank with the President."

In 1912, Theodore "Teddy" Roosevelt was ready to take back the reins of government from his former cabinet secretary. Teddy formed the independent Bull Moose Party. Although Roosevelt was still a member of the Tuskegee board of trustees, the board requested that Washington not play a role in the 1912 presidential campaign.

With 42 percent of the vote, Woodrow Wilson became one of only two Democrats to have been elected to the presidency since the election of the first Republican president, Abraham Lincoln, in 1860. The Party was founded in 1854 to counter the slavery movement and to bring forward the country's founding principles. Washington would tell a Boston colleague, "I fear the President's high-sounding phrases regarding justice do not include the Negro."

In his book *Up from Slavery*, Booker T. Washington wrote, "I would permit no man, no matter what his colour might be, to narrow and degrade my soul by making me hate him."

On November 14, 1915, the soul of Booker T. Washington was freed from the trials of this earth. His body was laid to rest on the grounds of the Tuskegee Institute.

How fascinating would it have been to have had a conversation with Booker T. Washington? Following are some of his more notable quotations:

> I have learned that success is to be measured not so much by the position that one has reached in life as by the obstacles which he has overcome while trying to succeed.

The slaveowner and his sons had mastered no special industry. They unconsciously had imbibed the feeling that manual labour was not the proper thing for them. On the other hand, the slaves, in many cases, had mastered some handicraft, and none were ashamed, and few unwilling, to labour.

The individual who can do something that the world wants done will, in the end, make his way regardless ...

But gradually, by patience and hard work, we brought order out of chaos, just as will be true of any problem if we stick to it with patience and wisdom and earnest effort.

I learned the lesson that great men cultivate love, and that only little men cherish a spirit of hatred. I learned that assistance given to the weak makes the one who gives it strong; and that oppression of the unfortunate makes one weak.

The average audience, I have come to believe, wants facts rather than generalities or sermonizing. Most people, I think, are able to draw proper conclusions if they are given the facts in an interesting form on which to base them.

The kind of reading that I have the greatest fondness for is biography.

In the long run, the world is going to have the best, and any difference in race, religion, or previous history will not long keep the world from what it wants.

No man who continues to add something to the material, intellectual, and moral well-being of the place in which he lives is long left without proper reward. This is a great human law which cannot be permanently nullified.

I pity from the bottom of my heart any individual who is so unfortunate as to get into the habit of holding race prejudice.

One might as well try to stop the progress of a mighty railroad train by throwing his body across the track, as to try to stop the growth of the world in the direction of giving mankind more intelligence, more culture, more skill, more liberty, and in the direction of extending more sympathy and more brotherly kindness.

In conclusion and respectful memory of a good and great man, here is a quote from the beginning sentences of chapter 1 of his book entitled *Character Building*

> There are quite a number of divisions into which life can be divided, but for the purposes of this evening I am going to speak of two: the bright side of life and the dark side.
>
> In thought, in talk, in action, I think you will find that you can separate life into these two divisions-the dark side and the bright side, the discouraging side and the encouraging side. You will find, too, that there are two classes of people, just as there are two divisions of the subject. There is one class that is schooling itself, and constantly training itself, to look upon the dark side of life; and there is another class, made up of people who are, consciously or unconsciously, constantly training themselves to look upon the bright side of life.

Now it is not wise to go too far in either direction. The person who schools himself to see the dark side of life is likely to make a mistake, and the person who schools himself to look only upon the bright side of life, forgetting all else, also is apt to make a mistake.

Notwithstanding, this, I think I am right in saying that persons who accomplish the most in this world, those to whom on account of their helpfulness the world looks most for service, those – who are most useful in every way – are those who are constantly seeing and appreciating the bright side as well as the dark side of life …

I want you to go out from this institution so trained and so developed that you will be constantly looking for the bright, encouraging, and beautiful things in life.

GEORGE WASHINGTON CARVER

A Professional

In the spring of 1896, a graduate student at Iowa Agricultural College in Ames, Iowa, received a letter from Booker T. Washington, of the famous Tuskegee Normal and Industrial Institute, inviting him to take a new position there as director of the new agricultural school and the state experiment station. Washington expected the school to be "the best equipped and only distinct agricultural school in the South for the benefit of the colored people."

George Washington Carver replied as follows: "It has always been the one great ideal of my life to be of the greatest good to the greatest number of 'my people' possible and to this end I have been preparing myself for these many years; feeling as I do that this line of education is the key to unlock the golden door of freedom to our people."

In confirming the agreement, he wrote, "I am looking forward to a very busy, pleasant and profitable time at your college and shall be glad to cooperate with you in doing all I can through Christ who strengtheneth me to better the condition of our people ... Providence permitting I will be there in November. God bless you and your work."

George Washington Carver was born a slave in Missouri, where divisions over slavery were bitter. Born prematurely in the Wild West in 1860, George was small and sickly with severe respiratory problems. He was kidnapped for a few days in 1863 during the Civil War. His mother was never seen again. His "owners," Uncle Mose and Aunt Sue, moved George and his brother Jim into their house to raise as their own.

Bronchitis and tubercular inflammation frequently kept him indoors. His chores were not demanding. He was fascinated by the garden and orchard and the cultivation of flowers. He developed a skill in cultivation. George could walk a mile to church on his own on Wednesdays and Sundays. He would also get up before daybreak and go into the woods at the edge of the yard. In the sparkling early light, he simply prayed earnestly, dedicating himself to doing God's will.

When George was in his teens, "Uncle Moses" Carver learned of a school that would accept black students some miles away. Finally, perhaps, George would get the education he longed for. He boarded with the Watkins's, who lived next to the school. They attended the African Methodist Episcopal Church. For Christmas, Mariah Watkins gave George a Bible, which he carried everywhere with him from that moment forward and read daily for the rest of his life. He received a graduation certificate on December 22, 1876.

George would then make his way to, a number, of locations, including Fort Smith, Minneapolis, and Omaha, in his efforts to continue his education, working several jobs, along the way. Self-employed and twenty years old, he enrolled into the eighth grade in Minneapolis. He would sometimes lose his voice for several days, and he suffered from colds and frequent coughing. A doctor once told him he should not expect to live to be twenty-one. Carver remembered that he simply "trusted God and pressed on." He also had witnessed a lynching and had often been refused meals at restaurants, even when with a friend.

At twenty-five, George was admitted to Highland University. On his way, he visited Locust Grove, his original home. His most healthy brother had passed away from smallpox in 1883. George left on a train, but only after a warm evening with friends and gospel. His application had already been accepted. However, when he arrived, he heard the words "… you didn't tell me you were a Negro. Highland college does not take Negroes."

Western Kansas was still the American frontier in the 1880s. George, too, would stake his claim to 160 acres of prairie and started building his "soddy," or sod hut. Neighbors were friendly on the frontier prairie. Carver readily made friends. He was talented with the accordion, and that was appreciated. He was quite a painter and even built a greenhouse. *The Ness City Times* elected Carver to be assistant editor of the literary society on December 15, 1887.

George decided to mortgage the homestead and make his way back east to Winterset, Iowa. He would find a home for his gifts of singing and artistry at the Baptist church.

He was encouraged to apply to Simpson College. One of his many college friends wrote, "In young Carver we saw so much beyond the color that we soon ceased to sense it at all …"

In college, George would write that God had special plans for him. "I am learning to trust and realize the blessed results from trusting Him every day … I realize that God has a great work for me to do." George's Art teacher, Miss Budd, also examined his plants with a practiced eye. Her father was a professor of horticulture at Iowa State College in Ames, Iowa. She examined some of his horticultural experiments, such as the plants he had grafted or cross-fertilized.

George loved the arts and science. He enrolled into Iowa State College in Ames, Iowa, to pursue the discipline of science. George would receive near-perfect grades in botany and horticulture. He also joined the college's Cadet Corps and was promoted to captain. He even participated as a trainer for the football team. One of his paintings was shown at the World's Fair in 1892.

His faith was the basis of his life.

> Oh, how I wish the people would awake up from their lethargy and come out soul and body for Christ. I am so anxious to get out and be doing something. I can hardly wait for the time to come. The more my ideas develop, the more, beautiful' and grand, seems the plan I have laid out to pursue, or rather the one God has destined for me. It is really all I see in a successful life. And let

> us hope that in the mysterious ways of the Lord, he will bring about these things we all so much hope for ... Let us pray that the Lord will completely guide us in all things, and that we may gladly be led by him ... (George Washington Carver)

George Washington Carver began to refer to God as "the Creator". Perceiving the intricate miracles of creation within nature, he would later credit his discoveries as much to divine revelation as to the scientific method. He was confident of his pursuit of a divine purpose and that science and religion were compatible in God's communication to mankind.

Carver became assistant director of the agricultural experiment station at Iowa State. He would finish his master's program before reporting to Tuskegee in October 1896.

Professor Carver made a habit of going out early each morning, in order, to collect plants to use as teaching tools. He explained the interconnectedness of nature to his students as all was derived from the same divine source. As every good teacher, he understood that his students learned and retained much more through their own discoveries and resisted simply being told what they ought to know. He encouraged the spirit of discovery.

An encyclopedic knowledge of plants and animals he had. Students would make a game of trying to stump him. One day a group constructed an insect made up of various bugs. After Carver examined the new specimen, he smiled, and identified it as a "hum-bug". Those who studied nature, and understood it, would be drawn closer to God, believed Professor Carver.

He wore a freshly picked flower every day on his lab coat. Slight in appearance, he was known to all as "the professor." When he gave a lecture at the Georgia Industrial College in Savannah, the chancellor there claimed that the professor's lecture on teaching agriculture was "the best he had ever heard." There were requests for reprints of Professor Carver's experiment station bulletins as far away as Cuba, Mexico, and India.

There were frustrations too. In 1904, Carver wrote to a friend and former Iowa professor—the then current secretary of agriculture, James Wilson—indicating an interest in leaving Tuskegee. Wilson replied firmly, "… in regard to leaving Tuskegee and going to … Don't do it … and the work you are doing in helping to educate future teachers is the best … But stay by Mr. Washington. He is doing a work that should be duplicated …"

Among George Washington Carver's accomplishments, he developed better planting methods that produced better cotton yields, as well as a strain of hybrid cotton that was able to produce yields in spite of the boll weevils spreading like a plague. Attentions were given in correspondence and ventures when the name of "Professor George W. Carver, the Chemist and Commissioner of Agriculture of the famous Tuskegee Normal and Industrial School of which Booker T. Washington is Principal" was invoked. George Washington Carver increasingly received invitations to submit scientific papers for publication both in America and abroad (chiefly in Germany, home of a world-renowned scientific community at the turn of the century), as well as requests to assess new seeds, farm machinery, and other products he had developed.

In his classroom presentations, Carver affirmed his belief that Christianity and science supported and reinforced each other. He would often use the name "Creator" instead of "God." In one of his Bible studies, he said, "our Creator never changes despite the names given Him by people here and in all parts of the world. Even if we gave Him no name at all, He would still be there, within us, waiting to give us good on this earth." The professor advised holding good thoughts for our fellow man, which then will bring one to a state of living of happiness, success, and peace—rather than the converse, which will bring the opposite result.

Professor Carver had an easy command of the classroom and the laboratory and a genuine interest in the spiritual welfare of his students. He had a natural way of combining science and faith: "To me nature in its varied forms are the little windows through which God permits me to commune with him, and to see much of his glory, by simply lifting the curtain, and looking in. I love to think of nature as wireless telegraph stations through which God speaks to us every day, every hour, and every moment of our lives."

He once addressed students as he was to begin a Bible class with these words:

> Your faces are beaming with happiness tonight. Your lives will be filled with happiness if you contact thy Creator and keep tuned in with Him.
>
> Each of you came to Tuskegee to learn a trade, to study the academic courses and graduate and then go out into the world. You are enthusiastic about that now, but if you do not know how to turn the key to the storehouse of happiness—how to contact and keep tuned in with our Creator—you are in for many unhappy situations.
>
> The advice of Solomon can come in handy here. With all thy getting, get understanding—understanding that our Creator is Law and he will give us the happiness our hearts desire, if we follow his Laws.

One Sunday night several students asked Carver to explain who and what the Creator is. "He is Spirit," Carver answered without hesitation, and he quoted John 4:24 from memory:

> "God is a Spirit, and they that worship him must worship him in spirit and in truth..... To refer to him as God or to call him our Creator is one and the same." Our Creator, being Spirit, is Principle— Law—and by keeping his laws, we get from him good, for he is good. The things we go to our Creator for must be good things; he has nothing else to give us and through us for the benefit of mankind— regardless of race—except good. Persons who attempt to contact him with a selfish

and mean motive in mind are defeated before they start and are driven from the temple in failure.

Many accolades came George Washington Carver's way. He served on the advisory board of the National Agricultural Society. In 1918, he was appointed to the US Department of Agriculture. In 1923, he would be the recipient of the Spingarn Medal for Distinguished Service in Agricultural Chemistry. He was elected a Fellow of the Royal Society for the Encouragement of Arts, Manufactures and Commerce in London. Carver received a presidential medal, and President Franklin D. Roosevelt visited him on the Tuskegee campus in 1939. Vice president Calvin Coolidge had already visited Carver on campus in 1923. The medal he received declared, "To a scientist humbly seeking the guidance of God and a liberator to men of the white race as well as the black."

At the request of the United Peanut Growers Association, on January 21, 1921, George Washington Carver addressed the US House Ways and Means Committee in Washington, DC, regarding proposed tariffs on imported peanuts. G. W. Carver expounded on the many, potential uses of the peanut. He was initially given ten minutes to speak. The chairman was so captivated by what Carver was describing that he simply said, "Go ahead Brother. Your time is unlimited!" George W. Carver spoke for an hour and forty-five minutes. He had discovered over three hundred uses for the peanut, over one hundred eighteen for the sweet potato, over sixty for the pecan, and dozens for the soybean. The committee chairman then slightly shook his head and said, "Dr. Carver how did you learn all these things?"

Carver answered: "From an old book."

"What book?" asked the chairman.

Carver replied, "The Bible."

"Does the Bible tell about peanuts?" the Chairman inquired.

"No Sir, but it tells about the God who made the peanut. I asked Him to show me what to do with the peanut, and He did."

In the 1920s, George Washington Carver eventually assumed the title "Wizard of Tuskegee." During the Great War, the inventor Thomas Edison had apparently offered Mr. Carver a job at a high salary. In

Success magazine, Carver said, "there was nothing to talk over, and I thanked Mr. Edison in a letter." He determined he would rather stay among "his people." Whatever the offer, it was further proof that his talents were appreciated. Other publications described him as "a man of international repute" acknowledged to be "one of the world's greatest scientists" and "a genius who lives in closest touch with nature."

Even a supporter of Mahatma Gandhi requested some of Carver's agricultural bulletins on behalf of Gandhi. Carver sent them and received a personal note from Gandhi. Carver wrote back saying he would pray for Gandhi "in the marvelous work [he was] doing."

In the 1930s, before Dr. Jonas Salk developed a successful vaccine, the feared disease of polio was killing thousands and leaving others with atrophied muscles and useless limbs. Dr. Carver developed a massage therapy using peanut oil that helped victims of polio and infantile paralysis regain the use of their limbs. A letter of his addressed to a mother read.

> My esteemed friend Mrs. Hardwick. Thank you so much for your beautiful card with its Greetings. I have not written to you in a long time, but my thoughts and prayers have been for you daily. Our patients have usurped almost all of my spare time, but my thoughts and prayers have been for you daily.
>
> God continues to speak through the oils in a truly marvelous way. I have patients who come to me on crutches, who are now walking 6 miles without tiring, without either crutch or cane. (one man).
>
> My last patient today was one of the sweetest little 5 year-old boys, who 3 months ago they had to carry in my room, being paralyzed from the waist down. When I had finished the massage today, much to our astonishment he dressed himself and stood up and walked across

the floor without any support. He is a handsome little fellow and so happy that he is improving, (and I too).

I said Our patients, because I feel that your prayers help to make it possible. Since last Dec.31st I have received 2020 letters, plus the people who come every day and almost every night for treatment. It is truly marvelous what God is doing.

Continue to pray for me that I may be a more fit medium through which He can Speak …

I am so gratefully yours,

G.W. Carver

Later in life, George Washington Carver became friends with Henry Ford, who genuinely admired Carver. Ford built a Carver cabin at his Greenfield village farm, set up a nutritional laboratory in his honor, and established the George Washington Carver School on his Georgia plantation, persuading Carver to attend the dedication. Ford personally escorted him throughout the day, just as he had, a number, of times in Dearborn. Henry also built George an elevator in Dorothy Hall so he could more easily make it down for meals and then return to his laboratory.

A prayer said by George Washington Carver before he would enter his laboratory in the morning went this way: "Open thou mine eyes that I may behold wondrous things out of thy law. My help cometh from the Lord who made heaven and earth, and all that in them is."

George Washington Carver would leave this earth on the fifth of January 1943. He would be buried near the grave of Booker T. Washington on the Tuskegee Campus.

President Franklin D. Roosevelt dedicated Carver's birthplace in Diamond, Missouri, as a national monument. This was the first national monument dedicated to someone other than a US president.

Henry A. Wallace served as vice president under Franklin D. Roosevelt and as secretary of agriculture. He was also a student of George W. Carver. He described Carver as the "kindliest, most patient teacher I ever knew."

Perhaps we may want just a bit more time with this genius and great man. Perhaps we might ask Dr. Carver to speak to us further before we, too, must leave.

> As a very small boy exploring the almost virgin woods of the old Carver place, I had the impression someone had just been there ahead of me. Things were so orderly, so clean, so harmoniously beautiful. A few years later, in this same woods, I was to understand the meaning of this boyish impression.
>
> Because I was practically overwhelmed with the sense of some Great Presence. Not only had someone been there. Someone was there ... Years later when I read in the Scriptures, "In Him we live and move and have our being," I knew what the writer meant. Never since have I been without this consciousness of the Creator speaking to me ... After I leave this world, I do not believe I am through. God would be a bigger fool than even a man if he did not conserve what seems to be the most important thing he has yet done in the universe. This kind of reasoning may aid the young. When you get your grip on the last rung of the ladder and look over the wall as I am now doing you don't need their proofs. You see. You know you will not die.
>
> God is going to reveal to us things He never revealed before if we put our hands in His. No books ever go into my laboratory. The thing I am to do and the way of doing it are revealed to me. I never have to grope for methods. The method is revealed to me the moment I

am inspired to create something new. Without God to draw aside the curtain I would be helpless.

More and more as we come closer and closer in touch with nature and its teachings are we able to see the Divine and are therefore fitted to interpret correctly the various languages spoken by all forms of nature about us.

[To a former student] As soon as you begin to read the great and loving God out of all forms of existence he has created, both animate and inanimate, then you will be able to Converse with him, anywhere, everywhere, and at-all-times. Oh, what fullness of joy will come to you. My dear friend, get the significance. God is speaking.

We doubt that there is a normal boy or girl in all Christendom endowed with the five senses who have not watched with increased interest and profit, the various forms, movements, and the gorgeous paintings of the butterfly, many do not know, but will study with increased enthusiasm the striking analogy its life bears to the human soul.

With insight, humor, and advice, George Washington Carver addressed a Young Men's Christian Association in the summer of 1920:

I always look forward to introductions as opportunities to learn something about myself …

Years ago, I went into my laboratory and said, "Dear Mr. Creator, please tell me what the universe was made for?"

The Great Creator answered, "You want to know too much for that little mind of yours. Ask for something more your size, little man."

Then I asked. "Please, Mr. Creator, tell me what man was made for."

Again, the Great Creator replied, "You are still asking too much. Cut down on the extent and improve the intent."

So then I asked, "Please, Mr. Creator, will you tell me why the peanut was made?"

"That's better, but even then it's infinite. What do you want to know about the peanut?"

"Mr. Creator, can I make milk out of the peanut?"

"What kind of milk do you want? Good Jersey milk or just plain boarding house milk?"

"Good Jersey milk." And then the Great Creator taught me to take the peanut apart and put it together again. And out of the process have come forth all these products!

George Washington Carver was asked more than once what the secret of his success was. He replied, "The secret of my success? It is simple. It is found in the Bible, 'In all thy ways acknowledge Him and He shall direct thy paths.'

MOTHER TERESA

A Joy

I am nothing but a little pencil in the hands of God. It is He who writes, it is He who thinks, it is He who decides.

—Mother Teresa

Mother Teresa always made clear that her work was driven by an absolute faith—that she was simply responding to Christ's boundless love for her and for every man, woman, and child on earth.

Born in Skopje in 1910 in, what was still the Ottoman Empire, Mother Teresa grew up in a Catholic community, hardly more than a tenth of all the Albanian people, which was composed also of Eastern Orthodox and Muslim. The Romans had subjugated the area in 167; the Ottomans, in 1385. The Albanians tell of a boy hostage of the Turkish sultan, who was later given to an army command. On learning that the Sultan had planned an onslaught on the Albanians, he crossed over to his own people and their Catholic faith. He unified the quarreling princes, and his armies never lost a battle. Following the death of Scanderberg, the absorption of Albania into the Ottoman Empire was completed. "There is, no compelling men in their inner belief" points out the Koran. Scanderberg's red banner, bearing a black double-headed eagle, became the flag under which Albanians of all creeds have struggled for freedom over the centuries.

"We were a very happy family" Mother Teresa once said of her upbringing. Her father, a merchant, supported her mother in her works of mercy. Their daughter Agnes would often accompany her mother in performing her charitable works. The poor would not be turned away at the Bojaxhius' door. Every evening, the family would gather in the living room and pray the rosary.

After the First World War, her father became involved in a movement to have the province of Kosovo joined to a greater Albania. While a vigorous man at forty-five, he traveled to attend a gathering. He returned home ill. He was so ill that Agnes looked for the parish priest. She was unable to find him. At the train station, she found a priest unfamiliar to the family to perform the last rites. It was the only time the family would see him. The hospital doctors were convinced their father, Nikola, had been poisoned. Drana, her mother, was paralyzed with grief, but she eventually set up an embroidery business.

The parish of the Sacred Heart was also a pivotal influence in the life of young Agnes Bojaxhiu. Like her mother, Agnes did not waste time, and she read many books from the parish library. Fr. Jambrenkovic introduced young people to the Sodality of the Blessed Virgin Mary, founded by students in 1563 in the Roman College of the Society of Jesus. "What have I done for Christ? What am I doing for Christ? What will I do for Christ?" Agnes and her sister Age were also members of the church choir and were known as the nightingales of the choir.

At the age of twelve, Agnes Bojaxhiu felt a call of vocation to minister to the poor. How could she know whether God was really calling her? The answer was that joy was the compass that pointed her direction in life and that joy would be the proof of the rightness of any endeavor. This was the answer provided by a local Jesuit of the Society of Jesus in Albania in 1922.

On the first of December 1928, Agnes Bojaxhiu, who would become Sister Mary Teresa of the Child Jesus—after Teresa of Lisieux, the "Little Flower"—would set sail for India via Paris and Dublin. On a port of call, she wrote these words:

> Many families live in the streets, along the city walls, even in places thronged with people. Day and night, they live out in the open on mats they have made from large palm leaves – or frequently on the bare ground. They are all virtually naked, wearing at best a ragged loincloth ... as we went along the street, we chanced upon one family gathered around a dead relation, wrapped in worn red rags, strewn with yellow flowers, his face painted in coloured stripes. It was a horrifying scene. If our people could only see all this, they would stop grumbling about their own misfortunes and offer thanks to God for blessing them with such abundance.
>
> I wanted to be a missionary, I wanted to go out and give the life of Christ to the people in the missionary countries. At that time, some missionaries had gone to India from Yugoslavia. They told me the Loreto nuns were doing work in Calcutta and other places. I offered myself to go out to the Bengal Mission, and from there they sent me to India in 1929.

Relating to the essence of her mission and Jesus's admonition that "Anyone who receives a child in my name, receives me," for Sister Teresa, there was an intimate and mysterious relationship between the vulnerable Christ and the suffering people.

On January 6, 1929, Agnes Gonxha Bojaxhjiu arrived in Calcutta, the capital of Bengal. She would not leave the province of Bengal for thirty-one years. For her training as a novice in the 'Sisters of Loreto', Agnes Gonxha was sent 450 miles north to the northern border town of Darjeeling, the city of the Thunderbolt. Darjeeling is situated at the foothills of the Himalayan range, and there one may sometimes see Mt. Everest. The novices pursued studies preparing them for the apostolate of teaching. The training was conducted in English, and the young women were also introduced to Hindi and Bengali.

Agnes Gonxha made her first vows as a Sister of Loreto on May 24, 1931, becoming Sister Teresa. Sister Teresa would then be sent to a school in the eastern district of Calcutta, where education was conducted by the Loreto Sisters. There she became a teacher of geography. Sister Teresa could now speak five languages. On May 14, 1937, Sister Teresa took her lifetime vows and became a professed nun.

Throughout the war years of the Second World War, the needs in Calcutta mounted. The year of 1943 brought a famine in which several million people would lose their lives. Many converged upon Calcutta in a quest for food or the means to earn their livelihood. Many, many "war babies" would be left on the doorsteps of Loreto. Mother Teresa chose to stay, while others would choose to leave. The year 1946 brought escalating conflict between Hindus and Muslims that preceded the partition and the independence of India. For a period, there were no teachers for children four to ten. Mother Teresa took them all. There would be no food, and she would risk all.

During that year, Mother Teresa herself became weak and ill. The Loreto Provincial was afraid she would be stricken with tuberculosis. She was directed to rest on her bed for three hours every afternoon. One familiar with the sister said that this was the only time he would see Mother Teresa cry: "It was very hard for her to be in bed and not to do the work." In the interest of her health, she was directed to undergo a period of spiritual renewal and have a physical break from the work.

Instead, as it transpired, she was to be called to another form of work and service within the religious life she had already chosen. On September 10, 1946, a date now celebrated by the Missionaries of Charity and Co-workers throughout the world as "Inspiration Day," on a dusty train, while on her way to the retreat, Mother Teresa would receive, as she would describe it, "the call within the call"—"The call of God to be a Missionary of Charity." "I was to leave the convent and help the poor while living among them." "[It] was a call within my vocation. It was a second calling. It was a vocation to give up even Loreto, where I was very happy and to go out in the streets to serve the poorest of the poor. It was in that train I heard the call to give up all and follow Him into the slums—to serve Him in the poorest of the poor ... I knew it was His will and that I had to follow Him. There was no doubt that it was going to be His work."

After the experience of the train ride came a period of silence, solitude, and prayer. At the retreat, Mother Teresa was even more deeply in prayer than usual. A Father at the retreat summarized the notes she was writing: "She was to start a new congregation. That congregation would work for the poorest of the poor in the slums in a spirit of poverty and cheerfulness. There would be a special vow of charity for the poor. There would be no institutions, hospitals, or big dispensaries. The work was to be among the abandoned, those with nobody, the very poorest."

Sister Teresa would pray for wisdom.

> "I had first to apply to the Archbishop of Calcutta. Then, with his approval, the Mother General of the Loreto nuns gave me permission to write to Rome. I had to do this because I was a nun who had taken final vows and nuns cannot be allowed to leave the convent. I wrote to the Holy Father, Pope Pius XII, and by return post I got the answer on the 12th of April. He said that I could go out and be an unenclosed nun. That means to live the life of a religious, but under obedience to the Archbishop of Calcutta."

The archbishop waited thoughtfully, contemplating the idea of a lone nun on the streets of Calcutta. "Loreto meant everything to me," said Teresa. "It was much harder to leave Loreto than to leave my family and my country to enter religious life."

Sister Teresa would write to the Medical Mission Sisters at the Holy Family Hospital in Patna. There she was able to learn basic skills of caring for the sick among the city's poor. On August 17, 1948, a lonely nun stepped off the train at Patna. Sister Elise Wynen, MD, recalled,

> In that way she became acquainted with fatal accidents, mothers dying on the delivery room table, children sick from being abandoned by hopelessly torn and desperate

families. She also attended cholera and smallpox patients. As I remember, nothing ever fazed her. She just wanted to know what was going on and what she could do to help. Soon, I would count on her to hold the patient's hand during painful procedures, to comfort a crying child, and to help the nurses whenever she could …During evening recreations, we would all talk together, and she would share her hopes and ideas with us. We did not spare her, and I think she welcomed our insights and criticisms …We all came to appreciate and admire Mother Teresa, and we visited her many times in Calcutta where her ideas were put into practice. While the city looked on in wonder, the poor came flocking. Nothing that has happened since then has ever surprised us. We knew her.

Sister Cyril Jacko, director of the nursing school, related:

We knew it was her period of transition for a future she was not sure of. In principle, yes, she was sure, but its shape was not clear to her. We welcomed her as a friend who needed help in preparing for a different life … I cannot forget how Mother Teresa helped a fifteen-year-old girl suffering from advanced tuberculosis—incurable as so many of the TB patients were then. From what I understood, the girl desired very much to join Mother Teresa in serving the poor. Toward the end of her stay, Mother Teresa somehow 'confirmed' her as an associate in her work. The young girl was able to say certain prayers for the work and, also, ministered to the other TB patients, talking with those unable to get out of bed. She died at Holy Family Hospital, a first follower of Mother Teresa.

Mother Teresa would stay for a short period with the Little Sisters of the Poor before transitioning into the abyss, so to speak, of her new life.

Mother Teresa reflected, "Today I learned a good lesson. The poverty of the poor is so hard."

The Missionaries of Charity would then begin. "I thirst" is inscribed on each of the society's chapels throughout the world. This relates to the text "… if any man thirst let him come to me and drink" and to Jesus's final words on the cross, from the Gospel of John: "Jesus knowing that all things were now accomplished, that the scripture might be fulfilled, said: I thirst."

As Mother Teresa herself would reflect, "We know that it is through Our Lady's pleading that the Society was born, has grown and will continue to grow in the Church and for the Church. It is through her special love, guidance, and intercession that the Missionaries of Charity will continue her role of contemplating, experiencing and satiating Jesus' Thirst for love and for souls in His Mystical Body – the Church."

After further clarifications, Mother Teresa would go to live in the slums. "Those who were not clean I gave a good wash at the tank. We had catechism after the first lesson in hygiene and their reading. We used the ground as a blackboard. After needlework class we went to visit the sick. I saw a woman dying on the street outside Campbell Hospital. I picked her up and took her to the hospital, but she was refused admission because she was poor. She died on the street. I knew then that I must make a home for the dying, a resting place for people going to heaven." The search for a house in which others might join her went on.

The first ten girls who would come work with her were former pupils. "As you did it to one of the least of these my brethren, you did it to me," states the Gospel of St. Matthew. "We had to start the work, we couldn't wait for money because life and poverty were everywhere," stated Mother Teresa. Yet somehow, where there was a need, the means of providing it was provided, and there was joy and peace to be derived from the experience, and a fresh appreciation of small things.

The first vows of the first group of Missionaries of Charity were taken on the twelfth of April 1953, exemplifying the exceptional growth and singular spirit of the mission. By the late 1950s, the archbishop would finally be heard to announce that "Manifestly the finger of God is here," referring to the work of the Missionaries of Charity.

For the dedicated Missionaries of Charity, the filth, vomit, humiliation, disease, misperception, and sacrifice given would not be for the ordinary mortal soul. All were welcomed to the work of the Missionaries of Charity, regardless of background or religion. No child was ever refused a home, even it meant that the babies slept three or more to a cot or were coaxed into life in a box heated by a lightbulb. "Do not be afraid to love until it hurts," Mother Teresa would say, "until it hurts because to give like that is easy, to give from the abundance is easy." Mother Teresa would go where others feared to tread, tending the nauseating wounds of the leper, or working at great personal risk in places of violence and pain.

In a period of just over five years of the sisters beginning their work, more than eight thousand, of the dying had been received by them. More than thirty-five hundred had perished. The Hindus would be taken to the nearby burning ghats. The Christians would be taken to their burial grounds, and the Muslims to theirs. Mother Teresa said that most died no matter what the sisters did, and then, in 1955 and 1956, about half of the dying lived. She further observed in a 1957 interview, "And now, more live than die." She added, "The foods of the American people have helped to bring these people back to life. America will be blessed for doing this thing. You must tell them and bring our thanks."

There was also mistrust and expressions of hostility toward the sisters. A group of young people, mostly students, feared that the Catholic sisters would convert people to Christianity and so came to protest. The leader of the group entered the Dharamshala, intending to get Mother Teresa out. When he saw the helpless, emaciated examples of humanity being cleaned and washed, and their sores being dressed by the sisters, he had a change of heart. He came back out to the protesters. He stated he would get Mother Teresa and the sisters out of town on one condition: they would have to get their mothers and sisters to come in and do the same work. The group left without returning.

At day's end, the sisters would recite an act of contrition, asking pardon of the Creator for anything done during the day that might have been an offense. Then it came time for sleep, perhaps by 10:00 p.m. That hour did not apply to Mother Teresa, and as the congregation kept growing, there would be more and more letters to be answered. Whether afterward it be midnight or past, she rose always at the appointed time, at the bell, which rang at 4:40 a.m. She kept to this schedule year after year, never giving in to fatigue, and never losing her recollection or her composure toward the multitudes who entered her life. Once asked about and lectured on the need for sleep, Mother Teresa simply gave a smile and said, "I sleep fast."

In September of 1957, Mother Teresa's first mobile leprosy clinic was opened. Any success, as Mother Teresa saw it, was entirely dependent on the recognition of Christ in the poor. Mother Teresa was firmly convinced that without this essential perspective, without the purity of heart vital to the seeing of God, and without the framework and grounding of the religious life, her sisters would be unable to bring peace to the dying, touch the open wounds of the leper, and nurture the tiny spark of life in babies whom others had abandoned. It was not possible to engage in the apostolate without being a soul at prayer.

Skeptical queries regarding the availability of resources were answered by Mother Teresa stating that God would provide. The Missionaries of Charity were not to wear gloves to touch the maggot-ridden bodies of the dying any more than they were to hold the lepers at arm's length, because they were tending the body of Christ. It would not be by efficiency or effectiveness that an action would be judged, but by the amount of love put into it. Mother Teresa sought to develop in the Missionaries of Charity "the constant awareness of the Divine Presence everywhere and in everyone, especially in our own hearts and in the hearts of our Sisters with whom we live, and in the poorest of the poor."

For ten years, as canon law would require, the Congregation of the Missionaries of Charity would do their work within the diocese of Calcutta. The sisters, eager to extend their mission throughout India, would begin to do so in 1959. In 1960, Mother Teresa would leave Calcutta on a trip that would lead to Rome. On the way, she made her first public appearance to the National Council of Catholic Women to say, "I have never spoken in public before. This is the first time, and to be here with you and to be able to tell you the love story of God's mercy for the poorest of the poor—it is a grace of God."

Mother Teresa would ask Pope John XXIII for pontifical recognition. There, also in Rome, she would see again the brother she had not seen since 1924. He, his wife, and his daughter were living there. Mother Teresa and her brother Lazar Bojaxhiu engaged in a topic of conversation common to all, across Europe at that time. Lazar said, "This is what is happening in Albania," and he related a story of a priest being shot for baptizing a baby. The priest was a distant relative. He had been imprisoned after the war as an anti-communist and then freed for good conduct. By 1965, over two thousand mosques, churches, and religious buildings, Orthodox and Catholic, were demolished or being used as warehouses or museums. The priest had protested the demolition of Catholic churches and was imprisoned again. A woman in the prison gave birth to a child and asked him to baptize the child. The priest was tried in a desecrated Catholic church by a "peoples tribune."

The Holy See conferred approval to the congregation in February of 1965. The expanding range of responses from the Missionaries of Charity included clinics for those suffering from tuberculosis; antenatal clinics; general dispensaries; mobile leprosy clinics; night shelters for homeless men; homes for abandoned children; homes for the dying and the destitute; nursery classes and crèches; primary schools; secondary schools; provision for further education; feeding programs; villages for lepers; commercial schools; training in carpentry, metalwork, embroidery, needlework or other skills; childcare and home management; and aid in the event of emergencies and disasters arising from riots, epidemics, famine, and flooding.

In July of 1965, Mother Teresa and five sisters would leave for Venezuela. In September of 1968, the sisters opened a house in Tanzania. In July of 1970, Mother Teresa and five other Missionaries of Charity sisters were welcomed to Jordan. Also in 1970, a home to train sisters was opened in London. In October 1970, a cyclone and tidal waves drowned more than three hundred thousand people in Bangladesh, formerly East Pakistan. The following year, an occupation by West Pakistan claimed a further three million lives. Two hundred thousand women were reported raped. About two hundred fifty thousand refugees pressed at the gates of Calcutta. One of the sisters said, "We went out by lorry early every morning and started our work. It was so hard to clean up those terrible places and make the people a bit clean. We have taken care of the sick and of the dying, but we could not get used to so many dying, especially the children. When I picked up the dead children, I could hardly feel their weight."

There also came to be Missionaries of Charity brothers. They were many fewer than the sisters, but there is one story of note involving them: On March 7, 1975, a Brother had written his final letter to his parents, brothers, and sisters explaining his decision to remain in Phnom Penh and continue the work he was doing, and his love for the Cambodian people. "Death doesn't seem to be made into such a big thing here as in the West. A number, of children here have died, and it is accepted like every other aspect of life. I can honestly say that in the saving truth of Christ's message that the death of a person's soul through resisting God's spirit is so much worse than the death of these children. I hope you're at peace ... I have been given God's peace and joy and I know that it is for you also." Brother Brian remained ministering to a flood of refugees from the visions of a "murderous utopia" inflicted on Cambodia under which estimates of two million perished.

Mother Teresa and her sisters were invited to places across the globe: to Belfast; to Gaza; to Yemen; to Lima, Peru; and to Guatemala after an earthquake. She would address the National Conference of Catholic Bishops in 1976. There was a procession of nearly five hundred thousand pilgrims. Later that year, Mother Teresa was in Singapore, speaking to three hundred representatives of over ten different world religions from seventeen Asian nations.

Early in 1977, Mother Teresa traveled to Manilla, Philippines, to open a novitiate. Then she traveled to Kerema in Papua, New Guinea. Seven houses would open outside of India in 1977, in London's East End; in Port-au-Prince, Haiti; in Rotterdam, Netherlands; in Dire Dawa, Ethiopia; and in Peru. One of the sisters in Guatemala expressed her sentiments: "God is overwhelmingly good to us. He answers our needs even before we have voiced them. It has been like that ever since we have come to this country. There is a miracle almost every day."

India's prime minister, Indira Gandhi, awarded Mother Teresa an honorary doctorate in 1980 from Visva-Bharati University, bestowing a mark of honor. The prime minister remarked, "She is so tiny to look at, but there is nothing small there."

Mahatma Gandhi himself put into practice the hard sayings of the Sermon on the Mount, making it known to millions the world over. He said, "When I read in the Sermon on the Mount such passages as 'Love your enemies and pray for them that persecute you, that ye may be sons of your Father which is in heaven,' I was overjoyed."

In her travels, Mother Teresa would not take herself too seriously and never stood on her dignity. She would squat unselfconsciously on the carpeted area at an airport terminal to have a chance to talk to the sisters as they sat around her.

One time, Mother Teresa decided to try to cut down on her schedule and requested that another sister make a phone call to cancel an appearance. The bishop from Vancouver on the other end of the line, with alarm in his voice, exclaimed, "What can I do? I have rented our fifteen-thousand-seat Pacific Coliseum! I can't get the money back!" Mother Teresa changed her mind and made the public appearance, along with other unadvertised visits to convents.

Mother Teresa would visit Boys Town, founded by Father Flanagan in Omaha, Nebraska, in 1917. Father Flanagan said, "They are children of God. I must protect them to the best of my ability." Even today, many boys and girls await a new beginning, longing to be rescued from abuse, abandonment, neglect, and pain. After her talk, she was presented a statue of a boy carrying another boy on his shoulders. Under it was the motto, "He ain't heavy, Father—he's my brother."

Mother Teresa took the statue back to Calcutta for the Missionaries of Charity brothers who were rescuing street boys. She often stated, "And this is for girls, for sisters, too."

Mother Teresa happened to be visiting sisters in July of 1974 when the twentieth anniversary of the Food for Peace program was being marked in Washington DC. Senator Hubert H. Humphrey had called a hearing of the Senate Committee on Foreign Relations inviting witnesses to testify on the accomplishments and challenges of the program. Mother Teresa was asked to appear as a "surprise witness" to open the hearing. Mother Teresa thanked Senator Humphrey for the opportunity. She opened by saying, "The poor are the hope of mankind ... for, in them, we see the hungry Christ looking up at us. Will we refuse Him?" She continued, "When the 'health cases' are cut off, and we have almost no food to give them, then we find that people stop coming for treatment. I mean, for example, the forty-six thousand lepers we are taking care of." Senator Humphrey thanked Mother Teresa, stating that her opening words were an invocation for the meeting. "I wanted very much to hear from someone who employs in her life the virtues of compassion, love and kindness, because governments sometimes become dehumanized."

Mother Teresa knew there was room for the miraculous. "There is a sort of miracle every day. There is not a day without some delicate attention of God, some sign of His love and care, like the time we ran out of food ... or, just the right medicine in a donation ..." This was her daily life—recognizing the Divine. Some moments were smaller. "That's a first-class miracle," she would say. One example is as follows:

> In Calcutta there were floods and we worked day and night cooking for five thousand people. The army gave us food. One day something told me to turn off the road towards an unknown area and we found a little village where people were being swept away. We got boats for them. We found out later that if we had come only two hours later, they would have been drowned. Then, I said to the bishop, that I was going to ask our novices to pray for the rain, which had been pouring down for many days, to stop. I told him, 'The novices are very earnest. They pray with great energy. It will be a strong expression.' So, we put them – 178 of them – in the church of our mission. Outside it was raining; inside they began to pray, and I brought out the Blessed Sacrament. After a while I went to the door of the church

and looked out. The rain had stopped and there was a patch of clear sky above us – yes, I believe in miracles.

Many examples of answered prayers from the Missionaries of Charity remained close to the hearts of the sisters, confirming Mother Teresa's faith in divine providence.

Not all, of the prayers of Mother Teresa were answered. Her mother, Drana Bojaxhiu, died on 12 July 1972 in Tirania, Albania. Mother Teresa never saw her mother again after she left home to join the Loreto Sisters at the age of eighteen. The Albanian government, a communist regime, would not permit Mother Teresa to enter the country, and all attempts to bring her mother and her sister, Age, out of the country were unsuccessful.

There were setbacks too. The sisters sometimes needed to leave places, but on the other hand, they found themselves welcomed to places—such as Ethiopia, during a famine, for instance. Mother Teresa would see a joyful private audience with Pope Paul VI in 1978. By the year 1980, there were 158 foundations scattered throughout the world, 1,187 professed sisters, 411 novices, and 120 postulants.

Mother Teresa prayed often and often prayed the Prayer of Peace of St. Francis of Assisi:

> Lord, make me a channel of thy peace,
> That where there is hatred, I may bring love;
> That where there is hatred, I may bring the spirit of forgiveness;
> That where there is discord, I may bring harmony;
> That where there is error, I may bring truth;
> That where there is doubt, I may bring truth;
> That where there is despair, I may bring hope
> That where there are shadows, I may bring light;
> That where there is sadness, I may bring joy.
> Lord, grant that I may seek rather to comfort than
> to be comforted;
> to understand rather than to be understood;

to love rather than be loved;
for it is by forgetting self that one finds;
it is by forgiving that one is forgiven;
it is by dying that one awakens to eternal life.

Mother Teresa also reflected on disintegrations of society, breakdowns of world peace, and the resulting miseries.

> Our Sisters are working around the world, and I have seen all the trouble, all the misery, all the suffering. From where did it come? It has come from lack of love and lack of prayer. There is no more of that coming together in the family, praying together, coming together, staying together.
>
> Love begins at home, prayer begins at home, and the family that prays together, stays together." Mother Teresa would add that "In spite of our defects, God is in love with us and keeps using you and me to be His light of love and compassion in the world. So, give Jesus a big smile and a hearty thank you.

Mother Teresa's contributions would be recognized, and she would receive numerous honors and awards from many countries. Upon receiving them, Mother Teresa never prepared a speech other than with prayer. Her aim was to touch the hearts of those to whom she spoke with a spiritual message, to bring them the Good News.

In 1979, Mother Teresa would be the recipient of the Nobel Peace Prize. She would say, "Let us then, use the occasion to do something beautiful for God." An ecumenical service was held at the Domkirche, the Lutheran Cathedral of Oslo. The vice chairman of the Nobel committee delivered a sermon.

> If there is something that our divided world without peace needs, it is people who in the name of Christ will

> cross boundaries to lessen his neighbor's need, regardless of standing and reputation. 'Blessed are the merciful,' said Jesus ... It is this care without boundaries, this understanding of the worth of man, this desire to heal the broken—it is this that after all lies at the bottom of all the peace-making work, regardless of where it is done, and by whom. That is why it is so natural that Mother Teresa and what she stands for would be honored with this year's Peace Prize.

And from the glorious cathedral choir burst the heavenly sound of the "Hallelujah Chorus" from Handel's *Messiah*.

Upon acceptance of the Nobel Prize, Mother Teresa asked everyone to join in praying the Prayer of St. Francis. About eight hundred voices intoned in unison. A simple reception was held rather than a formal banquet.

In 1980, Mother Teresa was honored in India at an official reception recognizing her receipt of the Nobel Prize.

A message to each and to all from Mother Teresa was a message of the joy of loving. One of her favorite stories was of a beggar. She told it this way:

> A beggar came up to me and he said, "Mother Teresa, everybody's giving you, I also want to give to you. But today, I just got (what do you call that-- ten pennies?) ten pennies, and the whole day I want to give it to you. Then I said to myself, if I take it, he may have to go to bed without eating; if I don't take it, I will hurt him, so I took. And I've never seen the joy on anybody's face who has given his money or food or thing as I saw on that man's face; that he, too, could give something for somebody. This is the joy of loving, and I will pray for you that you will experience that joy of loving and that you share that joy of loving first in your own family and with all you meet."

Pope John Paul II invited Mother Teresa to address the World Synod of Bishops in Rome in 1980. In 1986, Pope John Paul II visited Mother Teresa and the home for the dying in Calcutta. "This place represents a profound dignity of every human person," stated Pope John Paul II.

At those times when her physical strength faltered, it was as if "she ran on prayer," observed a fellow sister. The sister also observed that joy was the impression that Teresa left with those who met her.

When she received, an honorary Doctorate of Medicine from Rome's Catholic University, Teresa observed, "Abortion is nothing but the fear of the child— fear to have to feed one more child, to have to educate one more child, to have to love one more child. Therefore, the child must die."

A Red Cross official in Beirut commented that he thought Mother Teresa was "a cross between a military commander and St. Francis." Mother Teresa commented on that experience of man's inhumanity to man: "I have never been in a war before, but I have seen famine and death. I was asking myself what do people feel when they do these things? I don't understand. They are all children of God. Why do they do it? I don't understand."

There was a time when Pope John Paul II himself telephoned Mother Teresa to say, "The whole world needs you, so please enter the hospital and rest."

The sisters opened a house in Yugoslavia and, in 1981, a house in East Berlin—one of twenty-six opened that year. In 1983, another house was opened in East Germany, in Karl Marx Stadt. For Mother Teresa, the poverty of the people of communist countries was extreme, for they were deprived of that most vital of all riches: the knowledge of the love of God for all men. Her own ill health could not be allowed to stand in the way of endeavors to meet that need.

Regardless of health, Mother Teresa would continue her travels. For instance, in 1988 she and other sisters would go to South Africa. The sisters would remain to do their work. Her message there was that if people deepened their faith in prayer, they would see "there was no religion, no caste, no colour, no nationality, no riches and no poverty."

The *Cape Times* commented, "She did not sit on foreign sidelines condemning people or a situation in this country. She came in person, identified herself with those most in need of compassion, and set up a mission to help them. This has always been her method, ever since she started her first hospice in the slums of Calcutta. Her saintly credentials are so universally respected that they silence even the most rabid radicals – for once no one questioned a famous international figure's decision to visit South Africa."

What enabled her to continue? She would so often say, "It is the joy of bringing love into people's lives that keeps us all going." She would also say, "There will be plenty of time to rest in eternity. Here there is so much to do ..."

In April 1990, Pope John Paul II accepted the resignation of Mother Teresa as superior general of the Missionaries of Charity. Mother Teresa would write a letter to her entire family:

> This brings you my prayer and blessing for each one of you – my love and gratitude to each one of you for all you have been and have done all these forty years to share the joy of loving each other and the Poorest of the Poor.
>
> Your presence and the work you have done throughout the world for the glory of God and the good of the Poor has been a living miracle of love of God and yours in action. God has shown his greatness by using nothingness – so let us always remain in our nothingness – so as, to give God free hand to use us without consulting us. Let us accept whatever he gives and give whatever he gives and give whatever he takes with a big smile.

By 1990, the Missionaries of Charity had 3,068 professed sisters, 454 novices, and 140 candidates. The sisters had over four hundred houses in over ninety countries. From 1991 to 1997, 108 additional

Missionary of Charity houses outside India were founded. The bravery and dedication of the Missionaries of Charity have been recognized on every continent, including countries suffering the effects of localized persecutions, even genocides, such as the Rwandan Holocaust of the '90s. There had also come to be, in a smaller measure, the Missionary Fathers of Charity. The coworkers struggling to do small things with great love throughout the world numbered some three million. In Mother Teresa's words,

> I did not know that our work would grow so fast or go so far. I never doubted that it would live, but I did not think that it would be like this. Doubt I never had, because I had this conviction that if God blesses it, it will prosper. Humanly speaking, it is impossible, out of the question, because none of us has got the experience. None of us has got the things that the world looks for. This is the miracle of all those little Sisters and people all around the world. God is using them – they are just little instruments in his hands. But they have their conviction. As long, as any of us has this conviction, we are all right. The work will prosper.

Mother Teresa was then able to return to her childhood home of Albania. Albania was the poorest European country and the last bastion of communism in eastern Europe—a country, as Mother Teresa would put it, that was "legally atheist." Practicing religion meant a prison sentence of three to ten years. Nearly a thousand Orthodox and Catholic churches were being used for secular purposes. Of the 160 Catholic clergy there, 100 died in prison or labor camps. Schoolchildren had been encouraged to denounce parents who prayed or kept icons, Bibles, or crucifixes in their homes. Forty years of communism had undermined basic moral and spiritual values. God had been effectively banished from Albania.

Mother Teresa, however, had been quietly conducting a crusade of her own to bring Him back. She asked the president of Albania about opening a house. "The President told me that to open a house there, I would have to break the law. I told him, 'Then I am ready to break the law'." She confided such with mischievous satisfaction in February 1992. The idea of being a lawbreaker for God amused her.

Mother Teresa did succeed in obtaining permission to take her sisters to Albania. On the twenty-first of February 1991, jubilant crowds had sent toppling a towering statue of Enver Hoxha, a hated symbol of Albania's Stalinist past. Tens of thousands gathered in the capitol to call for democracy and greater freedom.

Originally the date for the arrival of Mother Teresa and her sisters into Albania had been fixed by the Albanian president for March 4, but he brought it forward to March 2—a fact that Mother Teresa saw as significant because it was the birthday of Pope Pius XII, the first pope to have given his blessing to her congregation. It was also the birthday of Cardinal James Knox, the bishop who had given so much encouragement to her and her sisters in the early years of the congregation. Before flying to Albania on March 2, Mother Teresa received a blessing from Pope John Paul II with his instructions: "Go and prepare the way."

Pope John Paul would later meet the new Albanian prime minister, and the ties between Albania and the Vatican, which had broken off in May 1945, would renew in September 1991. As the pope stated on October 19, 2003: "The witness of Mother Teresa's life reminds us all, that the Church's evangelizing mission is achieved through charity and is nourished through prayer and attentive listening to the Word of God."

In her later years, Mother Teresa could still be found handing out prayer cards, which she also referred to as "business cards." Printed on them were these words:

> The fruit of silence is prayer
> The fruit of prayer is faith
> The fruit of faith is love
> The fruit of love is service
> The fruit of service is peace.

On Friday September 5, 1997, Mother Teresa's heart beat its last. Her last appearance before the cameras was only days before. She had given an address on the untimely death of Diana, Princess of Wales, speaking of Diana's love for the poor and offering special prayers for her.

A week later, India afforded Mother Teresa a state funeral. The Missionaries of Charity accepted the offer. On September 13, Mother Teresa's body was borne through the streets of Calcutta on the same gun carriage that had carried the bodies of Mahatma Gandhi and Jawaharlal Nehru, as tens of thousands of people lined the route.

Mother Teresa had written the following:

> There are many poor people that need love and compassion; that need your hands to serve them; that need your hearts to love them ... people are not hungry just for bread, they are hungry for love. People are not naked only for a piece of cloth; they are naked for that human dignity. People are not only homeless for a room made of bricks; but they are homeless – being rejected, unwanted, unloved. Jesus says: "Love as I have loved you": I have wanted you. I have loved you and you love, as I have loved you. There is so much suffering everywhere. Suffering from hunger, from homelessness, from all kinds of diseases. But I still think that the greatest suffering is being lonely, being unwanted, being unloved, just having no one, having forgotten what it is like to have the human touch, human love, what it is to be wanted, what it is to be loved, what it is to have your own people.
>
> I feel more and more that the poor are the hope of salvation of mankind because, we are going to be judged at the hour of death with what we have been to them, what we have done for them. Jesus Christ said that on the judgment day, He is going to judge us with these

words – "I was hungry and you fed me, I was naked and you clothed me, I was homeless and you took me in."

Mother Teresa had nearly died in Rome in June of 1983. As her strength returned, she asked for a pen and paper to write the fruit of her meditations. Perhaps we, too, may learn how to do a good work.

After describing Jesus as the "The Joy to be shared" and "The Peace to be given," Mother Teresa wrote,

> The Leper—to wash his wounds.
> The Beggar—to give him a smile.
> The Drunkard—to listen to Him.
> The Mental—to protect Him.
> The Little One—to embrace Him.
> The Blind—to lead Him.
> The Dumb—to speak for Him.
> The Crippled—to walk with Him.
> The Drug Addict—to befriend Him.
> The Prostitute—to remove from danger and befriend her.
> The Prisoner—to be visited.
> The Old—to be served.

There are too many stories of Mother Teresa to be told in this brief annal. Perhaps we may leave with one heartfelt story told by Mother Teresa of a woman picked up on a Calcutta Street. Mother Teresa personally looked after the woman.

> I did for her all that my love can do. I put her in bed, and there was such a beautiful smile on her face. She took hold of my hand, as she said one word only, "Thank you", —and she died. I could not help examining my conscience before her, and I asked, what would I say if I was in her place. And my answer was very simple: I would have tried to draw a little attention to myself; I

would have said, "I am hungry, that I am dying, I am cold, I am in pain," or something, but she gave me much more— she gave me her grateful love. And she died with a smile on her face.

In all her prayers, in all her work, and in all her dedication, Mother Teresa always knew that all this was not about her. She said,

> My conviction that –the work is His—is more than reality. I have never doubted. It hurts me only when the people call me foundress because I know for certain He asked—Will you do this for Me? Everything was His—I had only to surrender myself to His plan—to His will. –Today His work has grown because it is, He, not I, that do[es] it through me. Of this I am so convinced— that I would give my life gladly to prove it.

To each of us she would counsel, "I pray that nothing may ever so fill you with pain and sorrow as to make you forget the joy of the Risen Jesus."

FRANCIS S. COLLINS

A Scientist

He told them another parable: "The kingdom of heaven is like a mustard seed, which a man took and planted in his field. Though it is the smallest of all seeds, yet when it grows, it is the largest of garden plants and becomes a tree, so that the birds come and perch in its branches."

—Matthew 13:31–32 NIV

Francis S. Collins is known as one of the country's leading geneticists and a longtime head of the Human Genome Project. The human genome consists of all human DNA and is known as the hereditary code of life. Simple enough.

In effect, the many years of research revealed a language—a new text, three billion letters long—written in a strange and cryptographic four-letter code. Such amazing complexity of information is carried within each cell of the human body. If this code were to be read at a rate of one letter per second, day and night, the reader would not sleep for thirty-one years. Printing out these letters in regular font and on normal bond paper would result in a tower the height of the Washington monument. Collins once stated, "For me, the experience of sequencing the human genome, and uncovering this most remarkable of all texts, was both a stunning scientific achievement and an occasion of worship."

But of course, the story of Francis Collins does not begin so simply and begins without recognition of any God, starting from his youth. "My early life was unconventional in many ways, but as the son of freethinkers, I had an upbringing that was quite conventionally modern in its attitude toward faith—it just wasn't very important."

Collins was raised on a farm in the Shenandoah Valley of Virginia. His parents had met in graduate school at Yale in 1931. They worked on a project with Eleanor Roosevelt during the Great Depression. They established the Oak Grove Theater. It was farm work, summer theater, and music for Francis Collins while growing up. Francis was homeschooled by a talented mother. "Faith was not an important part of my childhood. I was vaguely aware of the concept of God ..."

When Collins was age ten, the family moved to town, and he entered the public schools. There he was inspired by a chemistry teacher at age fourteen: "I discovered for the first time the intense satisfaction of the ordered nature of the universe. The fact that all matter was constructed of atoms and molecules that followed mathematical principles was an unexpected revelation, and the ability to use the tools of science to discover new things about nature struck me at once as something of which I wanted to be a part. ... I decided my goal in life would be to become a chemist."

Francis also studied biology. The subject, however, seemed to involve more memorization than elucidation of principles.

> The overwhelming complexity of life led me to the conclusion that biology was rather like existential philosophy: it just didn't make any sense. For my budding reductionist mind, there was not nearly enough logic in it to be appealing ... Graduating at sixteen, I went on to the University of Virginia, determined to major in chemistry and pursue a scientific career. Like most college freshmen, I found this new environment invigorating, with so many ideas bouncing off

> the classroom walls and in the dorm rooms late at night. Some of those questions invariably turned to the existence of God. In my early teens, I had had occasional moments of the experience of longing for something outside myself, often associated with the beauty of nature or a particularly profound musical experience. Nevertheless, my sense of the spiritual was very undeveloped and easily challenged by the one or two aggressive atheists one finds in almost every college dormitory. But a few months into my college career, I became convinced that while many religious faiths had inspired interesting traditions of art and culture, they held no foundational truth.

By definition then, Collins was agnostic, or in the "I don't know"—and really, "I don't want to know"—camp, or the state of "willful blindness," as it is referred to by C. S. Lewis.

> After graduation, Francis went on to a PhD program in physical chemistry at Yale, pursuing the mathematical elegance that had first drawn me to this branch of science ... My intellectual life was immersed in quantum mechanics and second-order differential equations, and my heroes were the giants of physics—Albert Einstein, Niels Bohr, Paul Dirac ... I gradually became convinced that everything in the universe could be explained, on the basis of equations and physical principles ... No thinking scientist could seriously entertain the possibility of God without committing some sort of intellectual suicide ... And so, I gradually shifted from agnosticism to atheism. I felt quite comfortable challenging the spiritual beliefs of anyone who mentioned them in my presence and discounted such perspectives as sentimentality and outmoded superstition.

Two years into the PhD program, the narrowly structured plan began to fall apart. Francis revisited the life sciences as biochemistry, studying the principles of DNA, RNA, and protein. Here he had the ability to apply rigorous intellectual principles, as well as the possibility of applying this knowledge for human benefit. Francis was astounded. Biology had mathematical elegance. Life made sense.

Now with a young child, Francis instead applied to medical school and was accepted to the University of North Carolina. Francis loved the intellectual stimulation there. As a doctor, one is thrust into the most intimate relationships imaginable. Bedside conversations with the good North Carolina people included the spiritual aspect of what many were going through. "Is there a God?"— "could there be a more important question in all of human existence?" Collins asked himself.

At first confident a full investigation would, reaffirm his atheism, Francis finally went down the street to visit a Methodist minister. He was given *Mere Christianity* by C. S. Lewis, the legendary Oxford scholar. Lewis himself had been an atheist who had set out to disprove faith, on the basis, of logical argument. The title of book one is "Right and Wrong as a Clue to the Meaning of the Universe." The concept of a moral law—a concept of right and wrong appearing to be universal among all members of the human species—is expanded upon in this book, with many examples.

To quote Lewis, "We want to know whether the universe simply happens to be what it is for no reason or whether there is a power behind it that makes it what it is. Since that power, if it exists, would be not one of the observed facts but a reality which makes them, no mere observation of the facts can find it. There is only one case in which we can know whether there is anything more, namely our own case. And in that case, we find there is. Or put it the other way round. If there was a controlling power outside the universe, it could not show itself to us as one of the facts inside the universe—no more than the architect of a house could actually be a wall or staircase or fireplace in that house. The only way in which we could expect it to show itself would be inside ourselves as an influence or a command trying to get us to behave in a certain way. And that, is just what we do find inside ourselves. Surely this ought to arouse suspicions?"

As Lewis also reflects, "atheism turns out to be too simple. If the whole universe has no meaning, we should never have found out that it has no meaning: just as, if there were no light in the universe and therefore no creatures with eyes, we should never know it was dark. Dark would be without meaning." On the other hand, Lewis says, "It is no good asking for a simple religion. After all, real things are not simple. They look, simple, but they are not. The table [I] am sitting at looks simple: but ask a scientist to tell you what it is really made of—all about the atoms and how the light waves rebound from them and hit [my] eye and what they do to the optic nerve and what it does to [my] brain—."

In an effort, to understand time in a paragraph, —Lewis writes, "If you picture Time as a straight line along which we have to travel, then you must picture God as the whole page on which the line is drawn. We come to the parts of the line one by one: we have to leave A behind before we get to B, and cannot reach C until we leave B behind. God, from above or outside or all round, contains the whole line, and sees it all."

To quote Collins, "If God is the Creator of all the universe, if God had a specific plan for the arrival of humankind on the scene, and if He had a desire for personal fellowship with humans, into whom He had instilled the Moral Law as a signpost toward Himself, then He can hardly be threatened by the efforts of our puny minds to understand the grandeur of His creation ... The elegance behind life's complexity is indeed reason for awe, and for belief in God."

And the creation of the universe itself? At the beginning of the twentieth century, most scientists assumed a universe with no beginning and no end, or a static universe. This created certain physical paradoxes, along with evidence of background noise and a precise kind of afterglow predicating evidence of the correctness of a big bang theory. Owing to these and other observations, physicists came into agreement that the universe began as an infinitely dense, dimensionless point of pure energy. The laws of physics, of course, break down at this point, referring to the circumstance as a "singularity." Physics is unable to interpret the very earliest events in the explosion that took place during the first 1043 seconds, or one tenth of a millionth of a millionth of a millionth of a millionth of a millionth of a millionth of a millionth of a second. After that we have the formation of stable atomic nuclei, the formation of atoms, and the infinite complexity and laws of the universe as we know them.

The existence of the big bang begs the question of what came before. It certainly demonstrates the limits of science as no other phenomenon has done. The consequences of the big bang theory are profound. According to the theory, the universe was created from "nothing."

Collins observes: "The sense of awe created by these realizations has caused more than a few agnostic scientists to sound downright theological."

In *God and the Astronomers*, astrophysicist Robert Jastrow writes,

> At this moment it seems as though science will never be able to raise the curtain on the mystery of creation. For the scientist who has lived by his faith in the power of reason, the story ends like a bad dream. He has scaled the mountains of ignorance; he is about to conquer the highest peak; as he pulls himself over the final rock, he is greeted by a band of theologians who have been sitting there for centuries." Collins notes there to be much to inspire mutual appreciation between theologians and scientists due to these recent discoveries of the origin of the universe.

Jastrow further writes,

> Now we see how the astronomical evidence leads to a biblical view of the origin of the world. The details differ, but the essential elements and the astronomical and biblical accounts of Genesis are the same; the chain of events leading to man commenced suddenly and

sharply at a definite moment in time, in a flash of light and energy ...

In agreement, Collins writes,

> I have to agree. The Big Bang cries out for a divine explanation. It forces the conclusion that nature had a defined beginning. I cannot see how nature could have created itself. Only a supernatural force that is outside of space and time could have done that. If you are compelled (as I am) by the existence of the Moral Law and the universal longing for God, if you sense there is a glowing signpost within our hearts, pointing toward a benevolent and loving presence ...

Then Francis S. Collins offers that work like his, supports belief in a creator.

The questions of Genesis and creation clearly are not new. Saint Augustine, a converted skeptic, and brilliant theologian, lived around AD 400. In his writings *The Meaning of Genesis*, *Confessions*, and *The City of God*, Augustine may provide more questions than answers. Augustine writes of the meaning of time and does conclude that God is outside of time and not bound to it. As 2 Peter 3:8 NIV states, "But do not forget this one thing, dear friends: With the Lord a day is like a thousand years, and a thousand years are like a day."

The Hebrew word used in Genesis 1 for day ("*y^om*") can be used both to describe a twenty-four-hour day and, also to describe a more symbolic representation. There are places in the Bible where "y^om" is utilized in a nonliteral context, such as "the day of the Lord." We might say "in my grandfather's day" without implying that Grandpa lived only twenty-four hours. Thus is the understanding. We learn as much about God's character.

For Collins, "If the existence of God is true (not just tradition, but, actually, true), and if certain scientific conclusions about the natural world are also true (not just in fashion, but objectively true), then they cannot contradict each other. A fully harmonious synthesis must be possible."

As to the inner workings of the cell, Collins was amazed and awed by the intricacies of the molecular machines that reside there. "There are elegant machines that translate RNA into protein, others that help the cell move around, and others that transmit signals from the cell surface to the nucleus, traveling along a cascading pathway of multiple components. It is not just the cell that provides amazement. Entire organs, made up of billions and trillions of cells, are constructed in a way that can only inspire awe. Consider, for instance, the human eye, a complex cameralike organ whose anatomy and physiology continue to impress even the most sophisticated student of optics." Asking your optometrist to explain, precisely, the whys and how's that allow vision may elicit a reference to God.

Collins also references another complexity: "A prominent example is the bacterial flagellum. Many different bacteria possess these flagella, which are little 'outboard motors' that propel cells in various directions. The structure of the flagellum, which consists of about thirty different proteins, is really, quite elegant. It includes miniature versions of a base anchor, a drive shaft, and a universal joint. All of this drives a filament propeller. The whole arrangement is a nanotechnology engineering marvel."

Collins "found this elegant evidence of the relatedness of all living things an occasion of awe and came to see this as the master plan of the same Almighty who caused the universe to come into being and set its physical parameters just precisely right to allow the creation of stars, planets, heavy elements, and life itself." Collins concludes that "the God of the Bible is also the God of the genome. He can be worshiped in the cathedral or in the laboratory. His creation is majestic, awesome, intricate, and beautiful—and it cannot be at war with itself. Only we imperfect humans can start such battles. And only we can end them."

Saint Augustine, in referring to the Creator and to creation, wrote: "yet would man praise Thee; he, but a particle of Thy creation. Thou awakest us to delight in Thy praise; for Thou madest us for Thyself, and our heart is restless until it repose in Thee."

GEORGE FRIDERIC HANDEL

A Chorus

It was the days of kings and queens, princes and princesses, electors and electresses, and dukes and duchesses. Into that world, George Frideric Handel was born in Halle, Germany, in 1685. It was his talent that shone forth and his work that we remember.

These were the days of subjects rather than citizens. History had not yet written the pages of struggles that would allow for a government of the people, by the people, and for the people. At times, the subjects fixated, ascribed, and projected all the people's hopes, dreams, aspirations, and protections onto ordinary mortals. Hopefully we will never retreat from this quest for liberty, freedom, and responsibility we have been so privileged to enjoy.

Many of us have had the distinct pleasure of singing or listening to Handel's *Messiah*. Although gifted with natural musical talent, he was discouraged from developing those talents in his youth by his father. The elder considered his becoming a lawyer or maybe a respected physician much better. His talents would surface, however, and in the tradition of Luther, who was one of the first to put Christian words to popular tunes, George Frederic would eventually receive encouragement and music lessons.

Some of what George was taught involved the importance of music. A thousand years before, the Venerable Bede (673–735) had written, "Music encourages us to bear the heaviest afflictions, administers consolation in every difficulty, refreshes the broken spirit, removes headaches and cures crossness and melancholy." George would learn that music had a long history. The ancients invented musical instruments. In time, systems of musical notation were developed. The invention of printing finally stopped the continual modification of the systems.

John Calvin, for instance, disliked the idea of writing fresh words for hymns. He taught that only the psalms of David should be sung. Many Christians in the earlier centuries preferred voices and choral arrangements to be sung in church. Organs would enter the churches in the tenth century.

Describing Handel's earliest days, one of his biographers wrote, "from his very childhood Handel had discovered such a strong propensity to Music, that his father, who always intended him for the study of the Civil Law, had reason to be alarmed." Doctor Handel "strictly forbad him to meddle with any musical instrument." There were stories of smuggling clavichords and of a certain innate stubbornness to reflect Handel's propensity toward music. On the other hand, it must also be said that a contemporary writer for Doctor Handel wrote, "In common life, he was friendly with everyone and modestly mild and good to the needy and to paupers."

One day, a young Handel wished to go with his father as he traveled to see the Duke. His father thought it improper for an eight-year-old. George Frideric was persistent. He ran behind the carriage, and his father finally let him come with. While the adults were in conversation, they heard the young Handel playing the organ. "Something there was in the manner of playing which drew his attention so strongly" was recorded of the duke's attention to Frederic's playing. Apparently, the Duke, too, loved music. He assisted in persuading George's father to allow this rising genius to follow his inclinations and provided a monetary gift to that end.

George Frideric Handel returned to Halle and to the tutelage of Friedrich Wilhelm Zachow, the organist of the *Marien Kirche*. Handel also studied languages, mathematics, and ethics. At the age of twelve, he lost his father. Handel wrote a heartfelt poem in his memory.

After his father's death, George Frideric returned to learn further at the Lutheran Gymnasium. In 1702, at the age of seventeen, George Frideric enrolled at the University of Haller. One of Handel's professors, a zealous man and a pietist, taught that although Christians were saved by faith alone, their faith should be accompanied by good works. The professor operated an orphanage, and Handel often went with to the orphanage.

George was offered and appointed chief organist of the Calvinist Church known as Dom-Kirche. As well as performing his duties, he was to lead a Christian and edifying life. The final paragraph of the agreement read, "In return for his trouble and performance he is promised and assigned as a stipend for the probationary year … fifty thalers, which he will draw from the Royal Purse of this province … in quarterly instalments of 12 thalers 12 gulden, beginning next Trinity Sunday, and in addition free lodging in the Moritzburg most generally assigned to organists by his Royal Highness. This appointment is given at Halle under the hands and seals of us, the Pastors and Elders …"

At that time in 1701, King Frederick began to make Germany a military state. In 1702, Queen Anne came to the British throne. She spent her reign firming the bloodless Glorious Revolution, making England officially Protestant. Extraordinary cares were taken in discovering who would assume the throne. Would the king wake the next morning and still find himself a king? Charles I was beheaded in 1649. History records show that he was not popular. James II was kindly escorted from the throne in 1688.

In 1703, George Frederic Handel would leave Halle for Hamburg, paying his own way. Hamburg was two hundred miles to the northwest of Halle; it was a prosperous city untouched by the Thirty Years' War. There, Georg Friedrich taught music and played in churches. Hamburg was home to a magnificent opera house, the Theatre am Gansemarkt. The largest in northern Europe, it was under the direction of Reinhard Keiser. A fellow by the name of Johann Mattheson is said to have introduced George to Keiser. Mattheson, son of a customs collector, was well educated. Mattheson recommended a student to Handel for music lessons. That student was the son of the British consul. The versatile

Handel quickly learned various musical instruments at the theater. Reinhard saw his potential. Handel, indeed, composed music for his first success, *Almira*.

Operas were said to be more than just a bit melodramatic. The associated drunkenness and obscene material prompted Handel to begin thinking of writing his own operas.

Christian Postel, who wrote librettos for Keiser, converted to Christianity, and stopped writing the off-color scripts. He asked Handel to write music to his new libretto. Keiser came on board, and the *The Passion of St. John* was played at the opera.

Mattheson had left for Holland, but they invited him to the opening. He obliged. Mattheson then composed music for another libretto, titled *Cleopatra*. It was a hit. Mattheson starred as a tenor. Handel directed from the harpsichord. After a particularly dramatic scene involving the death of his character, Mattheson thought he should hasten to the pit and replace George at the harpsichord. Mattheson became the star actor, star composer, star singer, and star musician too! That became too much humiliation for Handel to handle. Finally, at one performance, Handel refused to give up his seat at the harpsichord. After some glaring between the two and a "Get off the bench," Mattheson tried pulling Handel off, but Handel continued to play. After arguing, both began shouting. Mattheson, logically, challenged Handel to a duel. An animated audience followed outside.

Not having a sword of his own and never having truly used one in his life, but with all the acumen and judgment at his disposal as a keen violinist, Handel agreed to a fight to the death with swords. He borrowed one from a friend.

Amid the shouting crowd, the two circled, thrust, and parried. In the following years, Mattheson would always tell the same story. It was only a large button on Handel's coat that saved him from an accurate thrust of Mattheson's sword. That is the essence of the story. Yes, they did reconcile, and each felt guilty. Mattheson, in later reflections, said the duel "might have passed off very unfortunately for both of us, had God's guidance not graciously ordained that my blade, thrusting against my opponent's broad metal coat-button, should be shattered."

Handel, at twenty-one, continued to give lessons, playing the violin and harpsichord, but, with all the drama, he began feeling played out in Hamburg. Apparently, as recorded from more than one source, George, and Johann each decided to apply for an organist position in Lubeck. The current holder was a Danish composer. Bach, at one time, had also applied, but he had turned down the position. Handel and Mattheson traveled the countryside together on their way to Lubeck. They discovered that a condition and custom of the time at this location in baroque Germany was that the new organist, marry the previous organist's daughter. Handel was said to stutter now and then. This was one of those times. Each respectfully declined. Handel and Mattheson returned to Hamburg.

Handel continued his apprenticeship in Hamburg. Some of his talents were seen in the success of *Almira*. He met many people from across Europe. Within that circle, perhaps, was the Grand Duke of Tuscany, who invited Handel to Florence, Italy. Italy was the country that had invented operas, oratorios, and cantatas. It was, by far, the leading center of music.

Handel would spend the next four formative years of his altogether distinguished career in the company of the world's finest musicians. Some of his patrons would be the Medici family in Florence, Cardinal Ottoboni, and others. Ottoboni held Wednesday music meetings, offering musicians the opportunity to make contacts.

On January 14, 1707, the diarist Valesio noted that "there has arrived in this city a Saxon, a most excellent player on the harpsichord and composer, who today gave a flourish of his skill by playing the organ in the church of S. Giovanni, to the amazement of everyone present."

Handel became a workaholic in his discipline, producing a voluminous portfolio of compositions. A psalm Handel put to music was performed in Rome on Easter Sunday.

He would write over one hundred cantatas, many psalms, and motets. He would meet some of the greatest musicians, composers, and singers alive, such as Allesandro Scarlatti. He traveled to Venice, which was alive with as many as seven opera houses. As a sidenote, opera had previously been banned in Rome by the Pope.

In Venice, Handel composed several operas. *Aggrippina* was performed twenty-seven times in a single season. Cheers of *"Liva il caro sassone!"* ("Long live the beloved Saxon!") were heard. Though technically, perhaps, not a Saxon, Handel readily accepted the applause, nonetheless.

Having had success while hearing and working with Italy's best musicians, Handel decided it was time to return to Germany. He settled in Hanover. He had been invited to do so by Prince Ernst, the younger brother of Electress Sophia Charlotte and George Ludwig. This would prove to be a royal family Handel, at some level, would be connected for a lifetime. Sophia was duly impressed with Handel and thought him to be the greatest organist in the world. She called George Frederic Handel "a Saxon who surpasses everyone who has ever been heard in harpsichord-playing and composition."

Elector Georg Ludwig offered Handel the post of kapellmeister with a high annual salary. George Frederic, on the other hand, preferred to travel. Ludwig countered with an immediate leave of absence "for a twelve-month or more, if he chose it."

George Frederic Handel accepted this generous offer. He left Hanover in the autumn of 1710. On his way, he travelled to Halle to visit his mother, who was in extreme old age at fifty-nine. He also visited former teachers and friends. From Holland, he sailed north across the North Sea, up the Thames, and past the Tower of London. He viewed the newly constructed St. Paul's Cathedral. Some earlier developments had been interrupted by the Great Plague of 1666. In 1711, Parliament passed a commission to build fifty new churches— a goal not achieved.

Queen Anne was described as lonely and as having reluctantly assumed the throne. She had married Prince George of Denmark. They would have sixteen children, but all of them would die: most in infancy and many from illnesses.

English opera needed a boost. Handel was presented to the Queen. He collaborated with Giacomo Rossi on a new opera. Rossi would later say, "to my great wonder I saw an entire Opera put to music by that surprising genius, with the greatest degree of perfection, in just two weeks." *Rinaldo* was written in the Italian vein of *opera seria* (serious opera) as opposed to *opera buffa* (comedic opera). George Frideric Handel, with members of the opera, performed for the Queen on her birthday, February 6, 1711.

George Frideric, still officially kapellmeister, returned to Hanover, where he further studied his English. Handel already knew Latin, French, and Italian. He would return to His Electoral Highness, Georg Ludwig, to ask permission to return to England. He was once again given permission "on [the] condition that he engaged to return within a reasonable time." It may be speculated that, in his conversation with His Highness, Handel would have been asked how he liked Ludwig's second cousin, Queen Anne.

This very brief writing will not endeavor to enumerate the various works written and performed by Handel while in England. He returned to the courts of Queen Anne and was awarded an annual pension. He continued to compose and perform concerts. Queen Anne would pass away on August 1, 1714, at the age of forty-nine. Georg Ludwig of Hanover would become His Majesty King George I of England. The new king was not proficient in English and was wooden in public. It is said that he loathed the pageantry that accompanied the monarchy. His disinterest for English society and the workings of Parliament strengthened that Parliament in its own way. He was despised for his cruelty toward his wife in Germany, and he freely imported his mistresses to England. English boys and girls would recite the jingle

> Georgie Porgie, pudding and pie,
> Kissed the girls and made them cry;
> When the girls came out to play
> Georgie Porgie ran away.

George Frederic Handel became a British subject in February of 1727, the same year King George I passed away, to no one's dismay.

The son of King George I became King George II. George I and George II had not operated on the best of terms for many different reasons.

The new king, unlike his father, loved pomp and pageantry. The king wore velvet, trimmed with ermine and gold lace at his coronation. His train was borne by four young noblemen and the master of the robes. Queen Caroline's dress was adorned with millions of pounds' worth of precious stones. She also carried a scepter and an ivory rod. She complained of the weight of her dress as "the worst thing [she] had to bear." Handel composed the coronation anthems. Londoners were excited and hopeful for the prospects of their new king.

The prospect for the opera, however, seemed more tenuous. Economies were weak, and singers went unpaid. Some wondered if the operas would survive the winter. Some superstars returned to Italy. In 1729, a reduced Royal Academy was summoned to Court. It was decided that two opera composers, Heidegger and Handel, would be permitted to carry on for another five years. Opera attendance was unpredictable for Handel. However, when King George II and Queen Caroline attended, attendance increased dramatically, as Londoners wanted to be seen with their king.

After five years, Handel's contract was not renewed. Compensation from the king would continue as Handel moved to his new venue. George Frederic continued working many hours composing, but it seemed the operas were not of the consistent high quality as previous seasons.

On April 13, 1737, Handel woke to find he had lost the use of four fingers on his right hand. The stroke had also affected his arm. Dejected, he would finally follow the advice of his doctors and travel to the steam baths of Aix-la-Chapelle. A friend said that "it was with the utmost difficulty that he was persuaded to do what was proper."

Handel stayed in Aix-la-Chapelle for six weeks. A large Cathedral was nearby. He went to visit and was allowed to play the organ. His playing was recorded as being "so much beyond any they had ever been used to." It was further written that "his cure, from the manner as well as from the quickness, with which it was wrought, passed with the Nuns for a miracle." A nun may have mentioned the miracle to Handel as he left. Perhaps she asked, "Could it be that God has worked a special miracle because He has a special purpose?" George Frederic Handel then returned to England.

On November 20, 1737, Queen Caroline died at the age of fifty-four. Family tensions had always been high as it seemed one generation hated the other. Lord Hervey recalled, "The Queen often in her illness spoke of [her eldest son], and always with detestation …and as the King and Princess Caroline, both told me, the Queen would sometimes when she talked of dying cry: 'At least I shall have one comfort in having my eyes eternally closed – I shall never see that monster again.'"

In 1731, the Spanish had boarded an English ship and looted its cargo in the West Indies. They lopped off the captain's ear and told him to give it to his king. King George had ordered an investigation, without results. After seven years, the captain of the ship addressed Parliament and may have shown them his ear. Crowds of Londoners marched and shouted, "War with Spain!" England declared war on Spain on October 19, 1739. The war was known as the War of Jenkin's Ear. New taxes to pay for the cost of war were imposed. This had the effect of reducing attendance at the theater.

In July of 1741, Charles Jennens wrote to a friend, "Handel says he will do nothing next Winter, but I hope I shall perswade him to set another Scripture Collection I have made for him, & perform it for his own Benefit in Passion week. I hope he will lay out his whole Genius & Skill upon it, that the Composition may excel all his former Compositions, as the Subject excels every other Subject. The Subject is Messiah …"

Handel studied the libretto, *Alleluia: for the Lord God omnipotent reigneth*, from Revelations. He may have remembered his own father telling him this same truth.

On Saturday, August 22, 1741, Handel seated himself at his desk in a front room of his home. He bowed his head and prayed. He began to compose. Music began to flow within his mind like a living stream from heaven. Harmonies stirred his soul. Hour after hour, day after day, he filled sheet after sheet with Jesus Christ, the Messiah, and the fulfillment of prophecy. The oratorio *Messiah* was completed in just twenty-four days—a miracle of creativity.

Jennens could not believe Handel had responsibly completed the work that quickly. In his opinion, "[Handel's] Messiah has disappointed me; being set in great haste, tho' he said he would be a year about it, & make it the best of all his Compositions. I shall put no more Sacred Words into his hands, to be thus abus'd."

Jennens further stated, "What adds to my chagrin is, that if he makes (out his) Oratorio (to be) ever so perfect, there is a clamour about Town, to arise from the Bishops, against performing it." A newspaper published an opinion that "An Oratorio either is an 'Act of Religion', or it is not." With a change of plan, the *Messiah* would modestly debut in Dublin, Ireland, rather than London, England.

While in Ireland, Handel introduced the *Messiah* during Passion Week (Holy Week). Handel would perform the work for the benefit of three local charitable societies. The Dublin New-Letter proclaimed, "Mr. Handel's new sacred Oratorio ...in the opinion of the best Judges, far surpasses anything of the Nature, which has been performed in this or in any other Kingdom."

The three Dublin newspapers carried the following similar reports:

> Words are wanting to express the exquisite Delight it afforded to the admiring crouded Audience. The Sublime, the Grand and the Tender, adapted to the most elevated, majestic and moving Works, conspired to transport and charm the ravished Heart and Ear. It is but Justice to Mr. Handel, that the World should know, he generously gave the Money arising from this Grand Performance, to be equally shared by the Society for relieving Prisoners, the Charitable Infirmary, and Mercer's Hospital, for which they will ever grateful remember ...

Charles Burney, a writer of the day, wrote: "this great work has been heard in all parts of the kingdom with increasing reverence and delight; it has fed the hungry, clothed the naked, fostered the orphan ... more than any single production in this or any country."

Audiences everywhere, traditionally stand up as the "Hallelujah Chorus" is sung. During the Holy Week of 1759, a friend related, "I had the pleasure to reconcile him to his old friends: He saw them, and forgave them, and let all their legacies stand! ... It was apparently his hope to die, like his Maker, on Good Friday ... 'as he had lived – a good Christian, with a true sense of his duty to God and man, and in perfect charity with all the world."

As George Frederic Handel concluded the "Hallelujah Chorus," he wrote with tears, "I did think I did see all heaven before me and the great God himself."

MONSIGNOR GEORGES LEMAITRE

A Discoverer

Where to begin? Georges Lemaitre was born July 17, 1894, the eldest son in a Catholic family, in Charleroi, Belgium. His father was a director of a marble quarry and a glass factory. His mother was said to be joyful and courageous by nature, demanding toward homework and punctuality at mealtimes, with an unbounded affection for her son Georges. She was also a woman of deep faith. She is quoted as having said, "If I were a man, I would have been at the top of the Himalayas." Georges would carry with him a deep attachment to his family throughout his life.

Georges Lemaitre entered a Jesuit school named the College of Sacre-Coeur in Charloi, in September of 1904. He excelled in mathematics, physics, and chemistry. One of his early influences was a scholar and priest named Fr. Ernest Verreux. Georges discovered that one could live a true life of faith along with an active openness toward science. At the young age of nine, Georges had decided to become a scientist.

Georges also confided to his parents his desire to become a priest. Edouard Lemaitre, Georges's father, proud of his young son, with wisdom, asked him to continue his studies. In July of 1911, Georges entered university, registering for mining engineering studies and Thomistic philosophy. His academic interests would rise from the subterranean to the cosmic, but not till after the Great War, or the War to End All Wars—The First World War.

During the summer of 1914, Georges and his brother Jacques planned a bicycle trip in Tyrol. The invasion of Belgium in August 1914 transformed their trip into a long walk to the Yser Front. Each enlisted, and by October 13 they had been sent to help the Third Army. On the eighteenth of October began the Battle of Yser, better known as the Battle of Flanders. Georges Lemaitre took part, often on the front line, in the toughest moments in the Battle of the Yser. After nine months of infantry service, he was transferred into the artillery. He would finish the war as an adjutant, his brother, as an officer. Later in life he would say, "1914. I was committed. The Yser. The war was for everybody … I finished it as an adjutant. Why not an officer?" Then, with some laughter, he added, "Maybe because I had a bad character. Unless it was my Commanding Officer. Or maybe both." Some of George's deepest and longest friendships were forged in the trenches of that war. Along with the Bible, Georges Lemaitre also read topics relating to science. He retained a great serenity during that war, it is said, as he deepened his spiritual quest and cosmic interests.

We here in the USA remember "In Flanders Fields" by John McCrae with poppies sold each Memorial Day.

> In Flanders fields the poppies blow
> Between the crosses, row on row,
> That mark our place; and in the sky
> The larks, still bravely singing, fly
> Scarce heard amid the guns below
>
> We are the Dead. Short days ago
> We lived, felt dawn, saw sunset glow,
> Loved and were loved, and now we lie,
> In Flanders fields.

Take up our quarrel with the foe:
To you from failing hands we throw
The torch; be yours to hold it high.
If ye break faith with us who die
We shall not sleep, though poppies grow
In Flanders fields.

In January of 1919, Georges Lemaitre returned to the university in Louvain, abandoning his studies in engineering. Instead, he studied physics and mathematics and then went on to the seminary. The seminarian mathematician would be comfortable with a certain concordance between the first biblical verses and data from the physical sciences. For instance, Lemaitre interpreted "the earth was without form, and void" as being an image of nothingness. As Lemaitre would say, "… There was not even any light. It is impossible that any 'body' could subsist without radiating light, indeed every 'body' at a certain temperature emits radiation of all wavelengths (according to the theory of Blackbody Radiation). Physically, absolute obscurity is the nothingness. One cannot see how it would be possible to understand this Tenebrae otherwise than in this absolute sense preceding the 'Fiat lux'; there was absolutely no light, there was thus, absolutely nothing. There was only the Spirit of God that prepared to create in the empty immensity: 'Spiritus Dei ferebatur super aquas'."

Lemaitre would prepare a thesis on relativity and gravitation. He would introduce cosmological constants in equations describing an expanding universe and resolving some of the various differentiations of Newton and Einstein. Rather than concepts of infinite universes, Lemaitre believed the universe remains accessible to human knowledge and proportionate to it.

Georges Lemaitre received ordination on September 22, 1923. Having earned a fellowship, he would leave for the University of Cambridge England as a research student in October the very same year. There he would study under the likes of renowned physicist Ernest Rutherford, the father of nuclear physics; G. W. Hobson, on the calculus of variations; and renowned astronomer Arthur Stanley

Eddington, whose writings included *The Mathematical Theory of Relativity*. Discussions of relativity and problems of astronomy and astrophysics were an encouragement to Lemaitre to focus on their intersection. This fertile interplay would lead to his seminal 1927 work on the expanding universe. A personal synthesis of science and faith would also emerge.

After returning briefly to Belgium in 1924, Georges Lemaitre would travel to Canada to attend a series of scientific meetings. Once again, the beneficiary of a fellowship grant, he would begin the 1924–25 academic year at the Harvard College Observatory. In order, to gain a PhD, he would also register at the Massachusetts Institute of Technology (MIT). His scientific work concerned the study of variable stars, general relativity, and Eddington's unified theory of electromagnetism and gravity, based on extensions of Einstein's ideas. Lemaitre would develop a method that enabled the calculation of pulsating variable stars.

Georges Lemaitre would be in direct contact and conversation with the other significant personages of his time. For instance, as Georges would later write: "In the spring of 1925, sometime before my return (to Belgium), I had the chance to attend a meeting at the Academy in Washington and hear Hubble presenting the discovery of Cepheids in the Andromeda nebula, which definitively established its distance and, therefore, the general structure of the universe."

Georges Lemaitre would visit several observatories before his return to Belgium. Lemaitre would meet with Edwin Hubble at the California Institute of Technology, near Mount Wilson in California. There he would also meet with Albert Einstein, as well as Robert A. Millikan, a Nobel laureate who had coined the term "cosmic ray" to explain high-energy particles of extraterrestrial origin. He would visit the Lowell Observatory and meet with Vesto M. Slipher, who had observed the high radial speeds of spiral nebulae.

After, all of this information gathering and scientific brainstorming at these defining moments in history, Georges Lemaitre would then have the tools to develop his own cosmology. In his toolbox were concepts of an expanding universe, observational values of distances, relative velocities of nebulae and the extragalactic nature of the nebulae, the equations of a non-homogenous model with spherical symmetry, and the idea of extraterrestrial origins of cosmic rays.

In October 1925, Georges Lemaitre began his first year of teaching at the Universite Catholique de Louvain. In the recommendations to the university was one that stated the author "[considered] M. Lemaitre as a 'future genius of mathematics'." Msgr. Ladeuze would thereby grant all the permissions necessary for Georges Lemaitres's research projects, even reducing his teaching load. During the years 1925–1927, besides attending conferences, Lemaitre voraciously read everything he could about relativity and wave mechanics.

Two prevailing universe constructs were those from de Sitter and from Einstein. One needed, in Lemaitre's view, to construct a universe achieving an interpolation between that of Einstein and de Sitter—one both dynamic and massive. Rather than a solution corresponding to the constructs of static universes as described by both Einstein and de Sitter, which were accepted science, Lemaitre's stroke of genius was to surmount an inhibition that weighed on the entire astronomical community and chained it to the idea of a static universe. This was done only with trepidation and called for a fair amount of courage, as the fame of Einstein held sway on the side of a static solution of the equations relating to general relativity. Lemaitre would offer in 1963 that there were "some hesitations about considering non-statical solutions or as Robertson called them, 'dynamical solutions', but I was better prepared to accept them, encouraged by the opinion of Eddington."

The following paragraph offers an abbreviated measure of the thought and work of such cosmological genius:

> "Lemaitre had finally found a dynamic universe achieving the desired interpolation between Einstein and de Sitter. In Lemaitre's universe, light emitted from a remote source, such as a nebula, undergoes a red-shift, related to the expansion of the universe. Lemaitre derived a law lining the distance r of a source to its recessional speed: $v = a*r$ where the coefficient a depends on the relative rate of change of the universe's radius. This

coefficient prefigured what, after 1929, would be known as the Hubble constant. Aided by the measurement of the distances of galaxies published by Hubble in 1926 and by the average speeds of 43 extragalactic nebulae published by Gustaf Benjamin Stromberg in 1925, Lemaitre determined the actual value of the coefficient to be approximately 625 kilometres per second for the objects located at a distance of one megaparsec (625 km/sec/Mpc)."

Lemaitre had an opportunity to talk and walk with Albert Einstein in the company of Auguste Picard in the Alle'es of Leopold Park in Brussels during the Fifth Solvay Congress held in Brussels in October of 1927. Einstein made some favorable technical observations on the mathematical aspects of Lemaitre's paper. However, "he concluded by saying that, from the physics perspective, this seemed to him absolutely abominable." Edwin Hubble's survey of the heavens at the Mt. Wilson Observatory two years later seemed to confirm Lemaitre's theory. Mr. Hubble Invited Mr. Einstein to Mt. Wilson to check the results. Einstein and Lemaitre co-presented at a conference at Mt. Wilson in 1933. It would take years, but Einstein reputedly said at one point that it was the most beautiful and satisfactory explanation of creation to which he had ever listened.

In any event, there has come to be a scientific agreement on Lemaitre's theory. It would take some thirty years for the majority, of the scientific community to recognize Lemaitre's contributions. It has been confirmed since in a variety of different ways, making it one of the most comprehensive and rigorously established theories in contemporary cosmology.

More simply stated, if one were to start from the assumption that there is a constant energy that is distributed in quanta (minimal quantities of energy) throughout the universe and that the number of quanta is always increasing, then we must be able to trace back an ever-lower number of quanta up to the point at which we arrive at a unique quantum in which the entire universe was concentrated. This is how the hypothesis of the primeval atom was reached in 1931. It is a theory that is still accepted and is now known as the big bang theory. Now, as one can imagine, it was not Georges Lemaitre who invented the term "big bang"; that was British astronomer Fred Hoyle, a critic and steady-state theorist, who coined the expression during an interview on BBC radio in 1950.

From September 1934 to June 1935, Georges was a guest at the prestigious School of Mathematics of the Institute of Advanced Studies of Princeton, where Albert Einstein had settled. Einstein's initial theory of relativity allowed for, or predicted, an expanding universe. However, a "cosmological constant" was added that provided a "steady state" theory of the universe.

Lemaitre would be a guest, at, a number, of prestigious universities during the thirties, receiving numerous awards and accolades. His views would also be picked up by widely circulated newspapers in the US. One article printed by the *Tower* on December 7, 1933, stated, "The noted Belgian priest-scientist who is a guest professor at the Catholic University for the winter semester has made a profound impression on the scientists in this country at his every appearance. Two weeks ago, he spoke before the National Academy of Sciences meeting at Cambridge, Mass., and the story of his picturization of the universe was carried on front pages of the leading newspapers of the nation ..."

In his home country of Belgium, Lemaitre received the Francqui Prize from King Leopold on March 17, 1934. In his address to his academic colleges and to all present, he concluded, "I wish to take advantage of this occasion to reaffirm (to Msgr. Ladeuze) my resolution to continue with all my efforts, together with all of you, to serve science. Science is beautiful; it deserves to be loved for itself, as it is, a reflection of God's creative thought."

Georges Lemaitre would write, but withhold from publication, the following words: "I think that one who believes in a supreme being supporting every being and every action, also believes that God is essentially hidden and may be glad to see how present physics provide a veil hiding the creation." Lemaitre would assert that there is no physics without the presupposition of a reality that is "always already there" and as such

> ...is forever veiled to the eyes of a science that must not be confused with metaphysics." Lemaitre used to sometimes say, "I have too much respect for God to make Him a scientific hypothesis ... There are two ways of arriving at the truth. I decided to follow them both. Nothing in my working life, nothing I have ever learned in my studies of either science or religion has caused me to change that opinion. I have no conflict to reconcile. Science has not shaken my faith in religion and religion has never caused me to question the conclusions I reached by scientific methods.

Lemaitre would further reflect that it was not by studying equations and examining photographic plates from a telescope that one would learn something about the content of revelation but that the unity of science and faith is successful at-the-moment when the scientist, in solving equations or observing photographs of galaxies, entrusts his work to God and places it in His hands:

> His faith gives a supernatural dimension to his greatest as well as his smallest activities! He remains a child of God when he puts his eye to the microscope, and as well, in his morning prayer, where the entirety of his activity is to place himself under the protection of his Father in Heaven. When he thinks of the truths of faith, he knows that his knowledge of microbes, atoms or suns will neither be a benefit, nor a hindrance to approach the inaccessible light, and, as for any man, he would need to try to have the heart of a little child to enter the kingdom of heaven. Thus, faith and reason, without undue mixture or imaginary conflict, are unified in the unity of human activity.

Georges Lemaitre, like other Belgians, would suffer through another world war. He would put himself at some risk evacuating family members and others. Left behind by nuclear and particle physics research, his focus would now be computational studies of dynamical systems. These would have application regarding models of the formation of galaxies. By 1945, he had a schematic picture of the first stages of the formation of galaxies, which he then developed over the next sixteen years to, more fully understand their structures, evolution, and clustering patterns. For instance, in 1951 he found a way of translating the problem of the three equal masses located on a plane into one of characterizing the motion of a point moving in a force field described by a scalar and a vector potential, such as is found in electromagnetism. In 1951–52, he succeeded in extending, the aforementioned techniques to the general three-body problem and achieving in this context, the regularization of binary collisions.

On June 20, 1966, Georges Lemaitre passed away from this earth and into the heavens of eternity. On the sixteenth or seventeenth, a friend came to him with the news of the discovery of cosmic microwave background radiation (CMB)—that is, the fossil radiation confirming the validity of the theory of an explosive beginning of the universe. Msgr. Lemaitre finally had his "hieroglyphs" that bore witness to the initial state of the universe, just as he had predicted in 1931.

His friend related, "We had an hour-long discussion on the most recent astronomical discoveries and their consequences for cosmological theories. Despite, being very sick, he lucidly expressed his satisfaction regarding the discovery of a type of cosmic microwave radiation that seemed to confirm the idea of an explosive origin of the universe."

In summary, and in humility, in the spirit of Georges Lemaitre, he also leaves us with these thoughts:

> [The Christian seeker] knows that everything that has been done has been done by God, but he knows also that God does not supplant his creation. The omnipresent divine activity is essentially hidden everywhere. It can

> never be a question of reducing the Supreme Being to the rank of a scientific hypothesis.

The mind of LeMaitre, it is safe to say, easily exceeds that of this author, but not that of The Author.

> I hope to have shown you that the universe is not out of reach for humans. This is Eden, this garden that has been put at the disposal of humans, in order, for them to cultivate it, to look after it. The universe is not too big for human beings, it does not exceed the possibilities of science, nor the capacity of the human mind.

In humble contemplation—

> Christ Jesus is the new image of God; before anything came to be, he was. In him resides the fullness of power to restore all things: in heaven and on earth, visible and invisible. (Colossians 1:15 NAB)

> In the beginning was the Word, and the Word was with God, and the Word was God. He was with God in the beginning. Through him all things were made; without him nothing was made that has been made. In him was life, and that life was the light of all mankind. The light shines in the darkness, and the darkness has not overcome it. (John 1:1–5 NIV)

> Dear children, keep yourselves from idols. Amen.
> (1 John 5:21 NIV)

AFTERGLOW

It was Albert Einstein who observed, "Science without religion is lame; religion without science is blind." This he stated in a written contribution to a symposium held in New York in 1940 on how science, philosophy, and religion advance the cause of American democracy.

As the poet said,

> If E does equal MC squared
> Then there is nothing to be scared
> As you or I the Universe we did not create
> It is pleasing then we only contemplate

Not long-ago, even-Steven Hawking, as he considered the mathematical immeasurables and impossibles, wondered, "Why did the universe start out with so nearly the critical rate of expansion that separates models that re-collapse from those that go on expanding forever, that even now ... it is still expanding at nearly the critical rate. If the rate of expansion one second after the Big Bang had been smaller by even one part in 100 thousand million, million, the universe would have re-collapsed before it ever reached its present size." He further wrote, "The odds against a universe like ours emerging out of something like the Big Bang are enormous. I think there are clearly religious implications."

As another writer summed up, "If there is no God, why is there something rather than nothing?" In light of the evidence, we are left with only two options: either no one created something out of nothing, or else someone created something out of nothing. Which view is more reasonable? Nothing created something? Even Julie Andrews knew the answer when she sang, "Nothing comes from nothing. Nothing ever could!" And if you can't believe that nothing caused something, "then you don't have enough faith to be an atheist."

No less a figure in our time, Martin Luther King Jr. observed, "Science keeps religion from sinking into the valley of crippling irrationalism and paralyzing obscurantism. Religion prevents science from falling into the marsh of obsolete materialism and moral nihilism."

Many decades ago, famous astrophysicist Sir James Jeans reflected, "The universe begins to look more like a great thought than a great machine."

"I felt an overwhelming sense of the presence of God on the moon" remembered astronaut James Irwin.

Imagine ourselves in the shoes of Irwin, taking our first step on the moon.

>And yet space and time
>began in rhyme,
>imponderable to the human mind
>A creature creating
>as Creator before.
>What character do we display
>revealing goodness without dismay
>or do we draw within our minds
>the curtains and the blinds?

EDITH STEIN

A Saint

Edith Stein was born on October 12, 1891—Yom Kippur, the Jewish Day of Atonement—the youngest of eleven children. When she was only two years old, her father died. Her mother, Frau Auguste Stein, intelligent and energetic, accustomed to hard work from childhood, would put her trust in God. She would take over to run the family lumber business with all its debts. She had lost four children early in her marriage, and now, with unshakable determination, she would shoulder the entire responsibility of raising her seven children.

Frau Stein would retain an endearing memory of the little child Edith calling her father back one last time before he would set off to his work site in the woods on his final day. Mother and daughter would later regard the coincidence as a mark of election.

The eldest daughter, Else, assisted in the upbringing of the youngest, Edith. It would not always be a simple task. Despite the youngest having an affectionate nature, Edith was not always easy to control and threw her fair share of temper tantrums. As a little girl, Edith Stein remembered, she always had to "put in her two cents" in the grown-ups' conversations and impress them with her clever remarks. Edith recalled, "Right from early childhood, my relatives used two qualities to describe me. They scolded me—correctly— for being vain, and they called me 'Edith, the smart one' with an emphasis on 'smart'. Both, of these hurt me very much. The second, because I thought they were saying that I tended to exaggerate my own intelligence. Also, even as a little girl, I knew it was much more important to be good than to be smart."

Her mind seemed to awaken as she grew, to the point at which, it might be said, she was ahead of her own emotions. Yet she stated, "… very early on I acquired so much self-control that I could remain constantly even-tempered without any great struggle."

She was a smart little girl; she wanted to attend the Victoria School in Breslau. She was willing, at such a young age, to forgo birthday presents for her sixth birthday if she could enroll early. Attending kindergarten would have been beneath her dignity. Edith was admitted midyear and took only a few months to catch up. She would then maintain her position at the head of the class. Edith was described by a teacher thusly: "She was just as gifted as she was hard working, with a will of iron. Yet she was never competitive in the bad sense of the word. She was a good classmate, always ready to help out."

Surprisingly, at age thirteen, Edith Stein decided to drop out of school. Perhaps her somewhat frail constitution contributed to her decision. Edith would acknowledge years later that from age thirteen to twenty-one she could not believe in the existence of a personal God. She stayed with an older married sister for eight months, doing household chores. Her mother suggested she return to school. With enthusiasm, she returned to study mathematics and Latin. As to the study of Latin, she said, "It was like learning my native tongue. Back then I had no idea that it was the language of the Church and that someday I would be praying in it." She joyfully tutored classmates and thought to become a teacher.

On March 11, 1911, Edith Stein entered the University of Breslau, and enrolled in the required courses. She began attending psychology lectures. With this discipline, she hoped to discern the underlying coherence of human existence. Her impression was that she had discovered a "psychology without a soul," one that was determined to prove the soul did not exist. "Spirit, meaning and life" were subtracted from the equation if not deleted. It would be irrational to consider the possibility of spirit posited beneath the physical senses. Although she did claim to be an atheist, she decided to attend a Bach concert. As she listened to *A Mighty Fortress is our God*, she began to rise from the depths of a surrounding darkness.

Edith happened upon a book written by Edmund Husserl titled *Logical Investigations*. He was endeavoring to rediscover spirit. By the school of phenomenology, one might discover the essence of a purified knowledge through intuition without preconceived conceptions. Edith decided to enroll in philosophy at Gottingen University and into the ever more popular School of Phenomenology. She could then explore philosophical formulas with the aid of Husserl. While at Gottingen, she marched with the suffragettes. Later in life, she would write, "All who seek truth seek God, whether this is clear to them or not."

Husserl would state in his seminars that "knowledge, as the name implies, depends on knowing ... It is in knowing that we possess the truth." By "truth" Husserl meant the "luminous certainty" that something is or is not so, sharply distinct from ordinary opinion and blind conviction. A classmate and friend, Hedwig Conrad-Martius, observed,

> Our commonly held approach to thinking and investigating created a bond among Husserl's students that can only be described as the natural outgrowth of a common spirit. I don't mean, that we all had any private terminology or held to one individual system—not at all. It was, rather, our newly won insight into the intellectual attainability of Being in all its possible configurations that united us ... the ethos of objective purity and cleanliness ... which rubbed off on our attitude, character, and behavior ... This is what made it natural for all of us to become friends, without anyone giving a thought to somebody's social class, race, or religion. Edith Stein was a born phenomenologist. Her calm, clear and impartial thinking, her undistorted vision and her absolute objectivity all predestined her for it." Her instructors were impressed and assisted in her remaining in school and pursuing her doctoral dissertation.

Another professorial influence was Max Scheler. She began attending evening sessions on religious questions, such as the nature of the holy and belief in the eternal. Edith began to see the human person as one who by nature searches for God. Faith began to stir within her. She wrote, "The bars of the rationalist prejudices I had unconsciously grown up with collapsed, and there, standing in front of me, was a world of faith." Adolph Reinach was another influential teacher who also helped with her dissertation. Edith was invited to meet his wife and family at their home. Reinach and his wife later converted to Christianity.

World War I broke out in 1914. Edith Stein volunteered for duty in the military hospitals. She requested an assignment at a hospital for infectious diseases. She wrote, "My life isn't my own anymore. All my energy belongs to the great undertaking. When the war is over, if I'm still alive, then there'll be plenty of time to think about my own affairs again ... Naturally, I offered my services without restriction. If there was anything I wanted, it was to be sent out as soon and as far as possible, preferably to a field hospital on the front." Stein cared for soldiers suffering from typhus, dysentery, and cholera. Edith served bravely and was awarded the Medal of Valor. In this battle, she learned that dedication rather than knowledge is of ultimate importance.

She returned to her studies hoping for "a great love and a happy marriage." Edith Stein was offered a position of graduate assistant under Professor Husserl. She was awarded her doctoral degree summa cum laude.

In 1917 a key event happened in Edith Stein's search for meaning. She received tragic news that Adolph Reinach, her former teacher, had been killed in battle. His family asked her to come to Gottingen to put his papers in order. Without a concept of or belief in life after death, she hesitated, uncertain she could offer any comfort to the family. Frau Reinach, on the other hand, appeared to be filled with hope and was able to bring real peace and consolation to the rest of the family and friends. Stein was rather deeply affected by such faith. She wrote of this as her "first encounter with the Cross and the divine power that it bestows on those who carry it. For the first time, I was seeing with my very eyes the church, born from its redeemer's sufferings triumphant over the sting of death. That was the moment my unbelief collapsed, and Christ shone forth—in the mystery of the Cross."

Edith began reading the New Testament, reflecting on the possibility of becoming a Christian. Amid the pessimism following Germany's defeat in the war, she was able to "rest in God."

Edith's ambition was to become a professor. Husserl made his recommendation for such on Edith's behalf in 1919. Edith was turned down. Few women were employed as professors at this time. Another renowned German philosopher, Martin Heidegger, began working with Husserl at Freiburg University, publishing manuscripts Stein had worked on without giving her credit. He would have a positive influence in his teaching on Karl Rahner, a famous Jesuit theologian. A contemporary of Edith Stein named Adolf Hitler had also recently published a work. In 1908, as Edith had moved on to high school, this teenager failed an entrance exam to the Vienna Academy of Arts and then wandered the streets for some time while reading anti-Semitic literature. Now he had finally finished his first political manifesto. In it he determined that the cause of Germany's defeat in the Great War was the Jews. They were his scapegoat. Hitler had abandoned his Catholic faith and was now an atheist. Edith Stein had moved from atheism to a faith in God and would soon move toward Catholicism.

For the moment, let us proceed with the far more important story. Many of us, if not all of us, have grown up with and known entire generations worldwide who were profoundly affected by the completely evil insanity of that antichrist, as he was so kindly known. His presence would become known to Edith Stein soon enough, just as he would become known to us all.

Edith Stein had her own reflections after the First World War. Some of her reflections read as follows:

> If there's anything certain, it's that we stand at a turning point in mankind's spiritual development ... There's good and evil, sense and nonsense on all sides here, though of course nobody wants to see anything but the positive side of his own position and the negative

side of everyone else's (And that goes just as much for nations as political parties!). All of this has now been released into the atmosphere in a whirl of tremendous confusion, and who can tell when peace and tranquility can be expected again. Life is just far too complicated for anyone to figure it out with a brilliant world-improvement plan that will let us know how things are going to turn out in the future.

She also reflected, "A convinced atheist learns through personal experience that there actually is a God. Now faith can no longer be eluded. Yet he can still refuse to ground himself in it or to let it become effective in him, choosing instead to hold on to the 'scientific worldview' that he knows an unmitigated faith would be the end of ..."

Edith Stein continued her research at Breslau. Her interest in politics led to an active concern about current issues. The essays she wrote in 1920 about the individual and the community and about the state reveal the development of her thinking on these subjects. While discussing the reciprocal relations between individual and community, Edith also examined the pertinent religious questions. Most important was the restriction she placed on the state's competency in religious matters. Because the state cannot be the bearer of religious values, she argued, it cannot justifiably encroach on the individual's religious or personal existence. It seems as if even the events of the 1917 Russian Revolution gave her some premonition of the impending horrors the European atheistic dictatorships would cause. She concluded her research by asserting the "inextinguishable uniqueness" of the human person who lives, at the same time, in a state of spiritual "interconnectedness" with the rest of reality.

Edith Stein continued working on intellectual projects and gave private lessons. She continued to explore her own religious questions. On a trip to Frankfurt, an experience touched her deeply. "We went into the cathedral for a few moments, and as we stood there in respectful silence, a woman came in with her shopping basket and knelt down in one of the pews to say a short prayer. That was something completely new to me. In the synagogue, as in the Protestant churches I had visited, people only went in at the time of the service. But here was someone coming into the empty church in the middle of a day's work as if to talk with a friend. I have never been able to forget that."

One evening, Edith went through the bookshelves of a friend who had left for the evening. The book she chose to read was *The Life of Saint Teresa of Avila*. In Teresa's autobiography was a confirmation of her own experiences. She read through the entire night. When she put the book down in the morning, she said to herself, "This is the truth."

She recognized that God is not a God of knowledge; God is love. He does not reveal his mysteries to the deductive intelligence but rather to the heart that surrenders itself to him. As Teresa asserted, "It is just the people who at first passionately embrace the world that penetrate farthest into the depths of the soul. Once God's powerful hand has freed them from its allurements, they are taken into their innermost selves." Teresa's understanding of the soul went beyond "phenomena"— "the active upper layer of the soul's life." For her, will, intellect, memory, and the essence of the soul were all undeniable objects of experience. As for "the most interior and personal part" of the soul, for Teresa, that was no hypothetical entity scientists had posited in order to explain psychic data but was "something that could light up inside us and become actually perceptible, even if it always did remain mysterious." Edith Stein discovered this "lighting" herself the night that she read of the saint's life.

Edith Stein's experience with Teresa was no different from what had happened to Teresa herself four centuries earlier when reading the words of St. Augustine: "Thanks be to God for giving me the life that rescued me from such an awful death ... After all the kindness I had received from you, my God, the hardness of my soul was almost unbelievable. I seem to have been almost totally powerless, as if bound by chains that were keeping me from making a total surrender to God ... Then I began to understand that I wasn't living but wrestling with the shadow of death ... My soul was utterly worn out; all it wanted was rest."

It makes no difference, what, particular form this "shadow" assumes—sensuality, as with Augustine; worldly contacts, as with Teresa; or attachment to a rationalist worldview, as with Edith Stein.

All that is necessary for a conversion to take place is that the individual honestly comes to recognize that his "death" is depriving him of the freedom to offer himself to God. Honesty and freedom, to Edith Stein, had always constituted the two greatest challenges imposed on the human person. According to Teresa, interior prayer is the setting where this inner resistance begins to be healed and transformed. Edith Stein wondered why she had not cultivated this silent inward prayer more seriously. For Teresa, "there are many people who have practiced interior prayer for a long time without ever reaching the goal ... simply because they haven't embraced the cross from the beginning ... Once one has tasted a single drop of water of this kingdom, he is repelled by the taste of anything earthly. Imagine what it must be like to be completely immersed in it."

Edith decided to attend her first Mass. She could follow the liturgy and asked to be baptized. She was baptized on New Year's Day of 1922. From then on, she would attend Mass daily.

A family acquaintance wrote, "I'm convinced that what overpowered Frau Stein was the transformation she observed in Edith Stein that seemed to make a supernatural force radiate from her entire being. Being a God-fearing woman, she was able to feel, though not to comprehend, the holiness emanating from her daughter. For all her deadly anguish, she knew that she was powerless against the mystery of grace."

Edith, as Teresa of Avila, could proclaim, "[I understood now] what it means for a soul to abide in truth in the presence of Truth itself. In this divine Truth I have come to know truths of the utmost importance--far better than if many scholars had explained them to me ... The truth that I said was communicated to me is Truth in itself, truth without beginning or end. From it there spring all other truths, just as all love springs from this Love and all glory from this Glory. And compared to the clarity with which the Lord revealed it all to me, what I have just said is obscure indeed."

Edith Stein took a position teaching German in a Dominican convent school—St. Magdalena's in Speyer. She accepted compensation only to the extent that it would pay for expenses. She was an excellent teacher and a true friend to her students, walking with them, counseling them, and sometimes sharing a meal. She actively participated in helping the poor and needy in the village nearby and wrote, "There is a vocation to suffer with Christ and thereby cooperate with him in the work of salvation."

It is said that Edith Stein "rapidly won her students' hearts, serving us all as a shining example with an influence that has lasted down to the present day. Modest and unassuming, she went about her work basically unseen and unheard, always equally friendly and ready to be of help." A student of hers wrote, "With her you sensed you were in the presence of something pure, sublime, and noble, something that elevated you and brought you to its own level." Of her work, Father Przywara observed, "Edith Stein was not only the finest educator the students at St. Magdalena's had; thanks to a wise prioress, she, was also a formative influence on the sisters and those starting out in religious life. The best members of that community owe their vocation to Edith Stein. To this day they remember the extent to which she actually functioned as their novice mistress."

In 1925, a scholar friend helped move Edith Stein back into scholarly activity; she began translating John Henry Newman into German. She next translated Thomas Aquinas's *Disputed Questions on Truth*. She learned a connection between faith and reason, confirming that experience of God transcends all that we can think or say about God. "My desire for the truth was one sole prayer," she wrote.

Her philosophical writings and translations attracted the attention of the Association of Catholic Women Teachers and Catholic University Graduates. Regular lecture tours were set up on her behalf. Edith Stein wrote, "It is possible to worship God by doing scholarly research."

Edith began her own study of the feminine. She felt that women were uniquely made in the image of God. Educational systems should be designed to bring forward those gifts. Within her writings and lectures she, would note that "it seems right, therefore, that no legal barriers of any kind should exist. Rather, one can hope that a natural choice of vocation may be made thanks to an upbringing, education, and guidance in harmony with the individual's nature." She counseled women to sustain a strong spirituality and life of prayer so that they could balance work and home life. She pointed to the importance women held in Jesus's ministry, to the early church, and to all the deaconesses in church history.

Some of her lecture titles were as follows: "The Ethos of Woman's Vocation," "The Vocation of Man and Woman in the Order of Nature and Grace," "The Life of the Christian Woman," "Foundations of Women's Education" and "The Place of Women in guiding the Young to the Church." They formed an outline of a central idea she wished to develop regarding a woman's mature Christian life as a source of healing for the world.

Perhaps a better description of Edith Stein was written by a schoolteacher.

> I was expecting to hear an imposing, self-confident, female Jewish intellectual, like so many of the ones I had encountered through the liberal women's movement and various charitable organizations— and a fascinating speech of course. But instead of an imposing personality all set to captivate you with her method of presentation and her intellectual brilliance, there appeared a small, delicate, surprisingly unpretentious woman, simply and tastefully dressed, who clearly had no intention of impressing you by her demeanor and her dazzling wit. In fact, there was almost something childlike in the way she introduced herself. Yet within her penetrating eyes lay something mysterious and solemn, and the contrast between this and her simplicity created a certain awe— at least in me.

> She spoke unrhetorically, with quiet charm, using clear, attractive, unpretentious words. Despite this, you immediately sensed a tremendous strength of intellect, and an extremely rich, intensely disciplined interior life springing from absolute conviction … She neither accused, disputed nor threatened. She simply stated the

facts, and, in the course, of her presentation, the dangers facing our nation became startlingly clear ... Then she called out, "The nation ... doesn't simply need what we have. It needs what we are."

Among Edith Stein's statements and thoughts of the times were these:

> After the life and death struggle of a World War, the nations of Europe have collapsed alongside one another, having learned through the bitter lessons of adversity that only a common effort can make recovery possible. Whether a policy of international conciliation will gradually prevail against strong counter currents is impossible to predict with certainty. But one thing is clear: the issue involves women. If a woman's vocation is the protection of life and the preservation of the family, she cannot remain indifferent as to whether or not governments and nations assume forms which are favorable to the growth of the family and the well-being of the young.

> More than anything else today, what is needed is the baptism of spirit and fire. This alone can prepare those who shape human life to take their rightful place at the front lines in the great battle between Christ and Lucifer. There is no more urgent task than to be constantly armed and ready for this battle. For, "If the salt loses its savor, how can it be restored?"

In March of 1931, Edith Stein would leave St. Magdalena's in order, to write and lecture. She would again apply for a university professorship. In 1932 she finally accepted a teaching position at the German Institute for Scientific Pedagogy, in Munster. She attended conferences and maintained correspondence with her earlier academic contacts. The idea of sacrifice and the cross had not left her mind.

In 1933, she would look on with horror as university students began attacking Jews. That same year, Adolf Hitler was elected chancellor of Germany. Also in 1933, the institute had to remove Stein from her teaching post. At forty-two and at the peak of her power, Edith Stein turned to the cross. There would still be time to leave for Latin America or the United States, as had other academics, such as Protestant theologian Paul Tillich, scientist Albert Einstein, Sigmund Freud, and others. Edith Stein, on the other hand, decided to stay, saying that she was willing to accept the destiny of her people as her own. "Even before beginning my work in Munster, I had pleaded for permission to enter the convent ... On April 30 (Good Shepherd Sunday that year), I attended part of the Thirteen Hours devotion which St. Ludger's parish was celebrating in honor of its patronal feast. I arrived in the afternoon, determined not to leave until I found out if I could now enter Carmel. Just as the concluding blessing was being given, I felt the Good Shepherd giving me his consent."

"She ran to Carmel, singing for joy, like a child to its mother's arms, never doubting her almost blind enthusiasm for even an instant ..." With these words, Abbot Walzer expressed his surprise at the speed with which Edith Stein settled into her new environment. Her vocation as a Carmelite was genuine. She felt at home with her new sisters. "Best of all," she wrote, "the spirit of Carmel is love, and that spirit is very much alive in our community."

One of her fellow novices recalled, "One of the things that struck me most about her was her devotion to prayer ... My impression was that once she had entered into these intimate conversations with God, time and space ceased to exist." Edith Stein would receive her habit in a ceremony on April 15, 1934. Gerda Krabbel, president of the Woman's Federation, exclaimed when she met Edith in her wedding dress, "I'm so glad to be here to see you like this. It is absolutely right." Edith Stein chose the name "Sister Teresa Benedicta of the Cross" or "Teresa, Blessed by the Cross"

> The bride of Christ assumes a life of spiritual motherhood for all redeemed humanity. This is just as true whether she works directly with souls, or whether, by sacrifice alone, she brings forth fruit hidden from both herself and from everyone else. (Sister Teresa)

Like a bad storm, the politics within Hitler's Germany would only worsen. Many of Edith Stein's Jewish friends visited her in the convent, and some discussed their plans to emigrate. Edith returned to her writings. She completed an index for her translation of St. Thomas and contributed, to several periodicals. On Easter Sunday of 1935, Edith Stein professed her simple vows.

As a professed nun, her superiors appointed her the task of completing the manuscript *Act and Potency*, which she had begun in Speyer. The work was completed in 1936 and was ultimately entitled *Finite and Eternal Being*. Her mother would die before the work was completed. The following winter, Edith had the joy of seeing her sister Rosa enter the Catholic Church. A year after completing the manuscript, there was still not a publisher to be found.

Sister Teresa's joy in the Spirit was expressed in one of her poems written at Carmel:

> What are you, kindly light, who fill me now,
> And brighten all the darkness of my heart?
> ...
> Loosened from you, I fall in the abyss
> Of nothingness, from which you draw my life.
> Nearer to me than I, myself am,
>
> And more within me than my inmost self,
> You are outside my grasp, beyond my reach,
> ...
> You, Holy Spirit, you, eternal Love!

Sister Teresa Benedicta would make her solemn vows on Thursday of Holy Week, April 21, 1938. She soon learned in a letter from a fellow sister that her old mentor, Husserl, had been freed by his illness from all, of his earthly scholarly obligations. He was once again attracted to Christ and, on Holy Thursday, had given his soul to God. The sister further wrote to Edith that on Good Friday morning, he woke with happiness, expressing, "Good Friday! What a wonderful day. Christ has forgiven us everything." On April 27, shortly before his death, he exclaimed to a nurse, "Oh! I have seen something wonderful. Quick, write it down!" Before the nurse returned with a pencil, Husserl had entered eternity.

As Edith replied to Sister Adelgundis, who had written her the letter, she pondered, "It reminded me of the way my mother died at the very hour I renewed my vows. Don't take this to mean that I put so much stock in the power of my prayers, or worse still, in my own merits. It's only that I'm convinced that whenever God calls someone, it's not for the sake of that person alone, and that, every time he does call anyone, he's lavish in offering proofs of his love."

November 8, 1938 is a date that still sends chills down the spines of those remembering history. Kristallnacht was the night Hitler's SS began to create their hellish havoc using billy clubs, driving Jews from their homes, and burning their synagogues. The general German population remained quiet, as by that time they had been trained by the Gestapo to keep quiet.

News of those events made it to the convent in Cologne. It is said that Edith Stein listened "like someone numbed with pain." She expressed her thoughts in a letter to Mother Petra that December:

> One thing I should tell you: when I entered, I had already chosen the religious name I wanted, and I received it exactly as I had asked for it. "Of the Cross" I saw as referring to the fate of the people of God, which even then was beginning to reveal itself. As I understood it, anyone who recognized that this was the Cross of Christ had a responsibility to bear it in the

name of all. I know a little more now than I did then what it means to be betrothed to the Lord in the sign of the Cross. But it's not something that can ever be understood. It is a mystery.

"Edith decided it would be dangerous for the convent if she remained any longer," one sister would relate. Her superiors decided that Edith would be transferred to the Dutch convent in Echt, Holland for her safety. Palestine had discontinued further immigration of Jews. Under cover of darkness, she entered Holland on December 31, 1938.

She would write to her sisters in Cologne: "Ever since coming here, I find my predominant feeling has been gratitude: for being allowed to live here, for this being the kind of community it is. That doesn't mean I'm not constantly aware that here we have no lasting dwelling-place. But, as long as God's will is accomplished in me, I ask for nothing else … As for the people who have heavier burdens than I do, without the benefit of being solidly rooted in the Eternal, anyone who joins me in praying for them has my heartfelt gratitude too."

> During that year, Edith Stein composed three acts of self-oblation: one for the Jewish people, one for the averting of war, and one for the sanctification of her Carmelite family. One of her prayers was submitted to the prioress on Passion Sunday in 1939, shortly before the outbreak of the war: Dear Reverend Mother: Please permit me to offer myself to the Heart of Jesus as a sacrifice of atonement for true peace, that if possible, the reign of Antichrist might be broken without another world war and a new social order might be established. I would like to do it today, if I could, since it is already the final hour. I know, I myself am nothing, but Jesus desires it, and I am sure he is asking it of many others in these days.

Rosa Stein followed her sister to Echt in 1940 and was joyfully welcomed by Edith. Rosa had made the harrowing journey to Holland by way of Belgium. Other reports began to arrive, describing the dissolution of other Carmelite convents in Germany and Luxembourg.

Edith wrote to her sisters: "Let us be grateful for what we have: our unity in the kingdom where limits and boundaries, separations and distances, do not exist ... Nothing gives me greater joy than the hope I have in this future vision. It is faith in our hidden stories that ought to console us when what we see externally in ourselves and in others tends to depress us."

Sister Antonia would become the prioress for the Carmelite sisters in Echt. Pleased to employ the talents of her new sister, Sister Teresa was assigned to teach the new postulants Latin as well as train Rosa in the basics of Carmelite life. Edith was also asked to use her mind to write a book to commemorate the upcoming centenary of St. John of the Cross in 1942.

Edith Stein would write, "As a result of the work I'm engaged in, I find myself living almost continually in the world of our holy Father St. John. This is truly a great grace. Do pray, Reverend Mother, that I may produce something worthy of his celebration."

Not long after Edith and Rosa arrived, Holland was occupied by the Germans. By the beginning of 1942, it became evident that Rosa and Edith must try to find some way out of Holland for the sake of the convent and for themselves. Swiss visas were applied for. Some delays halted processing. One objective of National Socialism was to bring about the complete extermination of Jewish people. SS operations were thereby extended into the occupied countries. They began to make their presence known. Both Edith and Rosa were regularly called for interrogations before the SS in Maastricht and the Council for Jewish Affairs in Amsterdam. Jewish people were required to wear the yellow star, keep their distance, and stand three meters from their "sympathetic" interrogators. The interrogations would often last for hours. Many Dutch Christians began to wear the yellow Star of David themselves to show empathy and respect for the Jewish people.

Edith, determined, worked past the point of exhaustion to finish *The Science of the Cross*.

She explored John of the Cross's view that Jesus asks souls to share his cross and his redemption. "God has created human souls for himself and given them even on earth the immeasurable fullness and ineffable bliss of his own divine life. This is the goal to which he directs them and to which they are meant to tend with all their might. But the road is narrow, the ascent steep and laborious, and most people fall by the way." Years before entering Carmel, she had written that all sufferings are nothing "compared with the dark night of the soul, when the Divine light no longer shines, and the voice of the Lord no longer speaks. God is there, but He is hidden and silent." Hell, then, becomes the absence of God.

The citizens of Holland and the Catholic and Protestant church leaders would not be silenced. A joint telegram was sent to Reichskommisar Seyss-Inquart:

> The undersigned Dutch Churches, profoundly disturbed by the measures already taken against the Jews of the Netherlands by which they have become excluded from the ordinary life of the nation, have now learned with horror of the proposed action which would evacuate men, women, children, and entire families into German territory. The suffering this would cause to thousands of people, the awareness that these measures are contrary to the deepest convictions of the Dutch people, and, above all, the resistance that such a step would constitute to God's commands of justice and mercy, compel us to urgently petition you not to have this directive carried out. In the case of Christians of Jewish descent, we are moved by a further consideration: namely, such measures would sever them from participation in the life of the Church

The authorities replied that the "Jewish Christians" would not be molested. The bishop informed the convent of the reply. Their dishonest intentions would be proven. Deportations of most Jews continued.

Another joint pastoral letter on behalf of their congregations was sent. Seyss-Inquart dismissed the letter. The bishop of Utrecht informed the occupation that it had no right to intervene in ecclesiastical affairs:

A week later, all Jewish Catholics were put under arrest. On July 29, Edith wrote to the sisters in Germany: "It's still up in the air whether we will be given permission to emigrate; it looks like the process could still go on for quite some time."

On August 2, Edith Stein spent her Sunday as she had so many before, she prayed. In the afternoon, she touched up her not quite finished manuscript about John of the Cross. She wrote, "The saint had passed away unnoticed, while Brother Diego held him in his arms. Suddenly, he observed a kind or radiance around the bed … Our father has gone to heaven in this light," he said to those present. As he laid out the body along with Father and Brother Matthew, a sweet fragrance was perceived emanating from it."

At about 5pm the prioress was called to the parlor where there were two SS Officers wishing to speak with Edith Stein. Sister Antonia thought they were there to speak about emigration and sent for Edith.

Edith was given five minutes to pack. The writing was left on her desk. Residents, began to fill the streets, upset over this latest injustice. Edith asked the sisters for their prayers. Rosa, confused, was already waiting at the police car.

From here, do we need to discuss the indignities one human can disburse to another? There is right and there is wrong. Without recognizing a difference, we blithely walk into future histories. "History repeats itself all over again" has been said too frequently.

The car sped to the headquarters. All pretenses were abandoned, and all were shoved into sleeping quarters with fists and clubs. One of the released survivors would write, "What I still recall very clearly is the unworried, or perhaps even cheerful, way that [Edith Stein] and the other brothers and sisters accepted the situation. There was no way to tell that a few hours before, the police had caught them completely unaware. They even took care of some of the children. This was so different from the attitude of the other prisoners, who seemed paralyzed with fear—and with good reason."

Another survivor Julius Marcan of Cologne said,

> It was Edith Stein's complete calm and self-possession that marked her out from the rest of the prisoners. There was a spirit of indescribable misery in the camp; the new prisoners, especially, suffered from extreme anxiety. Edith Stein went among the women like an angel, comforting, helping, and consoling them. Many of the mothers were on the brink of insanity and had sat moaning for days, without giving any thought to their children. Edith Stein immediately set about taking care of these little ones. She washed them, combed their hair and tried to make sure they were fed and cared for.

On August 5, the nuns received a telegram through the Council of Jewish Affairs. Two local men volunteered to drive blankets, medicine, and other basics to Westerbork. They related Edith's gratitude for the kindness the council had shown. They said, "She hoped she could offer her suffering for the conversion of atheists, for her fellow-Jews, for the Nazi persecutors, and for all who no longer had the love of God in their hearts."

Before her martyr's death in Auschwitz, she related to her Jesuit confessor, Father Hirschmann, "You don't know what it means to me to be a daughter of the chosen people—to belong to Christ, not only spiritually, but according to the flesh."

In 1941, Sister Teresa completed and sent an article to the United States that was published in the *Thomist*, a prestigious philosophical magazine. It commented on negative theology, where one discovers what God is "not." It then spoke of positive theology, using analogies between the Creator and creatures as a prophet is "touched by the Divine Presence in one's innermost being."

The convent in Echt would be in the path of British and US bombers on their way to bomb Germany. When the nuns evacuated Echt for Carmel of Herkenbosch, they would bring the thousands of sheets of Sister Benedicta's writings with them. That building would be destroyed by a bomber attack at the end of 1944. Sister Benedicta's writings had been in the attic. Those thousands of pages were said to be "scattered everywhere." *The Science of the Cross* was planned for publication in 1942 but was published in 1950.

A previous generation of parents who had become soldiers and who had also directly confronted this evil in World War II said little of it but would be seen at church.

> Finally, be strong in the Lord and in his mighty power. Put on the full armor of God, so that you can take your stand against the devil's schemes. For our struggle is not against flesh and blood, but against the rulers, against the authorities, against the powers of this dark world and against the spiritual forces of evil in the heavenly realms.
>
> Therefore, put on the full armor of God, so that when the day of evil comes, you may be able to stand your ground, and after you have done everything, to stand. Stand firm then, with the belt of truth buckled around your waist, with the breastplate of righteousness in place, and with your feet fitted with the readiness that comes from the gospel of peace. (Ephesians 6:10–15 NIV)

FLORENCE NIGHTINGALE

A Nurse

Lord here I am, send me, has always been religion to me.

—Florence Nightingale

The talents of Florence Nightingale and her good use of them will be the subject of these all too brief annals of a woman who transformed the thinking of the field of nursing. Her undying persistence amid the dying inspires nursing even today.

Born May 12, 1820, into comfortable English circumstances was Florence Nightingale. The Napoleonic Wars had come to an end, and the wealthier Britons now traveled. She was named after her birthplace—Florence, Italy.

A grandfather of Florence had supported humanitarian causes. An uncle had been a member of Parliament and had supported abolitionists and the downtrodden. Florence's early education was given by governesses. By age twelve, her father had assumed the task of homeschooling Florence and her older sister, Parthenope. Florence was taught Latin, Greek, French, history, composition, and mathematics. From early youth, Florence had developed the habit of daydreaming. She displayed some "fear of doing something unlike other people." The bustling and busy rounds of family visits and the many domestic events—such as weddings, engagements, christenings, and birthdays, which so satisfied her mother and sister—began to seem rather wasteful to Florence.

She began to crave "some regular occupation, for something worth doing, instead of frittering time away on useless trifles." Florence was a copious writer of notes and would be her entire life. On one such note she wrote at the age of sixteen reads, "God spoke and called me to His service." It would be another sixteen years before she would find out what this service would be.

In 1838, the Nightingales continued to traveling Europe with large coaches accompanied by attendants. Attending operas and grand balls was a part of the entertainment and excitement enjoyed by the Nightingales. For Florence, she began compiling statistics, as well as notes about distances, local laws, and social conditions. The visual beauty of the Chartres Cathedral by moonlight kept Florence awake at her window on one evening.

In Paris, Florence became friends with a Mary Clarke. A vivacious and intelligent Mary had placed herself in the center of the exclusive Parisian intellectual elite. In this congenial atmosphere, Florence held her own and expressed herself in perfect French. The Nightingale sisters went to parties, museums, operas, and concerts. Her shyness overcome, Florence was admired by men, and a good marriage seemed assured, quite to the satisfaction of her family.

Returning to London's social life, Florence became best friends with her cousins Marianne Nicholson and Hilary Carter. Indeed, Marianne's brother, Henry, gave his heart to Florence; but six years later, he was finally refused. This refusal resulted in some discord between the families and introspection for Florence. In this atmosphere where one was "forever expected to be looking merry and saying something lively," she also managed a performance of *The Merchant of Venice* in 1841.

Rather than dining at the dinner table, Florence would sometimes be found at the bedside of a sick person. This interest would not meet with her family's, nor her mother's, approval. During this time, Florence would write to her friend Mary Clarke, "I had so much rather live than write – writing is only a substitute for living … I think one's feelings waste themselves in words, they ought to be distilled into actions and into actions which bring results."

Meanwhile, in the summer of 1842, Florence would have another suitor, Richard Monckton Milnes. Richard was "one of the ornaments of English society"—a linguist and a member of Parliament. Florence's family was more than approving. They shared many common interests and Florence would later describe him as "the man I adored."

That same year, Florence learned about the Institution of Deaconesses at Kaiserswerth on the Rhine. It was an orphanage, school, hospital, and penitentiary. It was one place Florence knew of that provided training for women in the general field of nursing. Florence felt that nursing should be more than kind words and a little nourishing soup. It should be a technique, as with any other profession. As Florence wrote, "I saw a poor woman die before my eyes this summer because there was nothing but fools to sit up with her, who poisoned her as much as if they had given her arsenic."

The American philanthropist Dr. Samuel Howe stayed with the Nightingales in the summer of 1844. Florence asked him if he thought it would be such a "dreadful thing" if she were to devote herself to nursing. "Not a dreadful thing at all. I think it would be a very-good thing. Go forward ... act up to your inspiration and you will find there is never anything unbecoming or unladylike in doing your duty for the good of others," replied Samuel.

Bucking mid-nineteenth-century upper-class convention, Florence attended Salisbury Infirmary for a few months "to learn the 'prax.'" She then nursed some at West Wellow. She wrote to her friend Hilary, "I do not much like talking about it, but I thought something like a Protestant Sisterhood, without vows, for women of educated feelings, might be established."

Florence's mother, Franny, was terrified. Franny's fears were not altogether unfounded. Florence herself wrote of those fears being not only about "the physically revolting parts of a hospital, but things about surgeons and nurses which you may guess." Those were the days before Pasteur's discoveries of germs spreading infections or Lister and the use of antiseptics. Just the hospitals' smells alone could induce nausea.

Infections and gangrene were prevalent. Surgeons went from one room to another, using the same knives and wearing the same bloody clothing. In general, there was no privacy nor sanitation. The patients suffered. Sometimes the gin or brandy smuggled into the hospital would be shared. It was widely perceived that almost all the nurses had loose morals, and most drank. Franny pointedly wrote, "It was preferred that the nurses should be women who have lost their characters ..." To allow Florence to begin nursing was unthinkable to her.

Family friends Charles and Selina would bring Florence along for a trip to Rome in 1848. "I never enjoyed any time in my life as much as my time in Rome," wrote Florence. She would spend a whole day in the Sistine Chapel, "looking up into that heaven of angels and prophets." There, in Rome, she would meet Sidney Herbert and his bride, Elizabeth. Sidney was a former secretary of war. He had good looks, wit, intelligence, and a genuine love of his fellow man.

Sidney Herbert would remain associated with the government and Parliament. He was especially rich and charitable. He was a devout Christian. He and his wife, Liz, and Florence would become close friends. Without Florence's positive impressions, there may not have been the Lady with a Lamp.

Returning to a boring sameness, Florence complained to Aunt Hannah, "How can it be to the glory of God when there is so much misery among the poor, which we might be curing instead of living in luxury?" If she would not be allowed to actively nurse in a hospital, then she could, at least, learn all she could about hospitals. She researched their organization, what may have been causing the mortalities, what may be improved, and so on. Friends in Paris and London helped by gathering reports from hospitals across Europe.

Florence enlisted influential friends, including Lord Ashley and others, to talk to her parents. Fanny reluctantly agreed that Florence could visit Kaiserswerth for a few weeks when the family would be staying in Frankfurt. However, disturbances and dangers began there, altering the Nightingales' plans, and their trip was cancelled. Florence returned to being near the depths of despair. But Richard Monckton Milnes, still in love with Florence Nightingale, could wait no longer for an answer to his proposal. The answer from Florence was no. Florence wrote, "I have an intellectual nature which requires satisfaction, and that would find it in him. I have a passionate nature which requires satisfaction, and that would find it in him. I have a moral and active nature, which requires satisfaction, and that would not find it in his life …"

Her family was upset with her. Friends came to the rescue, and off to Egypt and then to Athens she went. On the twelfth of May, Florence wrote, "Today I am thirty—the age Christ began his mission. Now no more childish things. No more love. No more marriage. Now Lord let me think only of Thy Will, what thou willest me to do. Oh Lord, Thy Will, Thy Will."

On the return trip to England, Florence's friends routed through Berlin to look at the hospitals and orphanages, and then, at long last, they visited Kaiserswerth. They didn't stay long, but Florence felt a "feeling so brave as if nothing could ever vex me again." After a stop off in Ghent, Belgium, Florence wrote her own pamphlet about Kaiserwerth. It was published anonymously.

Finally, Florence decided to take matters into her own hands. She made plans to return to Kaiserswerth for three months when the family would be at Carlsbad in 1851. Life at Kaiserswerth was spartan. Staff were up at 5:00 a.m. for a bowl of rye gruel and had a ten-minute break at noon. Florence recalled the food to be poor and the hygiene horrible, and as for the nursing part, it was "nil." Yet, there was that spirit of dedication, service, and love. Florence stated, "Pastor Fliedner's addresses were the very best I ever heard … The world here fills my life with interest and strengthens me in mind and body."

Florence returned to the boredom of the treadmill in England, but through a Cardinal Manning, she began, in February 1853, working at a hospital in Paris run by the Missionaries of Charity. In April of 1853, efforts were being made to reorganize the Institution for the Care of the Sick Gentlewomen in London. Florence's name was suggested. The committee accepted. Mr. Nightingale began a yearly allowance to Florence.

In August of 1853, Florence took over an empty house. For the next fourteen months, she organized everything, including pots, pans, and curtains. The comfort of the patients and the well-being of the nurses were her top priorities. She was an expert at introducing practical and useful ideas such as devices to assist in bringing the patients their meals and buying in bulk rather than smaller quantities. The ladies thought that they had met a human dynamo. Only members of the Church of England were admitted. Florence believed that any woman deserved to be admitted, regardless of her faith. They compromised. Florence loved the work.

Some feedback from some of her patients includes the following: "Thank you, thank you, darling Miss Nightingale" and "My dearest kind Miss Nightingale I send you a few lines of love." Florence remarked in her notes, "When I entered into service here, I determined that, happen what would, I never would intrigue among the committee. Now I perceive that I do all my business by intrigue. I propose in private to A, B or C the resolution I think A, B or C most capable of carrying in committee, and then leave it to them, and I always win."

In August of 1854, a cholera outbreak swept the slums of Soho. Florence volunteered to help. She found herself nursing dying prostitutes and "drunken bawds," holding them in her arms as they died. A friend of the family observed, "Her powers are astonishing ... She is, I think, too much for institutions, sisterhoods, and associations ... her utter unselfishness in serving and ministering ... She is so like a saint ... [her] gray eyes ... are generally pensive and drooping, but when they choose, can be the merriest eyes I ever saw."

The details of the Crimean War will not be detailed within this writing. One element of that war was the protection of Turkish transports in the Black Sea. Another concern was Russian expansion into the Balkans. In 1853, Russia took territory south of the Danube. Would they proceed further? In any event, the exercises of power and privilege were not seen in the contexts of democratic concerns. Russia was ruled by a tsar (king) with absolute power over a population of serfs, rather than citizens with rights and liberties. Turkey was hardly a democratic state either and countenanced slavery. We may have heard or read of the infamous "Charge of the Light Brigade" conducted in October of 1854.

In March of 1854, England and France had declared war on Russia. In June, the British army landed on the western shore of the Black Sea. They began their transport across the sea to the Peninsula of Crimea with the objective of capturing the Russian naval base at Sebastopol.

The soldiers disembarked from Kalamita Bay on September 14. On September 20, the Battle of the Alma began. It was a glorious but bloody battle. The casualties were high. By mid-October, dispatches reached London, indicating the lack of preparations made to handle the high casualty numbers.

Amid the chaos, Sidney Herbert wrote to Florence, "There is but one person in England that I know of who would be capable of organizing and superintending such a scheme," referring to a plan to send nurses into the conflict. On October 21, the ship *Vectis* departed port with nurses on board. Florence Nightingale was selected to lead a group of nurses on their way to the Crimea. Florence selected thirty-eight women "with a view to fitness and without reference to religious creed, whether Roman Catholic nuns, Dissenting Deaconesses, Protestant Hospital nurses or Anglican sisters." At last, she was realizing her calling. Of their journey, the nurses commented, "We never had so much care taken of our comforts before … we had no notion Miss N would slave herself for us," and, "She looked so calm and noble in it all." One of the letters Florence took with her was from Richard Monckton Milnes: "I cannot forget how you went to the East once before, and here am I writing quietly to you about what you are about to do now. You can undertake that when you could not undertake me. God bless you, dear Friend, wherever you go."

Prayers were needed. The *Vectis* proved to be barely seaworthy, and Florence would often lie seasick on the floor. They finally arrived at their destination, Scutari. A former army barracks had been made into Barrack Hospital. Wounded arrived from the battle of Balaclava that had been fought just ten days earlier.

There was a great dislike for the women butting into the affairs of the men and the hospital. The hospital was in even worse condition than anticipated. The body of a dead Russian general needed to be removed from a room where nurses would stay. Florence and two other nurses shared a ten-by-ten-foot room. There was a daily water allowance of one pint per head. There were no tables and nothing to cook with. The privies were stopped up. It was a filthy place with rats everywhere, and the place stank. Below them were homeless women with nowhere else to go. The homeless women sometimes drank and quarreled. They were essentially starving, and many were dying of cholera.

Under orders, the nurses were admitted into the hospital. Their services were not permitted. Florence kept her head and tasked out finding any available linen to make slings, pillows, and stump rests for amputated legs. She considered the arrangements made to feed the sick and wounded patients. Many were dying from consuming the poorly cooked solids fed to them. Others were starving to death. Doctors' requests went unfulfilled. There were only thirteen cooking coppers for a hospital that was meant to accommodate twenty-five hundred patients. The hospital would soon be filled past capacity.

As a cold, damp winter set in, there was no heating. By November 5, a new influx of casualties entered Barrack Hospital at Scutari. The Russians had repulsed an attack. The new patients had spent eight or nine days at sea, arriving from the Crimean Peninsula. They had endured the open, cold, and rolling decks of the ships without the benefit of drugs or dressings or even blankets. The Bird and her flock were finally given permission to administer to the sick. The nurses began to wash and dress the wounds of the injured. They also began stuffing mattresses.

On November 14, Florence wrote home:

> We are very lucky in our Heads. Two of them are brutes and four are angels – for this is a work which makes either angels or devils of men and women too ... As I went my night-rounds among the newly-wounded that first night, there was not one murmur, not one groan, the strictest discipline – the most absolute silence and quiet prevailed – only the steps of the Sentry – I heard

one man say, "I was dreaming of my friends at home" … These poor fellows bear pain and mutilation with an unshrinking heroism which is really superhuman, and die, or are cut up without a complaint.

A Reverend Osborne wrote, "As to Miss Nightingale and her companions, nothing can be said too strong in their praise; she works them wonderfully, and they are so useful that I have no hesitation in saying that some twenty more of the same sort would be a very great blessing to the establishment …" Additional nurses were sent.

The former barracks was no small hospital. Every night, Florence made her way through about four miles of corridors, bringing comfort to the patients. She carried a Turkish lantern lit by a single candle. The legend of the Lady with a Lamp was born. A companion nurse, Fanny Taylor, explained,

> In all the confusion and distress of Scutari hospital, military discipline was never lost sight of, and an infringement of its smallest observance was worse than letting twenty men die from neglect. To pace the corridor and hear perhaps the low voice of a fever patient, "Give me a drink for the love of God …" Dozens of burials every day, nearly one of four men loaded unto the ships bound for Constantinople and then Scutari were dead before arrival.

…It seemed an endless walk and was not easily forgotten. As we slowly passed along, the silence was profound; very seldom did a moan or cry from those multitudes of deeply suffering ones fall on our ears. A dim light burnt here and there. Miss Nightingale carried her lantern, which she would set down before she bent over any of the patients. I much admired Miss Nightingale's manner to the men – it was so tender and kind … The hospital was crowded to its fullest extent. The building, which has since been reckoned to hold, with comfort, seventeen hundred men, then held between three and four thousand. Miss Nightingale assigned me my work …

Henry Wadsworth Longfellow penned the following famous verse:

> Lo! In that hour of misery
> A lady with a lamp I see
> Pass through the glimmering gloom
> And flit from room to room.
> And slow, as in a dream of bliss
> The speechless sufferer turns to kiss
> Her shadow, as it falls
> Upon the darkening walls.

By the end of 1854, just over 25,000 of the British Amy's 39,000 soldiers were receiving medical treatment or were otherwise declared unfit for duty.

Florence wrote, "Calamity unparalleled in the history of calamity," as the calendar turned to 1855. It seemed the light in her room never went out at night. There were stacks of requests. Her stove was so poor, it was used as a desk. Florence continuously wrote her reports and her thoughts on improvements. Surgeons, nurses, and patients alike died of cholera, scurvy, dysentery, and other diseases. Florence never flinched from her rounds. She wrote, "The tears come into my eyes as I think how, amidst scenes of loathsome disease and death, there rose above it all the innate dignity, gentleness and chivalry of the men (for never surely was chivalry so strikingly exemplified) shining in the midst of what must be considered the lowest sinks of human misery and preventing instinctively the use of one expression which could distress a gentlewoman."

Another dilapidated barracks might have been made into a hospital. Florence appealed to Lady Stratford, who informed the ambassador, and work began. The work was paid for through a "times" fund and Florence's own pocket just in time. Two shiploads of "frost-bitten, demi-nude, starved, ragged men" arrived at port on January 19, 1855. Florence wrote that January, "I am a kind of General Dealer in socks, shirts, knives and forks, wooden spoons, tin baths, tables and forms, cabbages and carrots, operating tables, towels and soap, small toothcombs, scissors, bedpans and stump pillows. I will send you a picture of my Caravanserai, into which beasts come in and out. Indeed, the vermin might, if they had but 'unity of purpose', carry off the four miles of beds on their backs, and march with them into the War Office, Horse Guards."

Florence organized the washing of the bedding. She got army engineers to install boilers. For the first time, there was clean linen without lice. She instructed nurses not to use the same sponge on all the men but a lean piece of rag for each. She bought great quantities of shirts and linen. She bought mops, buckets, brushes, and soap. She worked tirelessly on improving the patients' diets.

In March of 1855, a commission arrived to assist the hospital. A clogged sewer under the hospital was cleared. A full-scale cleaning and washing of the floors and walls commenced. The old wooden platforms used as beds by the patients and as "dormitories" for the rats were destroyed and replaced. The contaminated water supply was addressed and repaired. To Florence, the Sanitary Commission had saved the British army in Crimea. By early summer, the mortality rate had dropped from about 40 percent to 2 percent.

Florence wrote to her mother, "Having been at Scutari six months today, am in sympathy with God, fulfilling the purpose I came into the world for. What the disappointments of the conclusion of these six months are no one can tell. But I am not dead, but alive."

In May, Florence set out to visit the other hospitals and their heads. While aboard the ship and on horseback, she visited many doctors, nurses, and hospital personnel. One observed that she carried herself with a martial air and wore "genteel amazon or riding habit." Days later, the "Crimean fever" laid Florence low. It became so serious that she entered into a state of delirium, and doctors thought she would not survive. Even in this state, she continued her endless writing. The doctors tried to convince her to return to England without success. "If I go, all this will fall to pieces," Florence wrote. After some compromises and doctors' directions, Florence Nightingale returned to Scutari. At that point, Florence was so weak she could not feed herself nor speak above a whisper. She would never fully recover her strength. Today the diagnosis would have been brucellosis, a disease generally transmitted among domesticated animals such as goats, sheep, or cows. Symptoms include headaches, backaches, weakness, and poor appetite. The aftereffects can be chronic with periods of remission.

By July, Florence had much improved, so she then resumed her duties. The crisis in the hospital had, in the main, passed, but a different sort needed to be addressed. Some of the men, now with nothing to do, spent their pay on drink. This they did on some rotgut brews, with some becoming literally dead drunk. Florence would not stand idly by. She had already opened a small reading room. With the aid of conversation, she began receiving money from men who wished to send some to their families. Florence wrote to a chaplain in England that she had "just seen Thomas Whybron, 12th Lancer, and that he has promised [her] that he will not only write his wife, but transmit money to her through [Florence] after 1st of next month ... [His wife] had better also write to him herself, and send her letter through [Florence] ... He is well but has been in debt."

A General Storks decided to equip a building for recreation. A Nightingale fund began sending crates of useful gifts. Florence's sister Parthe wrote, "How hard we worked to send off boxes for F's education of the army! We have sent a dose of a thousand copybooks, writing materials in proportion, diagrams, maps, Macbeth to read ... chess, footballs, other games, a magic lantern for dissolving views, a stereoscope (very fine!), plays for acting, music, etc."

There would be more wounded, more cholera, and more nursing; to wit, she now would focus only on administration. A daily walk around the wards with Mrs. Roberts was her only recreation. Mrs. Roberts would reflect,

> Suppose you could see us just now at 12:30 by the little black clock just about to strike its half-hour, you would see us back-to-back, Flo at her large table covered with papers, I at my little table with my tiny work. We speak

not a word. The wind roars, the rain patters; I don't think Flo is conscious of the bluster. I never saw a mind so continuously concentrated on her work. Is it a mind that belonged to some other planet? For it does not seem adapted to the human frame, though it has forced that frame to obedience.

The last patient would leave the Barrack Hospital in Scutari on July 16, 1856. Now came the time for praises and grateful recognitions of Florence toward her nurses. General Storks wrote to Florence that of all the tributes, he knew she would value most "the grateful recognition of the poor men you came to succour and to save. You will ever live in their remembrance, be assured of that." Florence had scribbled one of her many notes written in stressful moments, and one that she would think of the rest of her life: "Oh my poor men, I am a bad mother to come home and leave you in your Crimean graves—seventy-three percent in eight regiments in six months from disease alone—who thinks of that now?"

A man-of-war was ready to return Florence home to England. As it docked, she would have been welcomed with speeches and a military band. Florence preferred traveling incognito with her aunt Mai as Mrs. and Miss Smith. They would leave on July 28, 1856. She landed undetected. The first thing she did upon her return was visit the convent of the Bermondsey nuns. There, she prayed. The public praise could wait. She refused the many invitations and ceremony. She wrote, "I stand at the altar of the murdered men and while I live, I shall fight their cause."

She immediately wrote to Lord Panmure and Sidney Herbert, asking to meet and talk. The queen wished to listen to Florence. Florence was invited to meet with the queen by her royal physician.

Why was Florence successful? She analyzed, defined, and then knew what needed to be achieved. Florence wanted to see a "root-and-branch" reform of the medical services with the army. The queen was impressed and thought Florence to be a woman "after her own heart." The queen said of her interview, "She put before all the defects of our present military hospital system, and the reforms that are needed. We are much pleased with her; she is extremely modest."

There were limits to the powers of Royalty. Lord Panmure was to visit Balmoral. The queen wrote Florence and suggested she may like to meet the minister "under the royal roof."

Florence returned a note saying, "I don't but I am obliged to succumb,"

The queen replied, "Lord Panmure, will be much gratified and struck with Miss Nightingale—her powerful, clean head, and simple, modest manner."

Sidney Herbert, though, was not quite so sure, "not sanguine: for, tho' he [Panmure] has plenty of shrewd sense, there is a 'vis inertiae' in his hesitance which is very-difficult to overcome."

"You fairly overcame Pan," Sir James Clark's son wrote to Florence. "We found him with his mane absolutely silky, and a loving sadness pervading his whole being." Sidney Herbert wrote that "he was very much surprised at your physical appearance, as I think you must have been with his." It was agreed that there would be a royal commission. Florence would submit her recommendations. Her proposal for an army medical school was well received, and the Bison, Lord Panmure, offered to submit Florence's plans for the first general military hospital to be built in Britain.

Entirely reticent to enter the public domain, Florence would do so as needed, in order, to move forward the ideas of the commission with its many reforms. After many debates and public discussions, on the 5th of May 1857, the royal warrant was signed, and the approved commission, with Sidney Herbert as chairman, began work the following week. Florence devoted, all, of her energy to see successful outcomes for the Royal Commission, her brainchild.

Florence agreed to answer any question in writing and wrote a thousand-page document entitled *Notes on Matters Affecting the Health, Efficiency and Hospital Administration of the British Army*. A comment made about her work stated, "I regard it as a gift to the Army, and to the country, altogether priceless."

In 1856, Florence's health had been so poor according to her sister Parthe that she said, "I cannot believe [Florence] will live long." In November of 1857, Florence wrote to Sidney Herbert, "I hope you will not regret the manner of my death ... I am sorry not to stay alive to do the 'Nurses.'" Aunt Mai remarked that Florence would work "day after day, until she [was] almost fainting." In the late summer of 1859, Florence moved to Hampstead. After the work in the war office was finished for the day, Sidney Herbert would ride out to consult with Florence. In some ways, from that time forward, Florence became a permanent invalid; yet she would live another fifty years, spending much time in bed or on a sofa.

In 1860, Sidney Herbert would learn he was suffering from an incurable kidney disease. On August 2, 1861, he died peacefully. Among his last words were these: "Poor Florence! Poor Florence! Our joint work unfinished. I have tried to do my best." The mortality rate of the home army reduced by one half. The medical school officially opened in 1859. Gladstone asked for a short account of Herbert's work. Florence wrote the account. It was published as *Army Sanitary Administration and Its Reform under the Late Lord Herbert*.

Notes on Hospitals was published in 1859. Many British cities and boroughs submitted hospital plans for Florence's comments. Even the queen of Holland and the government of India did so as well. Each hospital had developed its own method of disease classification. With assistance from Dr. William Farr, Florence constructed a uniform system, which she then had printed.

Florence later turned her attention to the creation of a nursing service of a kind never known in the world before. The Nightingale Fund, begun in 1855 as a tribute to her own services, was used to help finance this new training in a school for female nurses. At the end of 1859, she put out a short book entitled *Notes on Nursing: What It Is, and What It Is Not*. The book became very popular and is still in print today. Her added emphasis on the psychological aspects of sickness was well ahead of her time. She could describe and elaborate based on her own personal experiences. Florence Nightingale referenced Shakespeare to find the best definition of a nurse:

So kind, so duteous, diligent,
So tender over his occasions, true,
So feat, so nurse-like. ————

And what is new? And what is old? And what may Florence say?

I would earnestly ask my sisters to keep clear of both the jargons now current everywhere, of the jargon, namely, about the "rights of women", which urges women to do all that men do, merely because men do it, and without regard to whether this is the best thing women can do; and the jargon which urges women to do nothing that men do, merely because they are women, and should be "recalled to a sense of their duty as women" … and "these are things women should not do", which is all assertion and nothing more. Surely woman should bring the best she has, whatever that is, to the work of God's world, without attending to either of these cries.

The Nightingale Training School for Nurses was opened at St. Thomas Hospital on June 24, 1860.

Florence Nightingale thought deeply, theologically, and philosophically. She privately printed three volumes that totaled 829 pages. "It is not the material presence only that we love in our fellow creatures. It is the spirit, which bespeaks the material presence, that we love. Shall we not then love the spirit of all that is lovable …?"

What might we learn in conversation with Florence? As she said, "God governs by His laws, but so do we when we have discovered them. If it were, otherwise, we could not learn from the past for the future."

Florence was also called to duty, as it were, concerning the troops in India. She felt that perhaps a royal commission of sorts might be of some positive importance to the subcontinent. With the assistance of Sutherland and Farr, Florence began compiling statistics. The results were two volumes, two thousand words of small print, published in

1863. Sir Edward Cook commented, "The greater part bears in one way or another the impress of Miss Nightingale. A great Commander was lost to her country when Florence Nightingale was born a woman."

Florence's view of those of influence with whom she worked closely was that they all shared the "one needful thing"—"the serving with all their souls and minds and without a thought of self their high idea of right."

Soon after the commission's report was published, the viceroy of India died. Sir John Lawrence was appointed to replace him. Lord Derby thought Sir John needed to be brought up to speed on the report. Who better than Florence Nightingale to bring forward the facts? Florence may have hesitated. However, Lord John wrote with encouragement, "Why should he not see you? The plans are in the main yours; no one can explain them better; you have been in frequent correspondence with him. I believe there will now be but little difficulty in India ... Let me repeat—you must manage to see Sir John Lawrence." Years later, Florence would write, "He came like a footman to my door without giving his name ... The interview was one never to be forgotten." Sir John was of a family of twelve and a devout Puritan. Each held similar beliefs, sympathies, and convictions. Within a month of his return, Sir John began setting up sanitary committees for Calcutta, Madras, and Bombay. He wrote to Florence, "I am doing what I can to put things in order here, but it is very uphill work."

Florence replied, "Oh that I could come out to Calcutta and organize at least the Hospital accommodation ..." But on an upbeat note, she thought Lawrence "conquering India anew by civilization, taking possession of the Empire for the first time by knowledge instead of by the sword."

Beside Florence's busy workload on workhouse reform, public health in India, and reorganizing the India Office, another area of inquiry and research, begun in 1867, was a study of mortality of women in childbirth. This three-year effort was published in 1871: *Introductory Notes on Lying-in Institutions*. It was also said that "of the sanitary improvements in India, three-fourths are due to Miss Nightingale."

The Franco-Prussian War began in July of 1870. The National Society for Aid to the Sick and Wounded (the precursor to the British Red Cross) was formed with Florence Nightingale's blessings. The founder of the Red Cross and delegate at the Geneva Convention, John Henri Dunant, said, "It is to an Englishwoman that all the honour of that Convention is due. What inspired me … was the work of Miss Florence Nightingale in the Crimea."

Florence Nightingale continued to communicate and correspond and influence until she at last fell asleep on the thirteenth of August 1910.

In 1907, the Order of Merit was conferred upon her. Burial in Westminster Abbey was proposed, but by her own choice, her funeral was a very simple one. At her request, her only memorial was a small cross bearing the letters *F* and *N* and the inscription "Born 1820. Died 1910."

To conclude, here is an excerpt from the preface to Florence Nightingale's *Notes on Nursing*:

> The following notes are by no means intended as a rule of thought by which nurses can teach themselves to nurse, still less as a manual to teach nurses to nurse. They are meant simply to give hints for thought to women who have personal charge of the health of others. Every woman, or at least almost every woman, in England has, at one time or another of her life, charge of the personal health of somebody, whether child or invalid,—in other words, every woman is a nurse. Every day sanitary knowledge, or the knowledge of nursing, or in other words, of how to put the constitution of such a state as that it will have no disease, or that it can recover from disease, takes a higher place. It is recognized as the knowledge which ever one ought to have— distinct from medical knowledge, which only a profession can have.

If, then, every woman must at some time or other of her life, become a nurse, i.e., have charge of somebody's health, how immense and how valuable would be the produce of her united experience if every woman would think how to nurse.

I do not intend to teach her how, I ask her to teach herself, and for this purpose I venture to give her some hints.

LIN ZHAO

A Future

From her jail cell, Lin Zhao wrote on November 24, 1963, "The pain of grief, heavy yet burning, like molten lead, poured into my heart. Sir, I learned of your assassination two hours ago from the newspaper." She entitled her piece "Mourning Inside a Jail Cell."

"I remember you saying: 'all men who fight for freedom are our brothers.' You said: 'Freedom is indivisible, and when one man is enslaved, all are not free!' ... You have revealed to us—contemporary young fighters against tyrannical rule in China—more profoundly and more broadly the rich meaning of the sacred concept of freedom. In this way you have encouraged us and inspired in us the resolve, perseverance, and courage to dedicate our lives to her!" It was John F. Kennedy who had delivered those words near the Berlin Wall on June 26, 1963.

Some years later, Lin Zhao, too, would be assassinated—or executed, if one prefers—for her beliefs in freedom.

Sometimes the wheels of history can make unexpected turns. Sometimes the directions they take depend upon the ground upon which they are traveling. Sometimes it is the unanticipated that steers those wheels. Sometimes it is those turns that result in futures blessed with greater freedoms and better lives for the passengers riding in the wagon's train of events.

Who is at the wheel? What is just beyond the horizon? Even in the world of today, relying on steadfast technical predictabilities, it remains the unseen into which we enter—and it is in this, as history has so often shown us, that we may only truly rely upon the goodness and nobility of our own actions to better determine the better courses of our futures.

And sometimes it can be those run over by the wheels that leave their memories on those continuing life's journeys, leaving it up to them, as to all of us, to continually right the course for the greater good and betterment of mankind. And so, as the wheels of histories inevitably turn, it will be up to individuals to sing a chorus of joyful exaltation: "Give me liberty or give me death!"

Lin was five years old in July of 1937, when the Japanese invaded China. Fifty million would flee coastal China, her family among them. Some three hundred thousand would be massacred. Her mother would return as an undercover agent. After the war, she would serve as a trustee of a local bank, become a director of a newspaper, cofound a transportation company, and successfully run for the national assembly in 1946. Lin's talented parents were able to provide a comfortable life and education.

Lin would enter the Laura Haygood Memorial School for Girls in the fall of 1947. Named Jinghai "in admiration of Haygood"—the first female foreign missionary of the Methodist Episcopal Church, South—it was known as an elite school offering "exceptional literary advantages." She would identify with and learn Christian concerns for justice.

At that same time, inflation skyrocketed as the war between the Nationalists and the Communists continued. A "new democracy" was promised by the Communists. It was to replace the authoritarian government of Chiang Kai-shek. During those civil war years, Lin's mother, Xu, joined the China Democratic League, a coalition of pro-democracy parties that had been formed in 1941. At the age of sixteen, Lin Zhao secretly decided to join the Chinese Communist Party (CCP). She would reflect later, "In my solemn reflections and painful self-reproach, I always saw my leftist leaning and my pursuit of communism during adolescence as a personal mistake … It could be attributed to both the trend of the time and family influence."

In the summer of 1948, the Communists were on the offensive. Later that year, Communist forces routed the Nationalists in three major battles and came to control almost all areas north of the Yangzi River. "No one will prophesy when the Communists, will cross the river, occupy Nanjing, and move on down the railroad to Soochow and Shanghai," wrote Annie Bradshaw, Lin Zhao's teacher at Laura Haygood, in December 1948. "People don't seem to care. There is so much chaos and deprivation now that I believe they would welcome a frying pan as escape from the fire, especially a frying pan so full of Utopian promises."

To Lin, the Communists more boldly addressed systemic evils of an unjust society. The ends may have been noble, but the means were violent, as Lin would learn. The director of Laura Haygood's religious education had sternly warned her students, "... you are all hot-blooded youths. Be careful and don't let yourselves be used by other people!" A decade and a half later, Lin Zhao would write, "Countless hot-blooded youths fell victim to the agitation ... They abandoned their studies, forsook honest work, got swept into the political whirlpool, and became the tools of political careerists!"

Lin Zhao mimeographed some CCP propaganda from the school. Two progressive teachers left. The party directed the two students involved to leave. As a daughter of a member of the national assembly, Lin considered herself safe and chose to stay. She lost her party membership, as a result, of this refusal to leave the school as directed.

The Nationalist capital Nanjing fell to the People's Liberation Army in late April 1949. That summer, Lin Zhao, a brilliant student, graduated. Her parents expected her to go to college. They were shocked to learn that Lin had secretly applied to the South Jiangsu Journalism Vocational School. It would seem to Lin to be a very ideal arrangement as no tuition was required and the room and board would be free. This new school of questionable academic standards was opened July 1949 by the CCP in order, to prepare journalists to learn how to propagandize for the revolution ahead.

Her father, Peng Guoyan, warned her, "... it is the utmost cruelty to use the innocent zeal of young people for political purposes." Lin Zhao had not been her given name. Nee Peng Lingzhao had abandoned her name from birth to join the communist revolution.

In ten months, they would be assigned by the party to the frontline of the propaganda war. During the fall term, the students were to live with peasants for three months. They would work hard to obtain "a diploma from the 'University of the Peasants'," as Lin Zhao put it.

The phrase "taking off the pants" referred to a self-scrutiny of the most unforgiving kind. All were required to keep "soul-searching notes," to lay bare their thoughts, and to renounce their former selves. A party committee then had the right to demand to read the notes without prior notice. One Comintern wrote, "The cruel method of psychological coercion that Mao calls moral purification has created a stifling atmosphere inside the party. ... A not negligible number of party activists in the region have committed suicide, have fled, or have become psychotic." At journalism school, Lin Zhao became a true believer. Now, as a member of a collective body and the revolution, one would always be ready to renounce the self.

Land reform and redistribution included denunciation meetings where farmers were encouraged to seek vigilante justice. Between one and two million were killed as rural reform got under way. Several more million were placed under penal control. The mass campaign of rural reform remade the countryside. "The mass movement has a huge tempering effect on people," observed Lin Zhao. Now, as a land reform work team member, she observed that her work in these reforms required a proletarian tough-mindedness she had not possessed before—that is, a disregard for civility and a contempt for the claims or the pain of individuals if they stood in the way of the righteous cause of making a new society. Mao glorified all the violent justice.

For all her work on behalf of the party, she would write to another party member in March of 1951, "I hope one day, I will be able to write to tell you: 'I have once again returned to the ranks of the party.'" Returning to the party would be a rather more tortuous journey than she may have imagined. One obstacle was her parents' political background. The moment she entered journalism school she was pressured to renounce her parents. "I don't understand; why do I have to sever ties with my family just to take a firm stand?" she said as she burst into tears. Another side campaign Mao had launched in 1950 was designed to ferret out those who might pose a threat to the new regime. From three quarters of a million to one million were executed to meet quotas set by Mao and the party's central committee. To even have held positions as members of the bourgeoise or an entity not in line with communism was considered an evil.

On December 21, 1951, at a ceremony held by the Rural Work Corps to mark a conclusion of their land reform work, those gaining party membership or joining the Communist Youth League of China were noted. "However, there are those, incapable of being reformed, such as Peng Lingzhao!"

"Have I really sunk to an unredeemable level?" she wondered in a letter to a friend. "Yes, I have let the party down, but I also suspect that somebody has let me down."

Lin Zhao had so much to learn. Milovan Djilas, a seasoned former Yugoslav communist leader who had "traveled the entire road of Communism," would say, "membership in the Communist Party before the Revolution meant sacrifice. Being a professional revolutionary was one of the highest honors. Now that the party has consolidated its power, party membership means that one belongs to a privileged class. And at the core of the party are the all-powerful exploiters and masters." If he were there to advise Peng, he may have added, as he also said, "Revolutionaries who accepted the ideas and slogans of the revolution literally, naively believing in their materialization, are usually liquidated."

In March of 1952, Lin Zhao would write, "My mood has continued to be melancholy." After concluding her land reform work, Lin was assigned as a junior editor and reporter to the *Changzhou Peoples News*. The CCP-trained journalists wrote, "We kept reminding ourselves that 'we were sent by the party and must do a good job propagating the party's "positions"'."

Two mass campaigns began in 1951 and 1952 to root out corruption. One was within the party. The other targeted the remnants of the capitalist class. Lin Zhao was put in charge of the campaign at a textile company. She often worked late, sometimes sleeping only two or three hours a day. She also had tuberculosis and at times was unable to continue working. She requested sick leave, intending to go home. "I feel confused and tormented," she told a friend. The local party secretary was adamant she should not leave.

Across China, some one hundred thousand people killed themselves during these twin campaigns. Even Lin Zhao was pressured to write up materials exposing her mother. Many years later, her sister would relate that Lin told her mother, "They drove me to my wit's end," and that they did not care "whether [she (Lin)] would jump to [her] death in a well or in the river." She added, "I had no choice but to satisfy them, and wrote up things that I was clueless about … I did not mean to falsely accuse you."

At that time, despite poor health, Lin Zhao was persuaded not to take sick leave. "We have not taken good care of you when you were sick, so that you were unable to feel the warmth in the revolutionary ranks," she was later told. That seemed to lift her chin just a bit and lift her out of dejection. "Whenever I see my comrades, the party's flag, the national flag, or a portrait of Mao, I no longer feel too ashamed to raise my head," wrote Lin Zhao. For Lin Zhao's generation of progressive youths, calling Chairman Mao "dear father" was common. To many, he was their spiritual father and the maker of a new China. For the next two years, Lin Zhao would produce news reports celebrating the dawn of a new China.

Lin would receive permission to apply to Peking University. Five years after choosing revolution over college, she found herself on the campus of the most prestigious university in China. She was twenty-two. Originally, the university was located near the imperial palace, but it was moved to the outskirts of Beijing, to what had been the picturesque campus of Yenching University. Yenching was the leading Christian University in pre-Communist China.

Lin Zhao was admitted as a journalism major. She would join a poetry club and serve as editor of the poetry journal as well as the university's official periodical. Although delicate in appearance, she would show a feisty personality in "bantering with others" and enjoyed "waging long verbal battles and scoring victories in jokes," as a friend remembered. A wry sense of humor she had. They were near Tiananmen, or the Gate of the Heavenly Peace.

As a junior, Lin was one of about a dozen named to the editorial board of the new student journal named *The Red Building*. In 1955, a noted literary theorist and a key member of the League of Left-Wing Writers in the 1930s was purged after being denounced by Mao. This member had advocated the "emancipation of individuality" in literary creations (a definite no-no). He was arrested in May of 1955. More than twenty-one hundred were denounced and considered to be members of what the party called the "Hu Feng Counterrevolutionary Clique."

This minor purge was followed by a major purge that would become known as the Elimination of Counterrevolutionaries Campaign. Mao instructed that Hu Feng and his imaginary clique were by no means the only "bad elements" to sneak into the CCP. Many had entered "deep into our liver" and made up about 5 percent of the people in the revolutionary ranks. This would be about 700,000 of the 14.3 million cadres in 1955. They would need to be weeded out. At least 300,000 were arrested, and the overall number of victims is unknown.

The repercussions would be felt on campus. As an example, a student was caught having corresponded with Hu Feng. Hundreds of students attended a session to denounce him. A hunt for "little Hu Fengs" found more than two hundred, who were incriminated and quarantined, tied up with ropes and beaten.

Lin Zhao was suspected. The campaign carried on well into 1956. She was denounced by some party members with a grudge against her, perhaps, for her having "incorrect views." She was put on a one-year probation as a member of the Communist Youth League of China—another slip in her journey to regain party membership. She later wrote of "the wound of the mental slavery that writer Hu Feng had spoken of."

Still, in the May issue of *The Red Building* was a poem by Lin Zhao addressed to one of the giant pair of stone lions guarding the entrance to Tiananmen:

Forty years of wind, frost, rain, and snow—and you are still here;

The red flags on Tiananmen flutter on this sunlit, festive day.

You watch the joyous procession swell past you like a wild tide,

And smile with wide-opened eyes at the free people who have cast their shackles away.

In 1956, Mao had cleverly launched what was known as the Hundred Flowers Movement. The slogan "Let a hundred flowers bloom and a hundred schools of thought contend" was intended to invite criticism and help improve the party's work. In February of 1957, Mao delivered an address to the Supreme State Conference entitled "On the Correct Handling of Contradictions among the People." He would advocate openness toward criticisms, such as different ideas expressed in the arts and sciences, as well as tolerance toward the skeptics of communism. Going forward, the only way to settle "controversial issues among the people" would be "by the democratic method, the method of discussion, criticism, persuasion and education." He said the method would be called "unity-criticism-unity."

At first unwilling to speak out, a few Peking University students became convinced they could do so without reprisal. Eventually hundreds of posters and poems appeared on a wall outside a dorm building. It became known as the democracy wall of Peking University. On the opposite side of the street was another wall, which became known as the apologist's forum, upon which the leftists posted their chastisements of the ideological heresies.

The violent crackdowns on democracy movements in Poland and Hungary in 1956 raised many questions about communist regimes. A friend of Lin Zhao posted a poem entitled "It Is Time": "It is time / Young people / Give full voice to your song! ... I call to my generation:

/ My brethren who sing to truth / raise the torch without delay / to cremate all the darkness under the sun!"

A different poem, written by a student party member, entitled "Our Song," denounced the so-called hysterics of "It Is Time." "It Is Time" had attacked the CCP's shortcomings. Lin Zhao was spurred to write her own poem, entitled "What Song is this?" Her poem was directed at the self-appointed defenders of the party. "The power of truth / never lies in / the arrogant air / of the guardians of truth."

Lin would write another poem, entitled "Party I call out to You." The same day, May 22, a nighttime debate pitted two democracy advocates against a large, organized group of leftist students. The two came under waves of angry denunciations. A debater recalled that "a girl student ascended the dining room table in the thick of dark." She spoke in a "vigorous voice," with a "graceful Suzhou accent" in her Mandarin Chinese. She reminded the crowd that the CCP had repeatedly called on nonparty members to make criticisms and asked why there was such an ideological crusade against the debater just because of a single poem? Someone from the crowd roared, "Who are you?"

"I am Lin Zhao," she shot back. She retorted with a question: "Who are you, that you should assume the tone of an interrogator?"

The answer she heard was "Make note of it! 'Lin' with the two trees, and 'Zhao' for 'the day when the knife is put to the mouth!'"

The movement gained steam, and some students formed their own independent clubs. The Hundred Flowers Society organized forums and debates. Pamphlets were published—the most influential of these being *The Square*. Lin decided not to join the editorial board. Ironically, she was alleged to be the actual "wire puller" and "strategist" by the counterrevolutionary journal.

In early May, Mao's hundred flowers began to bloom across the country. Leading members of China's powerless "democratic parties" joined the chorus of discontent. They called for implementing the "mutual supervision" between them and the CCP as Mao had publicly advocated. Hundreds of thousands of people spoke out, calling for respect of human rights, freedom of speech, an independent judiciary, and even a multiparty system to replace the CCP dictatorship.

Little did they know that Mao had laid a trap. He would later call it open conspiracy with the design of "enticing snakes out of their lairs." The Anti-Rightist Campaign officially began on June 8 and, on Peking's University campus, on June 16. In the months that followed, participants in the democracy wall movement were forced to recant and denounce themselves publicly. By August, some were arrested. Some cracked under the constant struggle sessions. Lin Zhao dodged the initial bullet. She was doing an internship at the *China Youth Daily*.

Across China, leading writers were denounced. Wives were pressured to divorce their husbands. Tens of thousands took their own lives during the purge. Others simply vanished.

Lin Zhao returned to the university in the fall of 1957. Yang Huarong, a classmate from the Jiangsu Journalism Vocational School had been labeled as a rightist. Lin did not avoid him. Yang remembered, "She was an innocent girl and was not familiar with the way of the world ... She was baffled by the Anti-Rightest struggle and the punishments for the Rightists and was deeply disaffected with the bad faith of some people, the insincere words of some teachers, and the mutual betrayal of some classmates and friends." The two traded jokes and talked on many topics. They became quite close. Yang wrote that when it came to religion, she grew serious. She had said, "... don't you belittle God. I am a Christian."

Late in 1957, another of Lin's friends and cofounder of *The Square* attempted to slip on board a foreign cargo ship leaving for Hong Kong. He was sentenced to fifteen years in a labor camp. Later, Lin was accused of helping plot his botched escape in order, to "collude with the imperialists." The friend called the accusation a fabrication.

Lin Zhao recalled after her arrest that the participants in the May 19 democracy movement believed they were in a position, to "reveal the reality of the totalitarian rule and the vicious political persecutions" to the outside world. Lin wrote, "... as long as the good earth of the motherland remains under deep darkness my spirit will never gain freedom. I preferred to keep watch over this land and endure the afflictions, torture, and even death together with my fellow countrymen!"

Mao had set minimum quotas of about 1.2 million for the cadres to meet in declaring rightists. Lin Zhao would be added to the prestigious list in January of 1958. She had just turned twenty-six. The indictment stated that she had been found a rightist for her antiparty and antisocialist activities. Lin would write later that the "correct way of putting it" should have been "In 1957, fueled by her youthful blood and driven by a conscience that had not yet perished, she became an activist in the 'May 19' democracy movement against tyranny!"

Lin stated, "Throughout the second half of 1957, I still held on to that ray of hope inside my heart, the hope that the party would stop before going too far and would wrap up the whole thing." She looked for any "trace of wisdom," only to find "Nothing! Nothing!" She added, "After all my hope was lost, I naturally had no choice but to opt for resistance!"

At a national meeting, a delegate made a comparison to the first emperor of China in the late third century BCE. Mao promptly disabused him. "Qin Shihuang is nothing. He only buried alive 468 scholars; we buried alive 46,000 scholars … We had a debate with people from the democratic parties. 'You curse us, calling us Qin Shihuang. That's incorrect. We exceed him a hundred times. You call us Qin Shihuang and dictator. We admit to all of that. But what you say is an understatement; we often need to make some additions.'" Mao's audience burst into laughter.

On March 10, a meeting with ten thousand people was held on campus at Peking University. Within three hours, some eighty thousand posters in revolutionary colors were produced. After three days, about two hundred eighty thousand had been produced. On March 15, thousands gathered at Tiananmen Square to hold a "meeting of democratic party figures and non-party figures to promote socialist self-reform." They chanted in unison, "Hand over the heart to the party; resolutely become a leftist." A fellow Peking University rightist recalled, "Almost all the Rightists made their self-criticisms … The only Rightist who refused to make self-criticism was Lin Zhao."

Lin Zhao's decreed punishment was three years of reeducation through labor—in simple terms, internment at a labor camp. The vice chair of the Chinese Department, concerned about Lin's tuberculosis, persuaded university authorities to allow her to remain on campus. She would undergo reform under the supervision of the revolutionary masses. In early 1958, at the start of Mao's Great Leap Forward, the government launched a campaign to exterminate "four pests": rats, flies, mosquitoes, and sparrows. Across China, groups were organized to beat pans and pots to scare the sparrows and keep them flying until they dropped from exhaustion. At Peking University, students, faculty, and staff were ordered to wet their washbasins with soap bubbles and use them to catch mosquitoes. After spending an entire day catching mosquitoes, Lin Zhao told her friend Tan Tianrong, "I couldn't help laughing inside me the whole day; I laughed at how this party is going crazy."

Overall, it was a bleak time. One by one, Lin Zhao's friends vanished into police custody or exile—for instance, Chen Fengxia, who had attempted escape to Hong Kong. Of seventy-five people sentenced to a group, only twenty-nine were still alive eight years later. Party leaders needed to come up with another two hundred or so to designate as rightists at the university, in order, to meet their quota. One such was Gan Cui. He worked in the library, as did Lin Zhao. He had been nice enough to get permission to place a coal burner and ventilation duct in Lin's room. After a time, Gan Cui began joining Lin Zhao for Sunday worship at Dengshikou Church, the largest church in Beijing. Sixty plus churches were forced to combine their worship services at four facilities. Surprisingly, young people made up the majority, of the congregation. He wrote, "Amid the myriad sufferings, they went there in search of spiritual sustenance ... The atmosphere was beautiful. It brought us into a transcendent realm in those depressing, gloomy days."

In August 1959, having finished his bachelor's degree, Gan requested permission from the department's party secretary to marry Lin Zhao. He also asked that he be assigned to a job near her. "What business does a Rightist have getting married?" the party secretary replied. On one last Sunday, Lin took Gan to worship at the iconic Shanghai Community Church. It would later be destroyed by the Red Guards during the Cultural Revolution, in which a generation of trained leaders, professors, diplomats, and experts were sent to the countryside to work and learn from the masses—a revolution designed to remove Chinese history from the minds of the youth. Gan would return and be sent to a twenty-year exile of forced labor. They would not see each other again.

In early 1960, Lin Zhao would return home and leave Beijing behind. As a writer and a poet, she privately wrote two lengthy poems. "Seagull" reads as follows:

> What crimes have the prisoners committed? There is only one: we see freedom as food, and as air to breath ...
>
> The tyrant wields his sword and rod, and puts us on trial,
>
> Because he fears freedom just as he fears fire.
>
> He is afraid that once we find freedom,
>
> His throne will be shaken, his fate will be dire." And then a young man leaning against the mast of a ship declares:
>
> "What am I thinking, this rebellious, disquieted heart of mine?"
>
> "Freedom, I cry out inside me, freedom!
>
> The thought of you has filled my heart with yearning, like a choking man gasping for air, like one dying of thirst lurching toward a spring.

In September 1959, she mailed a copy to a brother of a friend. An unprecedented famine in human history had overtaken the countryside as a result of the Great Leap Forward. A decline in food production and the breakdown in distribution had set off the famine. Demographic data in the 1980s revealed between sixteen million and twenty-seven million deaths. A small group was secretly meeting, discussing how they might stop Mao's policies. Their leader was a Korean War veteran. He had entered a university and witnessed some of the hundreds of thousands of earnest and sincere students who fell victim to Mao's so-called "open conspiracy." He visited Lin at her mother's home in Suzhou.

By 1957, the planned economy had been implemented and was firmly in place, controlling both means of production and the people's livelihoods. Some 120 million rural households had been herded into some twenty-six thousand five hundred "peoples communes." Families became unimportant. Mao was convinced he could soon overtake the United Kingdom in industrial production, particularly steel production. As a result, an estimated one hundred million people were mobilized nationwide to build a million steel furnaces in their backyards.

With the economic and social collapse of rural China, this group of rightist students saw no choice but to become self-appointed spokespersons for the masses. Their first periodical, *A Spark of Fire*, was published in January 1960. It dissected the "slavery" of Mao's rule. A new poem by Lin Zhao was included. Following essays described the state as imposing a military organization on the people, putting them into "slave-like collective labor." By September, nearly all the contributors had been arrested. On October 24, police showed up in Lin Zhao's home in Suzhou.

After her arrest, Lin Zhao was sent to the No. 2 Detention House of Shanghai. Her attitude appeared to soften, and she was given medical parole in March 1962. She wrote a letter to Lu Ping, the university president, requesting to bring back to campus those students who had been arrested and persecuted following the democracy movement of 1957 and to stand up to Communist "tyranny." She received a summons in August to appear in people's court. In early November, Lin Zhao was rearrested. She was sent to a psychiatric hospital. On December 23, she was sent to the Shanghai Municipal Prison and then to Tilanquao, where she spent thirty-six months in presentencing incarceration. She would engage in a month-long hunger strike. Her faith was becoming the backbone of her rebellion against CCP rule. She saw a "demonic political party."

On August 8, 1963, the authorities moved Lin Zhao to the Shanghai No. 1 Detention House for full regime interrogations. Another inmate remembers, "no sound in the hallway ... cannot feel any breeze except a dark coldness that seeps into your bone." A typical cell was three meters by five meters with up to fourteen inmates crammed into it. To this day, the interrogation records remain locked and classified. Along with taunts and hair pulling came a series of handcuffing of all sorts. Lin would also be placed in two pairs of behind-the-back cuffs. In her undestroyed prison documents, which were eventually returned to her family, she wrote, "Freedom—the most sacred, the most beautiful, and the most noble noun in the human language—always kindles the most fervent love ... in the souls of people, especially the young people!" Despite the "extremely reactionary" nature of her writings, no prison or public security bureaucrat apparently dared to risk a potentially costly political mistake by ordering their destruction. Instead, they were filed as part of criminal evidence. Her primary file remains locked at a secret location.

On February 5, 1964, Lin Zhao was so distraught that she swallowed medicated soap in a futile suicide attempt. She lamented that, as a wronged political prisoner, she had cried her eyes out over the sorrows of her homeland. Her "Self-Eulogy" was written in her own blood; this was the first of her many known blood writings. Her hands had been cuffed behind her back, and she had been deprived of stationery.

In the spring of 1964, the two pairs of handcuffs on her wrists and arms were finally removed after she wrote a statement of repentance on March 23. It appears to have mainly concerned her letter to Lu Ping as well as a writing entitled "We Are Innocent." On April 12, she wrote a letter to her uncle on the anniversary of his death. He had been a Communist activist killed in 1927. In her letter, she wrote of the overwhelming cruel irony of mourning his death "from a Red prison." In her writing, she stated, "If only you had known / the millions of compatriots for whom you sacrificed your life / are now but unfree sinners and famished slaves!" She also included a verse dedicated "To the Shackles." By May 20, she was back in handcuffs.

By August, less than three months before the people's indictment against Lin Zhao, her interrogations appeared to intensify, with accompanied beatings. Without stationary and with cuffed hands, she wrote in her own blood the words "Wronged" and "Where is justice" across her sleeves and the back of her shirt. On September 7, her shackles were removed. Pen and paper were given her, allowing her the opportunity to write confessions. Instead, she produced her own writings. She wrote simply that a decade before, Mao had been the "guiding red star" in her heart, and her dear father. She had clung to a hope that, somehow, he might repent. In 1963, after her rearrest, she had "prayed for his soul." She explained, "After all, I am a Christian," adding that she had "neither the right to offer forgiveness in the place of the Heavenly Father nor the right to prevent the Heavenly Father from forgiving him."

On November 4, 1964, the indictment was completed. She was accused of collaborating with her rightist friends in the publication of *A Spark of Fire*, "spreading rumors," and planning a "treasonous defection." According to the indictment, Lin Zhao had "engaged in a series of counterrevolutionary activities" in a "vain attempt to overthrow the people's democratic dictatorship, sabotage the socialist cause, and give counterrevolutionary dying kicks in collusion with the imperialists." It asked for "severe punishment."

On November 9, another nighttime "conversation" urging her to "examine her mistakes" drove her to teary protest. Citing "nonsensical misbehavior," the guards put the handcuffs back on her that night. This time the manacles would remain on her for the next six and a half months, until May 26, 1965. She was then handed over to the Shanghai Municipal Prison. Her comment was "I wonder whether I had the honor of breaking the national or even world record during this decade of the 1960s."

On May 31, 1965, Lin Zhao was tried in district people's court. She was sentenced to twenty years in prison as an "impenitent counterrevolutionary." By December 5, 1965, she was confined to a prison hospital bed. She would write, "As a Christian, my life belongs to my God ... I am willing—even hope—to receive medicine for my lung disease from the American missionaries who baptized me into the church when I was in high school."

She would write another play script in her own blood, but coagulation was a constant problem. She correctly predicted the murderous politics under Mao's rule. The Cultural Revolution, soon to launch, would prove her right. As for herself and her own mistreatment, she admitted that, as someone engaged in political struggle, she was prepared for battle wounds, so to speak, but not for the "savagery" she encountered: "What has your honorable No. 1 Detention House done to this youth … countless tricks just with the use of shackles … even when I was writhing in pain from gastritis during my hunger strike, and when I was in my menstrual period—that special … condition … they did not even let up on the abuse—such as removing one of the two pairs of shackles. Oh Heaven, Oh Heaven! Even hell cannot rival this. What a place is this human world!"

Lin Zhao would write, "[the reason Mao was able to commit] all kinds of outrage in defiance of both law and Heaven … is that your party and the so-called party Central committee have long yielded to this tyrant and have tolerated and overindulged him!" The Cultural Revolution would victimize more than twenty million individuals and their families and claim the lives of some two million people.

Lin Zhao would write, yet again, another letter never sent. She wrote that she and her generation refused to bear the "absurd 'obligation' to surrender human rights and descend into perpetual slavery." Writing in the third person, she confirmed that her revolt against slavery "constitutes the inner logic and the fundamental reason of Lin Zhao's decision to write this letter."

In that same letter, she invoked a story about Abraham Lincoln and a pig written in David Decamp Thompson's *Abraham Lincoln, the First American*, published in 1894. She most probably had read the book at Laura Haygood. She wrote that she would think back to that story whenever she felt overwhelmed by the futility of calling the Communist leadership to repentance.

In the story, Lincoln was on his way to a party when he came across a pig stuck in a swamp and struggling for its life. He wanted to help the pig. But when he looked down at his new clothes, he hesitated and rode on. Yet he could not get rid of the squealing of the pig in his ears, so he turned back. With great difficulty, Lincoln pulled the pig from the swamp and "almost turned into a statue of mud himself," as Lin Zhao wrote. "After that, people praised his deeds." But Lincoln replied, "It wasn't for the sake of the pig; I did it for my own conscience." Likewise, Lin Zhao added, "I am doing this not for the sake of the pig, but for my own conscience as a Christian who, once lost, has found her path again." Lin Zhao would fight to the end as an "independent, free person for the basic human rights endowed by Heaven."

On April 29, 1967, Lin Zhao would leave a hospital bed. The doctor treating her later recalled that her weight had dropped to seventy pounds but that her eyes still flashed with intensity. Soldiers stuffed a rubbery gag in her mouth. A monkey king cap—a tight rubber hood covering the entire face with slits for the eyes and nose—was placed over her head as a precaution to prevent her from ideologically contaminating anyone. As a further precaution, lest the gag malfunction, a thin plastic rope was also wound around her neck—to be tightened, if necessary, as a backup silencing device. She was brought to a choreographed "public sentencing" meeting at the one-thousand-seat prison auditorium. As shouts of revolutionary slogans reverberated, Lin Zhao stood soundless. The Communist government would collect a "bullet fee" from the family for the execution.

Tens of millions directly perished under the rule of the CCP.

Let us remember these words of Lin Zhao, lest we forget: "As long as there are people who are still enslaved, not only are the enslaved not free, those, who enslave others are likewise not free!"

Lin Zhao dared to say she was Christian. That was her sin. Lin Zhao dared to say she believed in democracy. That was her heresy. For this she was prepared to lose her life, and for this she did.

What of us, then—you and I, born in a country founded with the eye of Christian ideals, born within the privilege of a democratic republic? These principles were said to be an experiment. This experiment in democracy lives to this day. Americans in each generation have been willing to sacrifice all for these ideals. The experiment is precious. The fires of democracy and independence need to be fed and maintained within the hearts of every American. Would we—those born in the cradle of democracy—have this courage?

Years later, in 1989, protests for freedom were held in over 340 cities. From June 3 to 4, four hundred to eight hundred or more were killed at Tiananmen Square. Many others were imprisoned. George H. W. Bush wrote the Chinese leader: "I ask you as well to remember the principles on which my young country was founded. Those principles are democracy and freedom—freedom of speech, freedom of assemblage, freedom from arbitrary authority. It is reverence for those principles which inevitably affects the way Americans view and react to events in other countries. It is not a reaction of arrogance or of a desire to force others to our beliefs but of simple faith in the enduring value of those principles and their universal applicability."

As Lin would learn, one may not politely disagree with a communist or a fascist. First, there is no "one." All are defined as part of a class, a race, or some other description. The appreciation of an individual's rights and liberties, let alone pursuits of happiness, becomes the subject of crimes of opposition to the arbitrary social theories whose mandates only intensify. Within Stalin's version of Soviet Communism, no fewer than twenty million detractors or those who dared to disagree were relocated into forced-labor camps. There and other places, millions perished. Apologists explain away the above by invoking the necessities required to form a new economy, along with all the unforeseen circumstances in its formation. Those at the top, however, always, live in comfort, as any escapee will tell you.

Within our own traditions, our freedoms are often not fully appreciated, and history teaches that it is not until we are tested that we appreciate them. Freedom of speech is one of those key freedoms that has been nullified throughout the centuries. It is no figure of speech but is central to our own understanding of ourselves and the American Revolution.

One of the phrases we have often heard growing up—one that Lin's generation never heard, and one that rings of appreciation—is "I may disagree with what you say, but I shall defend to the death your right to say it." Who said it first? But as Lincoln would say, "I should never be the last."

But as Pastor Christian Fuhrer observed in his home of Germany. The first atheist dictatorship or tyranny was one based on race, and the second then, based on class. Tyranny, then, requires division but remains impossible with a free and unified people.

WILLIAM WILBERFORCE

A Force

> As for everyone who comes to me and hears my words and puts them into practice, I will show you what they are like. They are like a man building a house, who dug down deep and laid the foundation on rock. When a flood came, the torrent struck that house but could not shake it, because it was well built. But the one who hears my words and does not put them into practice is like a man who built a house on the ground without a foundation. The moment the torrent struck that house, it collapsed, and its destruction was complete.
>
> —Luke 6:47–49 NIV

William Wilberforce would write a book entitled *A Practical View of the Prevailing Religious System of Professed Christians, in the Higher and Middle Classes in This Country, Contrasted with Real Christianity*. He would not just write a book, though; William Wilberforce was to be a force of history itself.

This is someone who needs no introduction. This is someone so instrumental in changing the course of human history that we are all familiar with the story of his life. William would begin to pull the threads from the tapestry of human civilization. So engrained and so accepted since the beginnings of civilization were servitude and slavery that they had been as accepted as birth and marriage and death—even on August 24, 1759, the birthdate of William Wilberforce.

How could William change history? "An unusual thoughtfulness for others marked his youngest childhood" is how young William was remembered. "A temper eminently affectionate."

William Wilberforce was born into a prospering family of merchants. Their home, a mansion, overlooked the Hull River that flowed into the Humber and the North Sea. The merchant ships of the time were easily seen transporting timber, iron, and other hard goods along the rivers' shores.

As young William was born, it is said that he carried with him a light, tiny frame. His eyesight was not good, and he was prone to illness. After one illness in his adult life, he hardly weighed seventy-six pounds.

However, "… his elocution was so remarkable that we used to sit him on a table and make him read aloud as an example to other boys," so said his headmaster in grammar school.

When William was eight years old, an older sister died. Soon after followed his father. His mother gave birth to a baby girl and became ill. It was decided that William would live with his Uncle William and Aunt Hannah when he turned ten. He boarded a carriage to travel to Wimbledon.

William and Hannah had no children of their own. They welcomed their serious, yet charming, nephew with open arms. Neither young William nor his mother appreciated the family he had just entered.

Hull was a world for the wealthy and fashionable. Card parties, theater, and late nights imbibing various beverages were the norm for this mid-eighteenth-century England. Since the days of the Puritans and the religious conflicts of the previous century, it seemed the emphasis on spiritual and moral values had been put on the shelf within the prevailing Church of England.

Two of Uncle William's and Aunt Hannah's friends were George Whitefield and John Newton. Newton wrote the moving spiritual we have all heard, if not sung with a tear in the eye, "Amazing Grace."

He had captained a slave ship, before becoming a minister. He surely mentioned the topic of slavery to young William. George Whitefield was at the center of the Great Awakening—the spiritual reawakening and revival within the heart of England. Whitefield was the epicenter of this movement within the American colonies. He was even friends with Benjamin Franklin.

Three students had enrolled at Oxford University in the 1730s: John Wesley, his brother Charles, and George Whitefield. They formed a worship club. Some of the students thought of their early worship as being too "methodical" or "white knuckled" so to speak. They were nicknamed Methodists. Gradually, they and other students saw that only one was morally perfect: Jesus. Jesus was the answer. Only Jesus could save their souls. This new revelation changed lives. Not only theirs, but people of all faiths, denominations, and classes. They were finally able to think for themselves. This new movement came to be known as Evangelical. This new understanding, appreciation, and freedom was despised by the cultural elites of mid-eighteenth-century England. In his later years, William Wilberforce would say to his son Robert, "It is impossible for you to have any idea of the hatred in which the Methodists were held."

This was the household where young William was sent. A house located amid a new revival and equipped to nurture his gifts.

As time went on, William's mother, Elizabeth, became a little suspicious from her son's letters and infrequent visits home. She made the trip to Wimbledon to rescue her twelve-year-old son from such influences. William was not allowed to attend church for some time after. William later recalled, "The religious impressions which I had gained at Wimbledon continued for a considerable time, but my friends spared no pains to stifle them. ... I was naturally a high-spirited boy and fiery. This pushed me forward and made me talk a great deal and made me very vain."

From gravitas to levitas, by the time William entered Cambridge College in 1776, at the age of seventeen, he was just the kind of boy his mother and grandfather had hoped to raise.

Was Cambridge challenging? William recalled, "I was introduced, on the very first night of my arrival, to as licentious a set of men as can well be conceived. They drank hard, and their conversation was even worse than their lives." William also recalled that developing the habit of wasting time had created a challenge for personal self-discipline later in life. He further elaborated about "a long period as [Shakespeare] has so emphatically styled 'shapeless idleness'; the most valuable years of life wasted, and opportunities lost, which can never be recovered."

> O gentlemen! The time of life is short; To spend that shortness basely were too long. (William Shakespeare)

Thomas Gisborne, William's neighbor, observed, "By his talents, his wit, his kindness, his social powers, his universal acceptability, and his love of society, he speedily became the centre of attraction to all the clever and idle of his own college and of other colleges … His rooms swarmed with them from the time when he rose, generally very late, till he went to bed … He spent much of his time visiting." Gisborne would later become a minister in the Church of England. Wilberforce would often visit him at his country home.

William Wilberforce was becoming culturally educated as it were. The deaths of his grandfather and his dear uncle William in 1777 made Wilberforce a very wealthy young man.

Wilberforce had a special talent for making friends. One was William Pitt, the brilliant son of a former prime minister. They would meet in the House of Commons and watch debates. William Pitt, the elder and former Prime Minister, was also known as the "Great Commoner." He had warned against the government's policies toward the colonies.

In the spring of 1780, on a return visit to his home in Hull, the idea of running for the House of Commons entered William's mind at the ripe old age of twenty. He would be twenty-one and eligible by Election Day on September 11. However, the very idea of running for the House of Commons was, in no small measure, an expensive enterprise. Election to the House was often only for the uncommonly wealthy. William included a large roast on his way to the House. On October 31, 1780, William took his seat for the first time as a member of Parliament. His friend William Pitt and some other new parliamentarians from Cambridge were also present.

Wilberforce adopted a position against government's stance on the American colonies. On February 22, 1782, William was given the opportunity to show his eloquent oratorical skills in a lengthy critique of Lord North's administration. Little did William realize that it was the birthday of George Washington.

In September of 1783, Wilberforce, Pitt, and a friend decided to travel to France. While there, they would dine with the Marquis de Lafayette. To their surprise and delight, they were given the opportunity to meet Benjamin Franklin. Perhaps due to their tableside discussions, William Wilberforce would begin to fight for the abolition of the British slave trade four years later in 1787. The same year, Benjamin Franklin would serve as the new president of the Pennsylvania Abolition Society. Later the American House of Representatives would receive a signed petition from Benjamin Franklin and the Pennsylvania Abolition Society, calling for Congress to "take such measures in their wisdom, as the powers with which they are invested will authorize, for promoting the abolition of slavery, and discouraging every species of traffic in slaves."

In October, the young Pitt received word from the king to return home. Apparently, the king had grown unhappy with Lord North and the opportunism displayed by Fox within the administration with the East India Bill. William Pitt, at just twenty-four, became the youngest prime minister in British history. The top end of the Pitt's and Wilberforce's ambitions seemed limitless. Wilberforce ran for and won an even more prestigious seat representing Yorkshire. For Pitt, his friend had "The greatest natural eloquence of all the men I ever knew."

In the autumn of 1784, William traveled to the French Rivieras for his sister's health. Some friends didn't have the time to go. Isaac Milner, his young tutor from the Hull Grammar School, would have the time. At Cambridge, Isaac had been dubbed with the official title "incomparabilis" or "super genius." Milner was a giant, both physically and intellectually. A jocular and funny fellow too. But he was, scared of thunder—a rather unique combination. The two men occupied the first carriage for a long trip, and two women were in the second carriage.

One of the topics discussed during their journey crossing the Alps was church. William talked about his off and on attendance at a new Unitarian church. The pastor had basically renounced any standing of the divinity of Christ. William offered, as well, that he thought the Methodists had carried things "a bit too far." While in Nice, William received a letter from Pitt, requesting his return to London. Before departing the residence of his cousin, Bessie Smith, he perused a volume entitled *Rise and Progress of Religion in the Soul.*

"What do you think of it?" William asked Isaac.

"It is one of the best books ever written," replied Milner.

William later wrote of the book he read through the icy Alps that the writer had a "clear grasp of the intellectual heart of Christianity." To one of his sons, he wrote, "you cannot read a better book." To another, "I happened to meet with Doddridge's 'Rise and Progress of the Soul' by ... Providential arrangement at a very critical period of my life." William commented in this manner, saying, "The first years that I was in Parliament I did nothing—nothing I mean to any good purpose—my own distinction was my darling object."

On the return venture to England, he and Milner had additional discussions along with the silence of the journey. William wrote, "Began three or four days ago to get up very early. In the solitude and self-conversation of the morning had thoughts, which I trust will come to something. The deep guilt and black ingratitude of my past life forced itself upon me in the strongest colours, and I condemned myself for having wasted my precious time, and opportunities, and talents." He later wrote to a friend, "When I was first awakened to a sense ... of the importance of Divine things, the distress I felt was deep and poignant indeed." These reflections would not fade overnight for William. These considerations would take months of time.

He would write: "It was not so much my fear of punishment by which I was affected, as a sense of my great sinfulness in having so long neglected the unspeakable mercies of my God and Saviour; and such was the effect which this thought produced, that for months I was in a state of the deepest depression, from strong convictions of my guilt. Indeed, nothing which I have ever read in the accounts of others, exceeded what I then felt ... It is the universal corruption of profligacy of the times, which taking its rise among the rich and luxurious has now extended its baneful influence and spread its destructive poison through the whole body of the people." Wilberforce concluded that he would need to leave Parliament. He would write to Pitt expressing that he must leave politics altogether and "live now for God."

To whom could William turn? The truths discerned from all the discussions with Milner had also left Isaac wrestling with all they had discussed in their travels. Even at this young age, due to his poor vision, William would have someone read scripture to him. Wilberforce wrote, "Pride is my greatest stumbling block; and there is danger in it in two ways—lest it should make me desist from a Christian life, through fear of the world, my friends, &c; or if I persevere, lest it should make me vain of so doing." At last, and finally, he thought of visiting John Newton, whom he had not seen since he was a boy.

To John Newton, William wrote, "I wish to have some serious conversation with you and will take the liberty of calling on you for that purpose." In his diary, Wilberforce related that after meeting with Newton, "my mind was in a calm tranquil state, more humbled, looking more devoutly up to God." William further wrote that "Mr. Newton, in the interviews I had with him, advised me ... to keep up my connection with Pitt, and to continue in Parliament."

Years later, John Newton would write to William, "The joy that I felt and the hopes I conceived, when you called on me in the vestry of St. Mary's, I shall never forget." Newton wrote to a friend, "I judge he is now decidedly on the right track ... I hope the Lord will make him a blessing both as a Christian and a statesman. How seldom do these characters coincide! But they are not incompatible."

William wrote of his "great change" to a college friend in June 1795:

> It is scarce too strong to say, that I seem to myself to have awakened about nine or ten years ago from

a dream, to have recovered, as it were, the use of my reason after a delirium. In fact, till then I wanted first principles; those principles at least which alone deserve the character of wisdom or bear the impress of truth.

Emulation, and a desire of distinction, were my governing motives; and ardent after the applause of my fellow-creatures, I quite forgot that I was an accountable being; that I was hereafter to appear at the bar of God; that if Christianity were not a fable, it was infinitely important to study its precepts, and when known to obey them; that there was at least such a probability of its not being a fable, as to render it in the highest degree incumbent on me to examine into its authenticity diligently, anxiously, and without prejudice ...

I am not now, what I ought to be; yet I trust ... through the help of the gracious Being who has promised to assist our weak endeavors, to become more worthy of the name of Christian.

Wilberforce returned to the House of Commons in 1786 a different man. He would take greater care to be present for every debate. He volunteered to serve on countless numbers of committees. He sold the grand house he lived in to help feed the poor. He would now try to refrain from overeating and drinking. His world-class wit would not require a wounding sarcasm. He no longer felt the need to mimic others and be charming only to feed his personal and vain ambitions. He would study and read the classics in both Greek and Latin. Rather than the sometimes-ill-tempered William, a sunnier dispositioned son returned home to Hull to see his mother. A Mrs. Sykes said to Mrs. Wilberforce, "If this is madness, I hope he will bite us all."

On October 28, 1787, William Wilberforce would write in his diary, "God Almighty has placed before me two great objects, the suppression of the slave trade and the reformation of manners [morals]."

William saw the effects of a hundred years of religion retreating in the present social decay: epidemic alcoholism, child prostitution, child labor, frequent public executions for petty crimes, public dissections, burnings of executed criminals, and cruelty to animals, to name a few. "And all the cords of moral obligation were relaxed as the spirit of religion slumbered," recited the Wilberforce's in later years. Hopelessness could be exemplified by the 25 percent of unmarried women in London who were prostitutes. Life in general was most often unpleasant. Some initial parliamentary efforts were ineffective.

Wilberforce thought, "The barbarous custom of hanging has been tried too long, and with the success which might have been expected from it. The most effectual way to prevent greater crimes is by punishing the smaller, and by endeavoring to repress that general spirit of licentiousness, which is the parent of every species of vice." This single thought would become a cornerstone in the journey toward the Victorian Era. The first great object could not be tackled unless the second great object could be attained.

William looked to British history. William and Mary had acceded to the throne in 1692. They issued a document with the title "The Proclamation for the Encouragement of Piety and Virtue and for the Preventing of Vice, Profaneness and Immorality." They formed a "Proclamation Society," in effect deputizing society to put into effect what the proclamation proclaimed. It was quite effective. To the modern-day reader, this may sound like a lot of citizen arrests. Each new monarch would issue a proclamation "for the encouragement of Piety and virtue; and for the Preventing of Vice, Profaneness and Immorality," but it was often nothing more than a formality.

Support for a new issuance of a royal proclamation was garnered. On June 1, 1787, a new quest for "making goodness fashionable" began. When a local proclamation society was formed, everyone in the community was invited to participate, including the more prominent members. As the objective would be to raise local moral standards— which, in many cases, could be set with a low bar— then even the more prominent and influential could be seen raising their standards. The cascading effects of good examples became evident.

Voluntary societies were chosen because Wilberforce and others thought that the good obtained through political means had its limitations. William said, "it is peculiarly needful to obtain these ends by the agency of some voluntary association; for thus only can those moral principles be guarded."

Today we talk of legislating morality, but to Wilberforce, "Compulsion and Christianity! Why, the very terms are at variance with each other—the ideas are incompatible. In the language of Inspiration itself, Christianity has been called 'the law of liberty.' Her service in the excellent formularies of our Church has been truly denominated 'perfect freedom'; and they, let me add, will most advance her cause who contend for it in her own spirit and character."

As the Society for the Reformation of Manners grew, Wilberforce published a list of members to include every walk of life: merchants, tradesmen, aldermen, and members of Parliament. The Archbishop of Canterbury also put his name behind the society, and other bishops followed. Volunteer societies sprung up from 1780 to 1830, numbering in the hundreds. The many societies were dedicated to good causes, such as publishing and distributing Bibles, assisting the poor, educating the blind, sponsoring vaccination efforts, treating ailing seamen, animal welfare, and those in debtor's prison. Later, Wilberforce was effective in obtaining and initiating the first hospital ship.

Wilberforce was instrumental in founding the British and Foreign Bible Society in 1804. The American Bible Society, ABS, was formed in 1816. The early president of the ABS was John Jay. Jay was an important Founder and author of some of the Federalist Papers and a friend of Wilberforce. In May 1822, Jay addressed the ABS. He said of Wilberforce and his successful struggle ending the British slave trade, "Considerations of a higher class ... finally prevailed, and the parliament abolished that detestable trade. Well-merited honor was thereby reflected on that Legislature; and particularly on that excellent and celebrated member of it, whose pious zeal and unwearied perseverance were greatly and conspicuously instrumental to [its] removal."

The fifty-year period prefacing the start of the Victorian Era (1837–1901) was also known as "the age of Wilberforce." William stated,

"Let every, one, regulate his conduct ... by the golden rule of doing to others as in similar circumstances we would have them do to us; and the path of duty will be clear before him, and I will add, the decision of [a] legislature would scarcely any longer be doubtful."

Wilberforce also said, "As to the arguments in favor of the slave trade, deduced from the Holy Scriptures, [I am] not much disposed to enter into a discussion of them, because [I] can scarcely believe they are urged seriously."

Those who were not religious also had something to say about the second great objective. Machiiavelli had views about religion and society. Wilberforce said Machiiavelli "was not considered either as a religious or moral authority, but ... was eminently distinguished for political knowledge and sagacity. [He] stated, that 'the rulers of all states, whether kingdoms or commonwealths, should take care that religion should be honoured, and all its ceremonies preserved inviolate, for there was not a more certain symptom of the destruction of states, than a contempt for religion and morals.'"

At the age of fourteen, William Wilberforce had written a school essay decrying the business of slavery. He would later tell his sons of his opinion the year he entered Parliament at age twenty-one, "I had been strongly interested, for the West Indies slaves, and I expressed my hope, that I should redress the wrongs of those wretched beings."

Perhaps it was a nutty musician and avid Christian who had earlier got the ball rolling, as it were. Granville Sharp would name his seven children- Doey, Ray, Mimi, and so on. On the street one day, a bloodied seventeen-year-old pistol-whipped slave named Jonathan Strong was seen struggling down the street by Granville. Sharp took him to his brother, a king's surgeon, and admitted him to the hospital. They found Strong a job, which he held for two years. His previous owner then kidnapped Strong and brought him to jail. Word got to Sharp, and the Lord Mayor agreed Strong should be free.

Sharp went to work studying English Law. The book Granville Sharp was familiar with was the Bible. The old saying was that "all English Law springs from this just and noble soil." Granville was happy to do the Lord's work. He worked to free these souls one by one. In

1772, a slave brought to England from Virginia sought out Sharp. The judge did not want to rule on the case. On different English soils, there were fourteen thousand slaves. However, a careful ruling freed only the one African, named Somerset. Throughout the 1770s, little happened in any concerted way regarding the abolition of slavery or the slave trade. John Wesley let his sentiments favoring the abolition of slavery and the end of the slave trade be known in 1774.

Can we bear to, only briefly, read of the horrors and evils of the Middle Passage across the Atlantic? It was called the Middle Passage because it was the middle leg of the infamous "triangle trade." The first leg transported European goods to Africa. The second leg transported human cargo to the West Indies to be sold. The third leg carried the West Indian goods back to Europe.

The following is a description from one ship written by a man named Falconbridge:

> The men Negroes, on being brought aboard ship, are immediately fastened together, two and two, by handcuffs on their wrists and by irons rivetted on their legs ... They are frequently stowed so close, as to admit of no other position than lying on their sides. Nor will the height between decks, unless directly under the grating, permit the indulgence of an erect posture.
>
> [On these decks] are placed three or four large buckets, of a conical form, nearly two feet in diameter at the bottom and only one foot at the top and in depth of about twenty-eight inches, to which, when necessary, the Negroes have recourse. It often happens that those who are placed at a distance from the buckets, in endeavoring to get to them, tumble over their companions, in consequence of their being shackled ... becomes a fresh source of boils and disturbances and tends to render the condition of the poor captive wretches still more uncomfortable ...

> The hardships and inconveniences suffered by the Negroes during the passage are scarcely to be enumerated or conceived. They are far more violently affected by seasickness than Europeans. It frequently terminates in death, especially among the women. But the exclusion of fresh air is among the most intolerable. For the purpose of admitting this needful refreshment, most of the ships in the slave trade are provided, between the decks, with five or six airports on each side of the ship, of about five inches in length and four in breadth. But whenever the sea is rough and the rain heavy it becomes necessary to shut these and every other conveyance by which the air is admitted. The fresh air being thus excluded, the Negroes' rooms soon grow intolerable hot. The confined air, rendered noxious by the effluvia exhaled from their bodies and being repeatedly breathed, soon produces fevers and [diarrhea] which generally carries off great numbers of them.

"And that's not the half of it" is a phrase that does not even begin to capture the depths of the injustices rendered. Other incidences and events were beginning to be seen by a few who could not let them go. In 1783, Quaker abolitionists formed a committee. Granville Sharp, too, became involved. What did they really know about slavery? What did they really know about politics, and who did they know?

In that same year, 1783, William met with Dr. James Ramsey, a surgeon. He and Sir Charles Middleton—the same whose naval strategy at Trafalgar was instrumental in Admiral Nelson's victory and thereby Napoleon's defeat at Waterloo—were on board the *Arundel* in the waters near the British West Indies in 1859. Ramsey was ordered onto a captured French slave vessel. What Ramsey and Middleton witnessed so horrified both, of them that Ramsey later wrote and published an "Essay on the Treatment ... Slaves in the ... Sugar Colonies." In 1781, Sir Charles invited Ramsey home from the West Indies to become a vicar in his parish church. Lady Middleton and Bishop Porteus both urged

Ramsey to write his account. William and James discussed the accounts of Ramsey before he published them. James was greatly concerned with the potential effects of such a publishing. He also hoped that someone, perhaps Wilberforce, might take up the effort in Parliament. Lady Middleton had urged both her husband and William to do so. It was said that this account could be likened to turning a hose loose on a nest of hornets. Once published, the battle had, at long last, begun.

At the request of Lady Margaret, Sir Charles wrote Wilberforce, urging he initiate a parliamentary inquiry. Young William replied that "he felt the great importance of the subject." Although he "thought himself unequal to the task," he "would not positively decline it." William stated, "I had a "higher sense of the duties of my station."

On May 12, 1787, three young men (each twenty-seven), met at William Pitts's Holwood Estate under an ancient English oak tree: current Prime Minister Pitt, a future Prime Minister William Grenville, and William Wilberforce. They would set in motion this momentous cause with the intention of introducing the effort to end the British slave trade into Parliament.

William would write, "I had [by this time] acquired ... much information ... I began to talk the matter over with Pitt and Grenville. Pitt recommended me to undertake its conduct, as a subject suited to my character and talents. At length, I well remember, after a conversation in the open air at the root of an old [oak] tree at Holwood just above the steep descent into the vale, of Keston, I resolved to give notice on a fit occasion in the House of Commons of my intention to bring the subject forward."

On October 28, later that year, William Wilberforce met with John Newton again. On that day, he wrote in his diary, "God has set before me two great objects, the suppression of the slave trade and the reformation of manners."

The battles would begin. The new Committee for the Abolition of the Slave Trade was chaired by Granville Sharp. As much information as possible needed to be gathered. Clarkson planned to visit slave ports. He noted, "On whatever branch of the system I turned my eyes, I found it equally barbarous. The trade was, in short, one mass of iniquity from the beginning to the end." Clarkson would interview thousands of sailors.

In his analysis with Wilberforce, it became evident that the slave trade corrupted all who touched it. Many were unwillingly forced into it in order' to pay debts. Others were kidnapped to fill the needs of sailors. The lie was that all of this was good for the British Navy because it trained sailors on these ships. Clarkson found the sailors to be miserable, but they also feared the lash hardly more than the captive slaves. Clarkson estimated an unimagined 25 percent annual mortality rate among the sailors he talked with. This was a dirty and dangerous mission for Clarkson. Wilberforce commented that hardly being "a nursery of seamen, [it] may rather be termed their grave."

The French, the old enemy of the British, were always in the forefront of any national calculation. Without an agreement with France, this deserving cause would be hopeless. The first argument in Parliament would be that when the British abolished the trade, it would simply be picked up by the French. Would that happen? What assurances could be made, and by whom?

William Eden, a statesman who had been sent to the American colonies, would be sent to France to speak with the French foreign minister, Minister de Montmorin. Montmorin asked for more information. Wilberforce wrote him a long letter discussing the discovered details and misinformation. Who were the captured slaves? The trade said they were war captives or were being saved from execution. How many women and children were fighting wars? The slave traders had lost all scruples. Greed ruled. The traders were desperate to fill the ships with labor. Tribal chiefs, in turn, looked for huge profits. Even there, the dishonesty and graft in the goods given in exchange for human beings was beyond belief. Wilberforce felt a debt owed to Africa

By December 1787, Wilberforce believed that once the British slave trade was abolished, the French would be alongside. He felt abolition would happen very soon. He wrote to Eden, "As to our probability of success, I assure you I entertain no doubt of it ... The evidence, the glaring justice of the proposition itself; Mr. Pitt's support of the measure, and the Temper of the House ..."

Wilberforce and the abolition movement were young. The eighty-four-year-old John Wesley wrote a letter to Granville Sharp in October 1787. In it he said, "Ever since I heard of it first, I felt a perfect detestation of the horrid trade, therefore I cannot but do everything in my power, to forward the glorious Design of your Society ... All the opposition which can be made by men who are not encumbered by either Honour, Conscience or Humanity and will rush on ... through every possible means, to secure their great Goddess Interest. What a comfort it is to consider (unfashionable as it is) that there is a God! Yea, and that (as little as men think of it!), He still has all power, both in Heaven and on Earth! To Him I commit you and your Glorious Cause, and am, sir, Your affectionate servant, John Wesley." Wesley had lived those battles in his life. Young Wilberforce and the others would need prepare for those they would certainly face.

In December of 1787, Wilberforce announced his intention that he would put forward a motion to abolish the slave trade when Parliament resumed session. He received support from the veterans of the Parliament, like Fox. Petitions of support with thousands of signatures from towns across England were received. With all the burgeoning support for this noble cause, the measure would be sure to pass, would it not?

Wilberforce worked furiously through one of his frequent illnesses. The introduction was planned for early February, but it was not ready. On February 19, William fell seriously ill. Today's diagnosis may have been ulcerative colitis, a very painful and stress-induced condition of the digestive tract. The noted physician James Pitcairne attended William, as did Isaac Milner. In early March, the doctors diagnosed William with "an absolute decay of all the digestive tracts ... He has not the stamina to last a fortnight."

Believing his death to be eminent, William asked to see Prime Minister William Pitt and handed off the cause to him. The London Committee for the Abolition of the Slave Trade asked for direction. In April, Granville Sharp reported to the Prime Minister. On May 9, Pitt moved the House to a binding resolution to investigate the slave trade in the following session. He expressed his hope that Wilberforce would be able to "resume his charge." Pitt declared the trade "shocking to humanity" and "abominable to be carried on by any country." He further stated that it "reflects the greatest dishonor on the British senate and the British nation. The Trade, as the petitioners propose to carry it on, without any regulation, is contrary to every humane, to every Christian principle, to every sentiment that ought to inspire the breast of man."

One small victory was had in Parliament. A bill passed that limited the number of slaves that a ship would be allowed to carry. As more about the slave trade became known, it was said that the slave interests acted like children, switching stories.

What else? The first storied madness of King George appeared on November 5, 1788. Should King George be declared unfit, then a most unbecoming character in the likes of the prince would become king. Pitt and the prospect of abolition would be out. On November 22, it was stated that "H.M. [was] entirely deranged this morning in a quite good humoured way." Days later, Pitt received word that "His Majesty passed the whole day in a perfectly maniacal state." Pitt stalled. Time ran out. It was time for a new regency government. On February 27, 1789, the king regained his sanity.

By the spring of 1789, William Wilberforce had recovered. On May 12, two years to the day from that fabled meeting under the venerable oak tree, Wilberforce would speak for three and a half hours: "So much misery condensed in so little room is more than the human imagination has ever before conceived … So enormous, so dreadful, so irremediable did its wickedness appear, that my own mind was completely made up for the abolition. A trade founded on iniquity, and carried on as this was, must be abolished, let the price be what it might—let the consequences be what they would, I from this time determined that I would never rest till I had [secured] its abolition." As he ended his speech, he stated, "I mean not to accuse anyone, but to take the shame upon myself, in common indeed with the whole Parliament of Great Britain, for having suffered this horrid trade to be carried on under their authority. We are all guilty—we ought all, to plead guilty, and not to exculpate ourselves by throwing the blame on others."

Testimony was also taken, including that from the likes of John Newton. Edmund Burke, known as the finest of orators in that era, pronounced the "principles so admirable, laid down with so much order and force," that the speech was "equal to anything he had ever heard of in modern oratory; and perhaps not excelled by anything to be met with in Demosthenes." The debates finally ended. The only decision made was to "hear more evidence".

On July 14, 1789, the Bastille fell. France dived headfirst into violence. Wilberforce intended to travel to France but was convinced to remain in Britain. An optimistic Clarkson did make the trip "I should not be surprised if the French were to do themselves the honour of voting away this diabolical traffic in a night." He learned that the revolutionaries wanted nothing to do with abolition. They would not offend the port cities. Clarkson decided to meet with mulatto leaders from the French colonies. He learned there had been an insurrection. In England, James Ramsey, author of "An Essay on the Treatment of Slaves in the Sugar Colonies," died. His constitution had been tested past its limits from the relentless and vicious lies slung in his direction.

Early in 1790, the grandfather of Florence Nightingale, William Smith, became Wilberforce's chief partner on a select committee to hear evidence for and against the slave trade. That year, Wilberforce would be re-elected to Parliament, representing Yorkshire.

On April 18, 1791, the debate once again commenced for the bill for the abolition of the slave trade. Wilberforce, once more, spoke with profound eloquence for four hours. However, as William began his oration, Banaste Tarleton—that nasty British hero of the American Revolution and member of Parliament—put his paper and pen in the air, a common tactic to distract speakers. The understood message was "you don't want to cross swords with me." He had boasted killing more men than anyone living. Pitt similarly messaged Tarleton in defense of Wilberforce. Throughout Wilberforce's speech there were audible cries of "Hear him, Hear him."

Wilberforce wrote that in this battle he looked to God. He looked for "wisdom and strength and the power of persuasion ..." and went on to say, "... and may I surrender myself to Him as to the event with perfect submission and ascribe to Him all the praise if I succeed, and if I fail, say from the heart thy will be done ... Whatever may be its success, I attach my happiness to their cause and shall never relinquish it." The vote was taken at 3:30 a.m.; the noes, were 163, the ayes 88. Once again, abolition had been defeated in England.

Less than two months before, and only days before the death of John Wesley, William Wilberforce would receive a letter from Wesley containing the words he would recall often in the years and battles ahead. It begins,

"Dear Sir:"

> Unless the divine power has raised you up to be as Athanasius contra mundum, I see not how you can go through your glorious enterprise in opposing that execrable villainy, which is the scandal of religion, of England, and of human nature. Unless God has raised you up for this very thing, you will be worn out by the opposition of men and devils. But if God be for you, who can be against you? Are all of them together stronger than God? O be not weary of well doing! Go on, in the name of God and in the power of his might ...

The message was beginning to be heard. After the 1791 defeat, 517 petitions for abolition and four against it arrived in Parliament. When the scrolls were unrolled, the signatures of thousands of British subjects had made their way into Parliament for the first time. The idea that ordinary subjects might directly voice their opinion in Parliament was unprecedented, but they did this for the common cause of their fellow human beings.

On April 2, 1792, Wilberforce again moved to abolish the slave trade and with emotion exclaimed, "Africa! Africa! Your sufferings have been the theme that has arrested and engages my heart— your sufferings no tongue can express; no language impart." The home secretary proposed that the slave trade be abolished gradually rather than immediately. As morning sunlight lit the chambers, Pitt addressed the House in reply. He spoke for one and on-half hours. "How shall we hope to obtain, if it be possible, forgiveness from Heaven for the enormous evils we have committed if we refuse to make use of those means which the mercy of Providence has still reserved for us for wiping away the shame and guilt with which we are now covered? ... Shall we not count the days and hours that are suffered to intervene and to delay the accomplishment of such a work?" The House of Commons would vote to gradually abolish the trade by January 1, 1796.

Preceding this session of the House of Commons, the Parisian mobs had imprisoned their monarch in the Bastille. What had first seemed a rather charming freshness of American ideal in France had lost all innocence by that point. The revolutionaries seemed drunk with their new-found power. People feared that this swirling tornado of revolution would jump the straights and land squarely into jolly old England. A defense of British civilization needed to be made. The idea that the abolition movement was seen allied with France was damaging, whether, or not it was correct.

As Wesley had warned, the "Great Goddess Interests" became more real. Would they prevail? The last two lines of a poem from the day are an example of the typical slights and mockery. "Go Wilberforce, begone, for shame, thou dwarf with big resounding name." A distinguished member of the House of Lords, when speaking of the possessions of the West Indies, said that "neither in the field nor the senate shall their just rights be infringed, while [he had] an arm to fight in their defense or a tongue to launch [his] voice against the damnable doctrine of Wilberforce and his hypocritical allies."

Wilberforce would be challenged to a duel. He would be ridiculed as a coward hiding behind his Christianity in order, to escape defending his manhood. One person demanded a public apology. Another showed up at his door. A friend became his bodyguard. Wilberforce was a bachelor at the time, but a story held that he beat his wife, she, being a "Negress". And on it goes. Wilberforce seems eventually to have learned to laugh at what was being said about him, or at least to ignore it. In

1794, Thomas Clarkson would retire from the fight, ruined financially and for reasons of health. However, he would return some years later.

In February of 1793, France declared war on Great Britain. The French King Louis XVI was dragged to the guillotine. On February 26, the House of Commons refused to confirm the vote cast in 1792 for gradual abolition. Wilberforce continued to work toward abolition. He put forward a "Foreign Slave Bill." The implementation of the bill would disallow British ships from transporting slaves to foreign countries. He reintroduced the bill once again in 1794. That year, it passed in the House of Commons but was defeated in the House of Lords.

As the war with France continued, Wilberforce saw the possibility of Britain adding territories from France (namely the Sugar Islands of the West Indies) as increasing British slave trade. Wilberforce thought long and hard on the matter. He could lose William Pitt as a friend. Wilberforce had long discussions with his friends. On December 30, 1794, he put forward an amendment to the House of Commons in opposition of the war. Roundly criticized, many of his colleagues could not fathom his actions. The king "cut him dead" so to speak, no longer supporting abolition. The sons of William Wilberforce later wrote that "the politician who truly thinks for himself and takes his own stand, must be assailed with unwelcome judgements on every side."

On January 2, 1795, Wilberforce offered an amendment to supply the resources needed to carry on the war. After a time, a mutual friend helped in reconciling Wilberforce and Pitt. Throughout the year, discussions continued regarding proposals about the war with France, what conditions were to be had, and whether, or not peace might be reached. Wilberforce needed to win reelection from Yorkshire. William pointed out that some of the constituents were "violently incensed by [his] political conduct."

The war with France was not faring well. By fall, France was victorious in nearly every battle. Some Britons and French even called for the overthrow of the British government. The king was even mobbed on his way to open Parliament. A few cartoon prints depicted his guillotining. The French, however, could not defeat the British Navy.

Prospects in 1796 for the passage of abolition seemed brighter. William met with the king. He had defended the treason and sedition bills put forward by Pitt. On February 18, the bill to abolish the slave trade saw an unusually animated debate. The prevailing argument throughout the day was to wait for the never-ending war with France to end. Wilberforce thought he had spoken "warmly and well." Banaste Tarleton—who had carried on the Waxhaw massacre of Virginia Continentals—thought otherwise, and moved, to adjourn the debate. The debate and some rewriting of the bill continued in the days ahead.

On March 3, a second reading of the bill was introduced to a near-empty House by an opponent. Wilberforce and some of his supporters hurried to the House. The second reading passed the House 63–31. At long last, there were enough supporters to pass a final reading. That very night would be the momentous vote. Ah, but please let us not forget the opera with the composer Portugallo and the talented lead singer Vignoni. A few of the more "cultured" Parliamentarians favoring abolition found their way to the performance and away from their solemn parliamentary duties. The vote in favor was 70–74.

Wilberforce would write in his diary, "I am permanently hurt about the slave trade." He then became quite ill for some time. Isaac Milner rode down from Cambridge to assist William. In 1788, Wilberforce penned that his eyes were so bad "[he could scarcely] see how to direct [his] pen."

He had time for the first time in his career. It was then that Wilberforce became inspired to write his book *A Practical View of the Prevailing Religious System of Professed Christians, in the Higher and Middle Classes in This Country, Contrasted with Real Christianity*. The book was published in 1797. It became amazingly popular for the time, running five printings in its first six months. It was also translated into five languages.

It began,

> It has been my desire for several years to write to my countrymen on the subject of faith. I have been unable to do so until now because of the demands of my position

and my poor health ... The advance or decline of faith is so intimately connected to the welfare of a society that it should be of particular interest to a politician. ...

Bountiful as is the hand of Providence, its gifts are not so bestowed as to seduce us into indolence, but to rouse us to exertion ... We should cease to be deceived by superficial appearances, and to confound the Gospel of Christ with the systems of philosophers; we should become impressed with that weighty truth, so much forgotten, and never to be too strongly insisted on, that Christianity calls on us, as we value our immortal souls, not merely in general, to be religious and moral, but specially to believe the doctrines, and imbibe the principles, and practice the precepts of Christ.

Wilberforce learned that "Christianity has always thrived under persecution. For then it has no lukewarm professors." He further believed that Britain would be unable to countenance the slave trade when it would take its Christian faith to heart.

William met his bride-to-be on Holy Saturday. Eight days later, they would be engaged. A month after that, they would be married. Within ten years, they would have six children: four boys and two girls.

They would move to what became known as the Clapham community. William's friend Henry Thornton had put together the idea of a community in which many of similar evangelical beliefs and ideals were able to live and support each other. Among these were Granville Sharp, as well as James Stephan, a lawyer from St. Kitts of the West Indies. Many, including Pitt, visited.

Among the many ventures of the community was one called the Sierra Leone Company. The idea then and there was to create a beachhead of freedom and self-government. Much additional text might be written about the topic, but not within context of this writing.

Year after year, the fight to abolish the slave trade went on. In 1798 and 1799, the motions to abolish were again defeated. In 1800 and

1801, the motions were deferred. Both years, they anticipated a general European conference concerning the ongoing war against Napoleon's France. Addington negotiated for peace with France in 1802. The peace only lasted about a year. On May 16, 1803, the war with France began again. The ongoing war with France, involving Napoleon, Lord Nelson, and the battle of Trafalgar, with Nelson's final words being "Thank God, I have done my duty"—all this important history will also be overlooked in this writing.

In 1806, William Pitt would fall ill and die. He would do so not long after Napoleon's victory at Austerlitz. William Granville would now become the new prime minister. This William, as we recall, was the third man under the fabled oak tree.

William Wilberforce had entered Parliament as a young man of twenty-one. He was now forty-seven. He had lived the years in pain and discomfort. The opium prescribed for his ulcerative colitis had a negative effect on his eyesight; although, the dosage remained the same. His spine was beginning to curve. One friend observed the following of his physical appearance: "[Wilberforce] seemed the frailest and feeblest of mortals." A biographer of the time wrote, "He had grown up to be a very charming young man. He was small, [a] little over five feet ... and so slight that he inspired such whimsical descriptions as 'all Soul and no body.' None of his features were handsome, but they had a liveliness which was attractive. His movements were very fast, and he was seldom still. His conversation followed the same pattern." The encouragements of John Wesley and John Newton had kept his boat in the waters, seeking safe harbor.

This year, 1807, William Granville decided the bill should be introduced first to the House of Lords rather than the House of Commons. The bill "for the Abolition of the Slave Trade" had its first reading. Prime Minister Granville opened the debate by focusing on the moral questions rather than the fiscal. "Is it to be endured, that this detestable traffic is to be continued, and such a mass of human misery produced?" he asked. He ended his speech with a eulogy for Wilberforce, calling the abolition bill "a measure which will diffuse happiness among millions now in existence, and for which his memory will be blessed by millions yet unborn." This time, 1807, the bill would pass the House of Lords 100–36. After the final reading, the bill was taken up in the House of Commons, and there it passed that same evening. "Our Success altogether greatly surpassed my expectations," wrote Wilberforce.

During the readings of the bill, William Wilberforce wrote, "Never surely had I more cause for gratitude than now, when carrying the great object of my life, to which a gracious Providence directed my thoughts twenty-six or twenty-seven years ago, and led my endeavors in 1787 or 1788. O Lord let me praise Thee with my whole heart: for never surely was there any one so deeply indebted as myself, which way 'soever' I look, I am crowded with blessings. Oh, may my gratitude be in some degree proportionate."

The House decided 283–16 in favor of abolition. The young parliamentarians all leapt to their feet, wishing to speak. Lastly, the solicitor general Romilly spoke, making a point of contrast,

> When I look to the man at the head of the French monarchy, surrounded as he is with all the pomp of power and all the price of victory, distributing kingdoms to his family and principalities to his followers, seeming when he sits upon his throne to have reached the summit of human ambition and the pinnacle of earthly happiness—and when I compare with those pangs of remorse the feelings which must accompany my honourable friend from this house to his home, after the vote of this night shall have confirmed the object of his humane and unceasing labours; when he retires to the bosom of his happy and delighted family, when he lays himself down on his bed, reflecting on the innumerable voices that will be raised in every quarter of the world to bless him, how much more pure and perfect felicity must he enjoy, in the consciousness of having preserved so many millions of his fellow-creatures.

Wilberforce, now overcome and head in hands, wept. The chamber rose to its feet, cheering. Emotions and tears flooded the chamber. At that moment, the inner joy of freedom and the universal wish of freedom for all mankind,—reverberated into a crescendo of deafening cheers.

Describing the demeanor Wilberforce had displayed over the years, a friend said: "When he was in the House of Commons, he seemed to have the freshest mind of any man there. There was all the charm of youth about him."

Lord Carrington had expressed misgivings of joyful expression. Wilberforce had replied, "My grand objection to the religious system still held by many who declare themselves orthodox Churchmen ... is, that it tends to render Christianity so much a system of prohibitions rather than of privilege and hopes, and thus the injunction to rejoice, so strongly enforced in the New Testament, is practically neglected, and Religion is made to wear a forbidding and gloomy air and not one of peace and hope and joy."

Wilberforce made a comment concerning the "nominal Christian." He said,

> Pleasure and Religion are contradictory terms with the bulk of nominal Christians ... O! little do they know of the true measure of enjoyment, who can compare these delightful complacencies with the frivolous pleasures of dissipation, or the coarse gratifications of sensuality ... The nominal Christian ... knows not the sweetness of the delights with which true Christianity repays those trifling sacrifices (self-denial).

There were also many moments when William Wilberforce needed prayer in his trials. One prayer written into his notebook was the following: "Lord, thou knowest that no strength, wisdom or contrivance of human power can signify, or relieve me. It is in thy power alone to deliver me. I fly to thee for succor and support,

O Lord let it come speedily; give me full proof of thy Almighty power; I am in great troubles, insurmountable by me; but to thee slight and inconsiderable; look upon me O Lord with compassion and mercy, and restore me to rest, quietness, and comfort, in the world, or in another by removing me hence into a state of peace and happiness. Amen.

On December 21, 1807, John Newton passed-away. Thursday morning, July 25, 1833, the youngest son of William Wilberforce brought home to breakfast a young member of Parliament, William Gladstone. The twenty-three-year-old future prime minister had never met Mr. Wilberforce. His parents, both evangelicals, had. The young Gladstone would write, "… a beautiful picture of old age in sight of immortality. Heard him pray with his family. Blessings and honour are upon his head."

"I am like a clock almost run down," Wilberforce said to a friend. Only days before his death, Wilberforce received word Friday evening, July 26, that the House had just passed the bill to abolish slavery within the British Empire. In 1821, William had been recruited and persuaded to propose a last petition against slavery. He reflected, "I had never thought to appear in public again, but it shall never be said that William Wilberforce is silent while the slaves require his help." Three months later, Wilberforce recruited Thomas Fowell Buxton to carry forward the fight. William cheered him on and encouraged others from the sidelines.

Upon passing, some details of the Bill needed to be worked out. This required another two or three days of deliberation. Thomas Buxton declared: "It is a singular fact that on the very night on which we were successfully engaged in the House of Commons, in passing the clause of the Act of Emancipation—one of the most important clauses ever enacted … the spirit of our friend left the world. The day which was the termination of his labors was the termination of his life."

FREDERICK DOUGLASS

A Thought

History records that about eleven million Africans were transported as slaves to the New World by the seafaring Portuguese, British, Spanish, and French slave traders. Most were delivered to the cruel conditions of the sugar plantations of Brazil and the West Indies. There they would often soon die of disease and maltreatment. About five hundred thousand or fewer would arrive in British North America. The many descendants of these people would achieve greatness. Among the standout progeny of their earlier forbearers was one thoughtful and courageous individual. Frederick Douglass would perceive and act upon history from the inside out, and the converse as well. He would write of and explain the equality of mankind. His story, in many ways, is, all, of our stories.

"I was born in Tuckahoe, near Hillsborough, and about twelve miles from Easton, in Talbot country, Maryland. I have not accurate knowledge of my age, never having seen any authentic record containing it. By far the larger part of the slaves know as little of their ages as horses know of theirs, and it is the wish of most masters within my knowledge to keep their slaves thus ignorant. I do not remember to have ever met a slave who could tell of his birthday," wrote Frederick Douglass. The best estimate of his birth month, later determined, is February of 1818.

Frederick would live a life unfamiliar to today yet intimately familiar to each of us.

Frederick Bailey would begin his life in the care of Grandmamma Betty and his grandpa. His mother, Harriet, was required to work long hours in the fields; thus, Frederick was given to his grandma. He remembered but a few nights being put to sleep by his mother.

> The dwelling of my grandmother and grandfather had few pretensions. It was a log hut, or cabin, built of clay, wood, and straw. At a distance it resembled -- though it was much smaller, less commodious, and less substantial — the cabins erected in the western states by the first settlers. To my child's eye, however, it was a noble structure, admirably adapted to promote the comforts and conveniences of its inmates ... Living here, with my dear old grandmother and grandfather, it was a long time before I knew myself to be 'a slave'. I knew many other things before I knew that. Grandmother and grandfather were the greatest people in the world to me; and being with them so snugly in their own little cabin — I supposed it to be their own — knowing no other higher authority over me or the other children than the authority of grandmamma ... The slaveholder, having nothing to fear from impotent childhood, easily affords to refrain from cruel inflictions; and if cold and hunger do not pierce the tender frame, the first seven or eight years of the slave-boy's life are about as full of sweet content as those of the most favored and petted "white" children of the slaveholder. The slave boy escapes many troubles which befall and vex his white brother ... freed from all restraint ... the slave boy can be ... a genuine boy ... To be sure, he is occasionally reminded, when he stumbles in the path of his master—-and this he learns to avoid—-that he is eating his "white bread", and that he will be made to "see sights" by-and-by ... I learned by degrees the sad fact, that the "little hut," and the lot on which

it stood, belonged not to my dear old grandparents, but to some person who lived a great distance off, and who was called, by grandmother, "OLD MASTER." I further learned the sadder fact, that not only the house and lot, but that grandmother herself, (grandfather was free,) and all the little children around her, belonged to this mysterious personage ... I was told that this "old master," whose name seemed ever to be mentioned with fear and shuddering, only allowed the children to live with grandmother for a limited time, and that in fact as soon as they were big enough, they were promptly taken away, to live with the said "old master." These were distressing revelations, indeed; and though I was quite too young to comprehend the full import of the intelligence, and mostly spent my childhood days in gleesome sports with the other children, a shade of disquiet rested upon me.

There would be a day when Grandmamma and little (seven-year-old) Frederick would walk the twelve miles to the master's house; sometimes with Frederick riding on his grandmamma's shoulders. He was to be left at the house with many other little children. "Grandma looked sad." He did not see his beloved grandmamma leave and cried himself to sleep. "I remember as well as if it were yesterday ... The germs of affection with which the Almighty, in his wisdom and mercy, arms the helpless infant against the ills and vicissitudes of his lot, had been directed in their growth toward that loving old grandmother."

Little Frederick was now on Col. Lloyd's plantation.

> That plantation is a little nation of its own, having its own language, its own rules, regulations and customs. ... The overseer is generally accuser, judge, jury, advocate, and executioner ... There are no conflicting rights of property, for all the people are owned by one man. ... Religion and politics alike are

excluded ... In its isolation, seclusion, and self-reliant independence, Col. Lloyd's plantation resembles what the baronial domains were, during the Middle Ages in Europe. Grim, cold, and unapproachable by all genial influences from communities without, "there- it stands"; full three hundred years behind the age, in all that relates to humanity and morals.

Nature enveloped the plantation, and for a time young Frederick breathed the joyous life and beauty of the wild, such as the warbling notes and sounds of red-winged blackbirds. Frederick would observe, "There is no better material in the world for making a gentleman, than is furnished in the African." Needless to add, that was not the purpose of the plantation. "Want of food was my chief trouble the first summer at my old master's." Even as the notice of the switch and whip were becoming more commonplace, Frederick would also play with the youngest son of Col. Lloyd, the owner of many plantations. "'Never mind, honey—better day comin', was even then a solace, a cheering consolation to me and my troubles."

More directly to the old master Captain Anthony, Douglass wrote, "... but a few months were sufficient to convince one that mildness and gentleness were not the prevailing or governing traits of his character. He could be literally insensible to the claims of humanity. By nature, he was not worse than other men." But as a slaveholder, he was different: "The slaveholder, as well as the slave, is the victim of the slave system. A man's character greatly takes its hue and shape from the form and color of things about him. Under the whole heavens there is no relation more unfavorable to the development of honorable character, than that sustained by the slaveholder to the slave. Reason is imprisoned here, and passions run wild." To a child's eye, he was unhappy. "Most of his leisure was spent in walking, cursing, and gesticulating, like one possessed by a demon. Most evidently, he was a wretched man at war with his own soul." Any slave might receive a brutal flogging from any master or any overseer. Those seen by young eyes make for a most lasting impression.

This child would begin to think, "Why am I a slave? Why are some people slaves, and others, masters? Was there ever a time when this was not so? How did the relation commence?" These are perplexing questions for a young mind. "Besides, how did people know that God made black people to be slaves? Did they go up in the sky and learn it? or did He come down and tell them so?"

Further thinking on the subject, Douglass stated,

> Then, too, I found that there were puzzling exceptions to this theory of slavery on both sides, and in the middle. I knew of blacks who were "not" slaves; I knew of whites who were "not" slaveholders; and I knew of persons who were "nearly" white, who were slaves. "Color", therefore, was a very unsatisfactory basis for slavery ... Once, however, engaged in the inquiry, I was not very-long in finding out the true solution of the matter. It was not "color", but "crime", not God, but "man", that afforded the true explanation of the existence of slavery; nor was I long in finding out another important truth, viz: what man can make, man can unmake. The appalling darkness faded away, and I was master of the subject. There were slaves here, direct from Guinea; and there were many who could say that their fathers and mothers were stolen from Africa—-forced from their homes and compelled to serve as slaves. This, to me, was knowledge; but it was a kind of knowledge which filled me with a burning hatred of slavery, increased my suffering, and left me without the means of breaking away from my bondage. Yet it was knowledge quite worth possessing. I could not have been more than seven or eight years old, when I began to make this subject my study. It was with me in the woods and fields; along the shore of the river, and wherever my boyish wanderings led me; and though I was, at that time, quite ignorant of the existence of the free states, I distinctly remember

being, 'even then' most strongly impressed with the idea of being a free man some-day. This cheering assurance was an inborn dream of my human nature—a constant menace to slavery—and one which all the powers of slavery were unable to silence or extinguish.

What is the sound of slavery? Frederick would describe it in this way:

> Slaves are generally expected to sing as well as to work. A silent slave is not liked by masters or overseers. "Make a noise," "make a noise," and "bear a hand," are the words usually addressed to the slaves when there is silence among them. This may account for the almost constant singing heard in the southern states. There was, generally, more or less, singing among the teamsters (team of horses and wagon), as it was one means of letting the overseer know where they were, and that they were moving on with the work. But, on allowance day, those who visited the great house farm were peculiarly excited and noisy. While on their way, they would make the dense old woods, for miles around, reverberate with their wild notes. These were not always merry because they were wild. On the contrary, they were mostly of a plaintive cast, and told a tale of grief and sorrow. In the most boisterous outbursts of rapturous sentiment, there was ever a tinge of deep melancholy. I have never heard any songs like those anywhere since I left slavery, except when in Ireland. There, I heard the same 'wailing notes' and was much affected by them. It was during the famine of 1845-46 ...More slaves are whipped for oversleeping than for any other fault. ... The overseer generally rides about the field on horseback. A cowskin and a hickory stick are his constant companions ... Cowskins are the favorite slave whip.

Slaves, Douglass stated, "are far too scantily provided for, and are worked too steadily, to be much concerned for the quality of their food." After a brief lunch, the day went as follows: "... now, from twelve o'clock (mid-day) till dark, the human cattle are in motion, wielding their clumsy hoes; hurried on by no hope of reward, no sense of gratitude, no love of children, no prospect of bettering their condition; nothing, save the dread and terror of the slave-driver's lash. So goes one day, and so comes and goes another."

How can this vulgar coarseness and brutal cruelty flourish— that "where a vile wretch, in the shape of a man, rides, walks, or struts about, dealing blows, and leaving gashes on broken-spirited men and helpless women, for thirty dollars per month—a business so horrible, hardening, and disgraceful, that, rather than engage in it, a decent man would blow his own brains out"?

> May we consider the less repulsive aspects of slave life; where pride and pomp roll luxuriously at ease, where the toil of a thousand men supports a single family in easy idleness and sin. This is the great house; it is the home of the Lloyds [in this case] Some idea of its splendor has already been given—and, it is here that we shall find that height of poverty and physical wretchedness that we have just now been contemplating. But - there is this difference in the two extremes; viz: that in the case of the slave, the miseries and hardships of his lot are imposed by others, and, in the master's case, they are imposed by himself. The slave is a subject, subjected by others; the slaveholder is a subject, but he is the author of his own subjection. There is more truth in the saying, that slavery is a greater evil to the master than to the slave, than many, who utter it, suppose. The self-executing laws of eternal justice follow close on the heels of the evil-doer here, as well as elsewhere; making escape from all its penalties impossible.

For Frederick himself, he relates some of his own personal experience there.

> I have nothing cruel or shocking to relate ... while I remained on Col. Lloyd's plantation, at the home of my old master. An occasional cuff from Aunt Katy, and a regular whipping from old master, such as any heedless and mischievous boy might get from his father, is all that I can mention of this sort. I was not old enough to work in the field, and there being little else than field work to perform, I had much leisure. The most I had to do was drive up the cows in the evening, to keep the front yard clean, and to perform small errands for my young mistress, Lucretia Auld ... Then, too, I one day got into the wars with Uncle Abel's son, "Ike," and had got sadly worsted; in fact, the little rascal had struck me directly in the forehead with a sharp piece of cinder, fused with iron, from the old blacksmith's forge, which made a cross in my forehead very plainly to be seen now ... Lucretia ... came forward; and, in quite a different spirit from that manifested by Aunt Katy ... she quietly acted the good Samaritan. With her own soft hand, she washed the blood from my head and face, fetched her own balsam bottle, and with the balsam wetted a nice piece of white linen, and bound up my head. The balsam was not more healing to the wound in my head, than her kindness was healing to the wounds in my spirit ...

Frederick would reflect,

> I love to recall any instances of kindness, any sunbeams of humane treatment, which found way to my soul through the iron grating of my house of bondage. Such beams seem all the brighter from the general darkness

into which they penetrate, and the impression they make is vividly distinct and beautiful ... As I have before intimated ... I suffered little from the treatment I received, except from hunger and cold ... I had no bed. The pigs in the pen had leaves, and the horses in the stable had straw, but the children had no beds ... I sometimes got down the bag in which corn-meal was usually carried to the mill, and crawled into that ... As I grew older and more thoughtful, I was more and more filled with a sense of my wretchedness ... I was just as well-aware of the unjust, unnatural, and murderous character of slavery, when nine years old, as I am now. Without any appeal to books, to laws, or to authorities of any kind, it was enough to accept God as a father, to regard slavery as a crime ... I was not ten years old when I left Col. Lloyd's plantation for Baltimore. I left that plantation with inexpressible joy. I never shall forget the ecstasy with which I received the intelligence from my friend, Miss Lucretia, that my old master had determined to let me go to Baltimore to live with Mr. Hugh Auld, a brother to Mr. Thomas Auld, my old master's son-in-law. I received this information about three days before my departure. They were three of the happiest days of my childhood.

Looking back, Frederick would thoughtfully reflect on his change of circumstance:

I may say, here, that I regard my removal from Col. Lloyd's plantation as one of the most interesting and fortunate events of my life. Viewing it in the light of human likelihoods, it is quite probable that, but for the mere circumstance of being thus removed before the rigors of slavery had fastened upon me; before my young spirit had been crushed under the iron control of the slave-driver, instead of being, to-tad, a FREE-MAN, I might have been wearing the galling chains of slavery. I have sometimes felt, however, that there is something more certain than 'luck', to be seen in the circumstance. If I have made any progress in knowledge; If I have cherished any honorable aspirations, or have, in any manner, worthily discharged the duties of a member of an oppressed people; this little circumstance must be allowed its due weight in giving my life that direction. I have ever regarded it as the first plain manifestation of the "Divinity that shapes our ends, Rough hew them as we will" ... I may be deemed superstitious and egotistical, in regarding this event as a special interposition of Divine Providence in my favor; but the thought is a part of my history, and I should be false to the earliest and most cherished sentiments of my soul, if I suppressed, or hesitated to avow that opinion, although it may be characterized as irrational by the wise, and ridiculous by the scoffer. From my earliest recollections of serious matters, I date the entertainment of something like an ineffaceable conviction, that slavery would not always be able to hold me within its foul embrace; and this conviction, like a work of living faith, strengthened me through the darkest trials of my lot. This good spirit was from God; and to him I offer thanksgiving and praise.

Sophia, Hugh Auld's wife, had never owned a slave before and was unfamiliar with the "proper" way to treat one. She disliked the servile manners Frederick had been taught on the plantation, and she told him to look her in the eye when he spoke to her. His only two jobs were to run errands and care for the Auld's infant son. "Feddy" and little Thomas got well along. "Mrs. Auld was not only a kind-hearted woman, but she was remarkably pious." Mr. Auld "cared very little about religion ... and was more of the world." Auld would become "a successful ship builder, in that city of ship building."

"Tommy, and I, and his mother, got on swimmingly together, for a time." Mrs. Auld had regarded Frederick simply as a child, as they would any child. Frederick asked her to teach him how to read. Without hesitation she began the task. She was proud of "Freddy's" progress. She exultingly told her husband of the aptness of her pupil. "Here arose the first cloud over my Baltimore prospects, the precursor of drenching rains and chilling blasts," recalled Frederick.

"Master Hugh was amazed at the simplicity of his spouse," Frederick would recall, "and, probably for the first time, he unfolded to her the true philosophy of slavery, and the peculiar rules necessary to be observed by masters and mistresses, in the management of their human chattels ... His discourse was the first decidedly anti-slavery lecture to which it had been my lot to listen." And he began thinking—an act which he was so capable of. "[It] but awakened within me a slumbering train of vital thought. It was a new and special revelation, dispelling a painful mystery, against which my youthful understanding had struggled, and struggled in vain, to wit: the 'white' man's power to perpetuate the enslavement of the 'black' man. 'Very well,' thought I; 'knowledge unfits a child to be a slave.' I instinctively assented to the proposition; and from that moment I understood the direct pathway from slavery to freedom. This was just what I needed; and I got it at a time, and from a source, whence I least expected it."

Frederick made friends on his errands with poor white children. They became his tutors, and he would pay for his reading lessons with pieces of bread. Slavery was a delicate subject for adults. Frederick and his play fellows freely talked about the subject: "I wish I could be free, as you will be when you get to be men." "You will be free, you know, as soon as you are twenty-one, and can go where you like, but I am a slave for life. Have I not as good a right to be free as you have?" "I do not remember ever to have met with a 'boy' while I was in slavery, who defended the slave system; but I have often had boys to console me, with the hope that something would yet occur, by which I might be made free. Over and over again, they have told me, that 'they believed I had as good a right to be free as they had;' and that 'they did not believe God ever made any one to be a slave.'"

By about thirteen years of age, Frederick had succeeded in learning to read. With some money earned doing errands, he purchased a copy of *The Columbian Orator*. "Once awakened by the silver trump of knowledge, my spirit was roused to eternal wakefulness. Liberty!"

Frederick became all ears whenever the topic of slavery was mentioned. "Every little while, I could overhear Master Hugh, or some of his company, speaking with much warmth and excitement about 'abolitionists.'" The dictionary was of little help. In a newspaper, Frederick learned of petitions presented to Congress praying for the abolition of slavery.

Here, once again, Frederick is honest:

> Previous to my contemplation of the anti-slavery movement, and its probable results, my mind had been seriously awakened to the subject of religion. I was not more than thirteen years old, when I felt the need of God, as a father and protector. My religious nature was awakened by the preaching of a white Methodist minister, named Hanson ... I knew that I could pray for light. I consulted a good colored man, named Charles Johnson; and, in tones-of holy affection, he told me to pray, and what to pray for ... I finally found that changed of heart which come by "casting all one's care" upon God, and by having faith in Jesus Christ, as the Redeemer, Friend, and Savior of those who diligently seek Him. After this, I saw the world in a new light. I seemed to live in a new world, surrounded by new objects, and to be animated by new hopes and desires. I loved all mankind—slave-holders not excepted; though I abhorred slavery more than ever ... I became acquainted with a good old colored man named Lawson. A more devout man than he, I never saw ... His life was a life of prayer, and his words, were about a better world ... The

old man could read a little ... I could teach him "the letter", but he could teach me "the spirit." The good old man had told me, that the "Lord had a great work for me to do;" and I must prepare to do it; and that he had been shown that I must preach the gospel. His words made a deep impression on my mind, and I verily felt that some such work was before me, though I could not see how I should ever engage in its performance. "The good Lord," he said, "would bring it to pass in his own good time," and that I must go on reading and studying the scriptures."

Frederick would ask, "How can these things be—and what can I do?" the man's simple reply was "Trust in the Lord."

Douglass goes on: "When I told him I was a slave, and a slave FOR LIFE," he said, 'the Lord can make you free, my dear. All things are possible with him, only "have faith in God." "Ask, and it shall be given." If you want liberty,' said the good old man, 'ask the Lord for it, in faith, AND HE WILL GIVE IT TO YOU.'

Frederick was old enough now to begin to work in the shipyard. He began to learn to write. With his playmates for teachers, fences and pavements for copy, and chalk for writing, Frederick finally learned the art of writing.

Owing to death and circumstances, Frederick was sent back for valuation and division of slaves among contending heirs. There were bitter tears. "Horses and men—cattle and women—pigs and children—all holding the same rank in the scale of social existence." Frederick fell, thankfully, to the portion of Mrs. Lucretia, who had bound his head years before. It was decided Frederick would return to Baltimore. However, within a year, Lucretia died. The two Auld brothers, Hugh and Thomas, got into a dispute. In March of 1832, after seven years, Frederick would return to live at Thomas Auld's new farm, which was just a few miles from the Lloyd plantation. Frederick had become a teacher to a group of other young blacks in Baltimore. Thoughts of freedom must wait. The memories of Irish sailors urging him to escape would, for now, only be memories.

Master Thomas Auld "came into possession of all his slaves by marriage; and of all men, adopted slaveholders are the worst. He was cruel but cowardly ... Bad as all slaveholders are, we seldom meet one destitute of every element of character commanding respect. My master was one of this rare sort. I do not know of one single noble act ever performed by him. The leading trait of his character was meanness; and if there were any other element in his nature, it was made subject to this ... Not to give a slave enough to eat, is regarded as the most aggravated development of meanness even among slaveholders." Frederick and three others were given less than half a bushel of cornmeal per week. He and they had to beg and steal from neighbors. Mrs. Auld wished to have her husband to be called "Master." He would generally be called "Captain Auld," and none were hardly disposed to grant him any title whatsoever; but he was never to be called "Master."

Frederick's master attended a camp meeting and experienced some religion. Some meetings were held at the house. A Mr. George Cookman—a very rich slaveholder—attended sometimes. "We, slaves loved Mr. Cookman ... When he was at our house, we were sure to be called in to prayers." The impression was that he was laboring to affect the emancipation of slaves. Unfortunately, as an understatement, Captain Auld would receive only some of the message but not all of the message, and thereby his undue punishments exaggerated any entire understanding of the Word, underlining a bloody, hypocritical example of faith.

"My master and myself had quite a number of differences. He found me unsuitable to his purpose." One of Frederick's faults was letting Auld's horse run away to his father-in-law's house. However, Frederick could always pick up a meal or something to eat there. After nine months, and, a number, of severe whippings, Auld resolved to put Frederick out to have him broken. He would give Frederick to a Mr. Covey, a renter with a reputation for breaking young slaves, for one year.

Frederick went to live with Mr. Covey on January 1, 1833.

GOOD LEADERS

"I was now, for the first time in my life, a field hand. In my new employment, I found myself even more awkward than a country boy appeared to be in a large city ... We were worked fully up to the point of endurance. Long before day we were up, our horses fed, and by the first approach of day we were off to the field with our hoes and ploughing teams. Mr. Covey gave us enough to eat, but scarce time to eat it. We were often in the field from the first approach of day till its last lingering ray had left us ... Mr. Covey's forte consisted in his power to deceive. His life was devoted to planning and perpetrating the grossest deceptions. Everything he possessed in the shape of learning or religion, he made conform to his disposition to deceive. He seemed to think himself equal to deceiving the Almighty ... I lived with Mr. Covey one year. During the first six months, of that year, scarce a week passed without his whipping me ... Our house stood within a few rods of the Chesapeake Bay whose broad bosom was ever white with sails from every quarter of the habitable globe ... I have often, in the deep stillness of a summer's Sabbath, stood all alone upon the lofty banks of the noble bay, and traced, with saddened heart and tearful eye, the countless number of sails moving off to the mighty ocean.

Frederick Bailey would become a free man. One day he would have it out with Mr. Covey for two hours.

He only can understand the deep satisfaction which I experienced, who has himself repelled by force the bloody arm of slavery. I felt as I never felt before. It was a glorious resurrection, from the tomb of slavery, to the heaven of freedom. My long-crushed spirit rose, cowardice departed, bold defiance took its place; and

> I now resolved that, however long I might remain a slave in form, the day had passed forever when I could be a slave in fact. I did not hesitate to let it be known of me, that the white man who expected to succeed in whipping, must also succeed in killing me. From this time, I was never again what might be called 'fairly whipped', though I remained a slave four years afterwards. I had several fights but was never whipped.

Frederick considered that Covey did not have Bailey taken to the constable, perhaps to save his own reputation.

In January of 1834, Frederick left Covey and went to live with a Mr. William Freeland. "I soon found Mr. Freeland, a very, different man from Mr. Covey. Though not rich, he was what would be called an educated southern gentleman ... seemed to possess some regard for honor, some reverence for justice and some respect for humanity." He also made no pretense of religion. Frederick began a Sabbath school. "[It was devoted to] teaching these my loved fellow-slaves how to read ... It was necessary to keep our religious masters at St. Michael's unacquainted with the fact, that, instead of spending the Sabbath in wrestling, boxing, and drinking whiskey, we were trying to learn how to read the will of God. I can say, I never loved any or confided in any people more than my fellow-slaves, and especially those with whom I lived at Mr. Freeland's."

Frederick was rehired for by Mr. Freeland for 1835. Frederick resolved the year should not pass without an attempt to secure his liberty. He devised a plan with some of his fellows. Regarding their determination to run away, Douglass wrote, "... we did more than, Patrick Henry, when he resolved upon liberty or death. With us it was a doubtful liberty at most, and almost certain death if we failed." The plan would include a canoe. On the day they were to paddle toward an unknown freedom, someone turned them in. Frederick would eventually find himself alone in a jail cell. Captain Auld, his master, surprisingly came to the jail and released Frederick, intending to send him to Alabama.

Ultimately, however, he concluded he would send Frederick "back to Baltimore, to live again with his brother Hugh, and to learn a trade."

So, after three years, Frederick returned to Baltimore. Master Hugh hired him to a shipbuilder to learn how to caulk. He would be at many a beck and call on board ship for about eight months. Frederick was unjustly assaulted. Master Hugh listened, expressed his unhappiness, and took the matter to court without resolution. He then took Frederick into the shipyard where he was foreman. Within one year, Frederick commanded the highest wages. He brought home six to nine dollars a week to Master Hugh. Frederick thought it piracy, in, its own right.

In the next paragraphs, Fredrick will finally succeed in escaping slavery. In Frederick's writings, he would not "give a minute statement of all the facts." He would not wish to put a guard on a door of "some dear brother," keeping him from escaping his "galling chains." In fact, he stated, "I have never approved of the very public manner in which some of our western friends have conducted what they call the 'underground railroad,' but which, I think, by their open declarations, has been made most emphatically the 'upperground railroad' … They do nothing toward enlightening the slave, whilst they do much toward enlightening the master … Let us render the tyrant no aid; let us not hold the light by which he can trace the footprints of our flying brother." Even as history tends to repeat itself, Frederick Douglas would have been understood as a brother to those escaping from behind the iron curtain and to others seeking no less than freedom.

It was 1838, and Frederick applied to Master Hugh "for the privilege of hiring [his] time." Frederick would find his own employment with a set weekly financial obligation to his master. He would buy his own clothes and caulking tools. This would not be easy, but with "untiring perseverance and industry," he might lay up a little money of his own.

> The wretchedness of slavery, and the blessedness of freedom, were perpetually before me. It was life and death with me … On the third day of September 1838, I left my chains, and succeeded in reaching New York without the slightest interruption of any kind … The

flight was a bold and perilous one ... The dreams of my childhood and the purposes of my manhood were now fulfilled ... A free state around me, and a free earth under my feet! What a moment was this to me! A whole year pressed into a single day. A new world burst upon my agitated vision. I have often been asked ... It was a moment of joyous excitement, which no words can describe ... I had very little money—enough to buy me a few loaves of bread, but not enough to pay board, outside a lumber yard. ... I kept my secret as long as I could, and at last was forced to go in search of an honest man—a man sufficiently "human" not to betray me into the hands of slave-catchers..; I found my man in the person of one who said his name was Stewart. He was a sailor, warm-hearted and generous, and he listened to my story with a brother's interest. I told him I was running for my freedom—knew not where to go—money almost gone—was hungry—thought it unsafe to go to the shipyards for work; and needed a friend. Stewart promptly put me in the way of getting out of my trouble. He took me to his house, and went in search of the late David Ruggles, who was then the secretary of the New York vigilance Committee, and, a very active man, in all anti-slavery works.

Frederick would send for his fiancée, Anna Murray. The two were married on September 15, 1838. Anna and Frederick took a steamer north to New Bedford, Massachusetts. There he might find work as a caulker. Frederick Bailey chose a new name, Frederick Douglass. Frederick Douglass had expected to find his new neighbors to be as poor as those in the South without slaves. On the contrary, most were wealthier than even the slaveholders. Why, five men and an ox did what it might take twenty to do at a Southern port, depending not on enslaved human muscle but industry.

A Mr. Johnson, himself a colored man, befriended Frederick. Mr. Johnson lived in a better house, had better furnishings and better dining, owned more books, and was more conversant about the conditions of the day "than nine-tenths of all the slaveholders in Talbot County." Douglass wrote that "the black man's children ... went to school side by side with white children ... Mr. Johnson assured me that no slaveholder could take a slave from New Bedford; that there were men who would lay down their lives ..."

He further wrote,

> Once assured of my safety ... I put on the habiliments of a common laborer and went on the wharf in search of work. I had no notion of living on the honest and generous sympathy of my colored brother, Johnson, or that of the abolitionists ... "Oh! Only give me work." Happily, for me, I was not long in searching. I found employment, the third day of my arrival ... in stowing a sloop ... I went at it with a glad heart and a willing hand. I was now my own master--a tremendous fact — and the rapturous excitement with which I seized the job, may not easily be understood ... The thoughts "I can work! I can work for a living; I am not afraid of work; I have no Master Hugh to rob me of my earnings ... placed me in a state of independence, beyond seeking friendship or support of any man. That day's work I considered the real starting point of something like a new existence.

Four or five months after reaching New Bedford, Frederick was introduced to and subscribed to the *Liberator*, which was edited by William Lloyd Garrison.

> His paper took its place with me next to the bible ... the Liberator was a paper after my own heart. It detested slavery—exposed hypocrisy and wickedness in high

places—made no truce with the traffickers in the bodies and souls of men; it preached human brotherhood, denounced oppression, and, with all the solemnity of God's word, demanded the complete emancipation of my race. I not only liked—I 'loved' this paper, and its editor ... Few men evinced a more genuine or a more exalted piety. The bible was his textbook—held sacred, as the word of the Eternal Father—sinless perfection ... Never loud or noisy—calm and serene as a summer sky, and as pure. "You are the man, the Moses, raised up by God, to deliver his modern Israel from bondage," was the spontaneous feeling of my heart, as I sat way back in the hall and listened to his mighty words; mighty in truth ... I had not long been a reader ... and listener ... before I got a clear apprehension of the principles of the anti-slavery movement ... My acquaintance ... increased my hope for the ultimate freedom of my race, and I united with it from a sense of delight, as well as duty ... All the anti-slavery meetings held in New Bedford I promptly attended ... Thus, passed the first three years of my residence in New Bedford ... I had not then dreamed of the possibility of my becoming a public advocate.

"In the summer of 1841, a grand anti-slavery convention was held in Nantucket, under the auspices of Mr. Garrison and his friends." Having taken no holiday since his escape, and needing a day or two of rest, Frederick attended, never supposing he would take part. William Coffin, a prominent abolitionist, sought him out in the crowd and invited Frederick to say a few words. "... excited and convulsed as I was, the audience, though remarkably quiet before, became as much excited as myself. Mr. Garrison followed me, taking me as his text ... It was an effort of unequaled power, sweeping down, like a very tornado, every opposing barrier, whether of sentiment or opinion." At the close of the meeting, Frederick was urgently solicited to become an agent of the Massachusetts Anti-Slavery Society, and a public advocate. Among Frederick's reasons for reticence and unease to accept was the belief that his joining would put him at risk of public exposure and possible arrest. He agreed to three months, thinking that would be the end of his story and usefulness. Frederick would become introduced by Mr. Collins as a "graduate from the peculiar institution with my diploma on my back."

Frederick Douglass would later reflect,

> Now what shall I say of this fourteen years' experience as a public advocate of the cause of my enslaved brothers and sisters? The time is but as a speck, yet large enough to justify a pause for retrospection— and a pause it must only be ... Young, ardent, and hopeful, I entered upon this new life in the full gush of unsuspecting enthusiasm. The cause was good; the men engaged in it were good; the means to attain its triumph, good; Heaven's blessing must attend all, and freedom must soon be given to the pining millions under a ruthless bondage. My whole heart went with the holy cause, and my most fervent prayer to the Almighty Disposer of the hearts of men, were continually offered for its early triumph, "Who or what," thought I, "can withstand a cause so good, so holy, so indescribably glorious. The God of Israel is with us. The might of the Eternal is on our side. Now let but the truth be spoken, and a notion will start forth at the sound!" In this enthusiastic spirit, I dropped into the ranks of freedom's friends, and went forth into battle ... At last the apprehended trouble came. People doubted if I had ever been a slave. They said I did not talk like a slave, look like a slave, nor act like a slave, and that they believed I had never been south of Mason and Dixon's line ... Besides, he is educated ... I was, in a pretty fair way, to be denounced as an impostor. The ... Society knew all the facts ... and agreed with me in the prudence of keeping them private.

In less than four years after becoming a public lecturer, Frederick was "induced to write out the leading facts connected with [his] experience in slavery, giving names of person, places, and dates." This he did, writing *The Narrative of the Life of Frederick Douglass*. "I was still tormented with the liability of losing my liberty."

The pamphlet was written in the spring of 1845. As considered among "the allotments of Providence," Frederick would seek refuge in monarchical England. "I have spent some of the happiest moments of my life since landing in this country. I seem to have undergone a transformation. I live a new life ... I visited and lectured in nearly all the large towns and cities in the United Kingdom." Before returning, his friends raised an amount sufficient to purchase freedom for Frederick Douglass. The papers of manumission were placed in his hands. The sum paid was one hundred fifty pounds sterling.

Frederick would be asked why he should not confine his efforts to the United States.

> My answer is, first, slavery is the common enemy of mankind, and all mankind should be made acquainted with its abominable character. My next answer is -- that the slave is a man, and, as such, is entitled to your sympathy as a brother. All the feelings, all the susceptibilities, all the capacities, which you have, he has. He is a part of the human family ... It is a system of such gigantic evil, so strong, so overwhelming in its power, that no one nation is equal to its removal. It requires the humanity of Christianity, the morality of the world to remove it. Hence, I call upon the people of Britain to look at this matter ...

Frederick Douglas would say more than once,

> I love the religion of our blessed Savior. I love that religion that comes from above, in the "wisdom of God, which is first pure, then peaceable, gentle, and easy to

be entreated, full of mercy and good fruits, without partiality and without hypocrisy." I love that religion that sends its votaries to bind up the wounds of him that has fallen among thieves.

I love that religion that makes it the duty of its disciples to visit the fatherless and the widow in their affliction. I love that religion that is based upon the glorious principle, of love to God and love to man, which makes its followers do unto others as they themselves would be done by. If you demand liberty to yourself, it says, grant it to your neighbors. If you claim a right to think for yourself, it says, allow your neighbors the same right. It is because I live this religion that I hate the slaveholding, the woman-whipping, the mind-darkening, the soul-destroying religion that exists in the southern states of America. It is because I regard the one as good, and pure, and holy, that I cannot but regard the other bad, corrupt, and wicked. Loving the one I must hate the other; holding to the one I must reject the other.

After a successful nearly two years, Frederick would return to America. He would continue lecturing with Lloyd Garrison for a time. On December 3, 1847, Frederick Douglass published the first issue of his weekly newspaper, the *North Star*, from his new home in Rochester, New York. The motto was, "Right is of no sex—Truth is of no color—God is the Father of us all, and we are all Brethren." The paper would continue as a weekly until 1860 and as a monthly for another three years. In 1848, he would lend a voice at the first women's rights convention, which included the likes of Elizabeth Cady Stanton and Susan B. Anthony. Frederick and his wife, Anna, had five children together: Rosetta, Lewis, Frederick, Charles, and Annie. Douglass campaigned to end segregation in Rochester's school system, and in 1857 his efforts succeeded.

Frederick would begin to incline to approve of political action. John Brown was among the abolitionists with whom he met. He attended a convention held by the Free-Soil Party in 1848, a party battling to stop the spread of slavery west of the Mississippi River. He attended many conventions of black abolitionists. The Missouri Compromise of 1820, authorizing a slave state to be added for every new free state added to the Union, held the Union together till 1850. The Compromise of 1850 perilously maintained the Union, adding California but also including the Fugitive Slave Act. In 1854, Congress passed the Kansas-Nebraska Act, allowing slavery into the northern territories of the west if approved by the citizens of new states. The Republican Party was formed as a result.

Frederick Douglass became involved in the Underground Railroad himself. Since the Douglass home in Rochester was near the Canadian border, it became an important stop. Sometimes he would find fugitives at his newspaper office when he arrived. Over the years, he and Anna sheltered hundreds in their home.

About three weeks before the raid on Harper's Ferry, John Brown wrote to Frederick, asking him to meet in an old stone quarry. Frederick observed,

> His face wore an anxious expression, and he was much worn by thought and exposure. I felt that I was on a dangerous mission, and was as little desirous of discovery as himself, though no reward had been offered for me ... The taking of Harper's Ferry, of which Captain Brown had merely hinted before, was now declared as his settled purpose, and he wanted to know what I thought of it. I at once opposed the measure with all the arguments at my command. To me such a measure would be fatal to running off slaves (as was the original plan), and fatal to all engaged in doing so. It would be an attack upon the federal government and would array the whole country against us ... He did not at all object to rousing the nation ... just what the nation needed ... I looked at him with some astonishment ... that Virginia would blow him and his hostages sky high ... we spent the most of Saturday and a part of

> Sunday in this debate— Brown for Harper's Ferry, and I against it.

At a lecture, Frederick Douglass was told of the news of Brown's raid. Frederick knew that letters and other evidence would implicate him too closely. A trial in Virginia at this time would augur a less-than-favorable outcome.

> On the 12th of November 1859, I took passage from Quebec ... the fact that I was now in danger of arrest on the ground of complicity with [John Brown] made what I had intended a pleasure a necessity ... England had given me shelter and protection before ... Slavery seemed to be at the very top of its power ... So I started on my voyage with feelings far from cheerful. No one who has not himself been compelled to leave his home and country and go into permanent banishment can well imagine the state of mind and heart which such a condition brings. The voyage out was by the north passage, and at this season, as usual, it was cold, dark, and stormy. Before quitting the coast of Labrador, we had four degrees below zero ... Our great ship was dashed about upon the surface of the sea as though she had been the smallest "dugout."

Frederick landed in England, where there was much interest in Harper's Ferry and the events of the time. Six months out, Frederick received news of the death of his beloved daughter Annie, whom he described as "the light and life of my house." He resolved to return home regardless of the peril and so did. He remained in his house for a month as the events of the day passed on and passed him by without charges.

> Through this disappointing sadness came an enabling to participate in the most important and memorable presidential canvass ever witnessed in the United States,

and to labor for the election of a man who in the order of events was destined to do a greater service to his country and mankind than any man who had gone before him in the presidential office. It is something to couple one's name with great occasions, and it was a great thing to me to be permitted to bear some humble part in this … It was a great thing to achieve American independence when we numbered three millions, but it was a greater thing to save this country from dismemberment and ruin when it numbered thirty millions. He alone of all our Presidents was to have the opportunity to destroy slavery, and to lift into manhood millions of his countrymen.

Abraham Lincoln would say: "What is it that we hold most dear among us? Our own liberty and prosperity. What has ever threatened our liberty and prosperity, save and except this institution of slavery."
Frederick Douglas would say of President Lincoln,

He did not hesitate, he did not doubt, he did not falter; but at once resolved that at whatever peril, at whatever cost, the union of the States would be preserved. A patriot himself, his faith was strong and unwavering in the patriotism of his countrymen. But, in the midst, of all this tumult and timidity, and against all this, Abraham Lincoln was clear in his duty, and had an oath in heaven. He calmly and bravely heard the voice of doubt and fear all around him; but he had an oath in heaven and there was not power enough on the earth to make this honest boatman, backwoodsman, and broad-handed splitter of rails evade or violate that sacred oath.

Charles Sumner, a Republican senator of Massachusetts and a friend of Abraham Lincoln, said, "But the inevitable topic to which he returned with the most frequency, and to which he clung with all the grasp of his soul, was the practical character of the Declaration of Independence in announcing the Liberty and Equality of all men."

Frederick Douglas also said of Lincoln,

> His great mission was to accomplish two things: first, to save his country from dismemberment and ruin; and second, to free his country from the great crime of slavery. To do one or the other, or both, he must have the earnest sympathy and the powerful cooperation of his loyal fellow-countrymen. Without this primary and essential condition to success, his efforts must have been vain and utterly fruitless. Had he put the abolition of slavery before the salvation of the Union, he would have inevitably driven from him a powerful class of the American people and rendered resistance to rebellion impossible. Viewed from the genuine abolition ground, Mr. Lincoln seemed tardy, cold, dull, and indifferent; but measuring him by the sentiment of his country, a sentiment he was bound as a statesman to consult, he was swift, zealous, radical, and determined.

All three of Frederick Douglass's sons—Lewis, Frederick, and Charles—would join Union forces along with another over two hundred thousand black soldiers. Thirty-eight thousand black soldiers were killed or wounded in Civil War battles. Via his newspaper and other efforts made, Frederick Douglass assisted in recruiting. Attending Lincoln's second inaugural address, Douglas felt himself to be "a man among men." When he was declined entry into the White House reception, Frederick sent word to Lincoln, and he was quickly ushered in. "Here comes my friend Douglass," greeted Abraham.

Douglass once stated, "I have often said elsewhere what I wish to repeat here, that Mr. Lincoln was not only a great President, but a GREAT MAN—-too great to be small in anything."

With the ratification of the Thirteenth Amendment in December of 1865, slavery was officially abolished. Many abolitionists would soon retire. Frederick, too, considered a quieter life. Senators Stevens and Sumner joined with abolitionists supporting voting rights. Douglass traveled throughout the North, speaking out for black suffrage. In 1866, Congress passed the Civil Rights Bill, granting full citizenship. Also in 1866, Douglass attended as a delegate from New York and spoke in favor of suffrage at a Republican convention in Philadelphia. There he spotted Amanda Sears, the daughter of Lucretia Auld. Amanda and her two daughters had traveled the distance just to see Frederick Douglass. President Johnson continued trying to block Reconstruction efforts by Congress. Impeachment efforts failed by one vote.

During the 1868 presidential contest, Douglass campaigned for the Republican candidate, Ulysses S. Grant, former commander of the Union Army. The fifteenth amendment, guaranteeing all citizens, regardless of race, the right to vote, passed. With a successful campaign for state ratification, President Grant declared the amendment adopted on March 30, 1870. By 1870, the Southern states had been readmitted into the Union. Large numbers of blacks were elected to state legislatures. Blacks also won seats in Congress. In 1870, Frederick Douglass was asked to serve as editor of a newspaper based in Washington, DC, named the *New National Era*. The goal of the paper was to herald the progress of blacks throughout the country.

Douglass also campaigned hard for the reelection of President Grant in 1872. Grant won easily. Frederick was chosen as one of two electors-at-large from New York. Considered by many to be one of the world's greatest speakers, Douglass continued, on the lecture circuit. When he encountered, as he would, discrimination in restaurants, hotels, or railway cars, he wrote letters. In 1875, a civil rights bill to give blacks the right of equal treatment in theaters, inns, and other public places cheered him.

On April 14, 1876, Frederick Douglass was invited to speak, on the occasion, of the unveiling of the Freedmen's Monument in memory of Abraham Lincoln:

> Few facts could better illustrate the vast and wonderful change which has taken place in our condition as a

people, than the fact of our assembling here for the purpose we have today. Harmless, beautiful, proper, and praiseworthy as this demonstration is, I cannot forget that no such demonstration would have been tolerated here twenty years ago. The spirit of slavery and barbarism, which still lingers to blight and destroy in some dark and distant parts of our country, would have made our assembling here the signal and excuse for opening upon us all the floodgates of wrath and violence. That we are here in peace today is a compliment and a credit to American civilization, and a prophecy of still greater national enlightenment and progress in the future.

After the inauguration of the new Republican president, Rutherford B. Hayes, in 1877, Fredrick Douglass was appointed as US marshal for Washington DC. For good and for bad, the bulk of federal troops would soon begin to be removed from the South.

Then there came a surreal moment—a "striking illustration of the trite saying that "truth is stranger than fiction," reflected Frederick. It was one that "might well enough be dramatized for the stage." Frederick returned that year to St. Michaels.

> My return ... in peace, to this place ... was strange enough in itself; but that I should, when there, be formally invited by Captain Thomas Auld, then over eighty years old, to come to the side of his dying bed, evidently with a view to a friendly talk over our past relations, was a fact still more strange, and one which, until its occurrence, I could never have thought possible. To me, Captain Auld had sustained the relation of master—a relation which I had held in extremest abhorrence, and which for forty years I had denounced in all bitterness of spirit and fierceness of speech ... I had by my writings made his name and his deeds

familiar to the world in four different languages, yet here we were, after four decades, once more face-to-face—he on his bed, aged and tremulous, drawing near the sunset of life, and I, his former slave, United States Marshal of the District of Columbia, holding his hand and in friendly conversation with him in a sort of final settlement of past differences preparatory to his stepping into his grave, where all distinctions are at an end, and where the great and the small, the slave and his master, are reduced to the same level ... But now that slavery was destroyed, and the slave and the master stood upon equal ground, I was not only willing to meet him, but was very glad to do so. The conditions were favorable for remembrance of all his good deeds, and generous extenuation of all his evil ones. He was to me no longer a slaveholder either in fact or in spirit, and I regarded him as I did myself, a victim of the circumstances of birth, education, law, and custom ... Our courses had been determined for us, not by us. We had both been flung, by powers that did not ask our consent, upon a mighty current of life, which we could neither resist nor control. By this current he was a master, and I a slave; but now our lives were verging toward a point where differences disappear, where even the constancy of hate breaks down and where the clouds of pride, passion and selfishness vanish before the brightness of infinite light. At such a time, and in such a place, when a man is about closing his eyes on this world and ready to step into the eternal unknown, no word of reproach or bitterness should reach him or fall from his lips; and on the occasion there was to this rule no transgression on either side.

On September 19, 1881, the day of the interment of James A. Garfield, twentieth president of the United States, Frederick Douglass addressed a gathering in the Fifteenth Street Presbyterian Church. Frederick called the day of his assassination "a day of gloom long to be remembered as the closing scene in one of the most tragic and startling dramas ever witnessed."

Frederick Douglass addressed the gathering with these words:

Friends and fellow citizens:

To-day our common mother Earth has closed over the mortal remains of James A. Garfield, at Cleveland, Ohio. The light of no day in our national history has brought to the American people a more intense bereavement, a deeper sorrow, or a more profound sense of humiliation. It seems only as yesterday, that, in my quality as United States Marshal of the District of Columbia, it was made my duty and privilege to walk at the head of the column in advance of this our President-elect, from the crowded senate Chamber of the national capitol, through the long corridors and the grand rotunda, beneath the majestic dome, to the platform on the portico, where, amid a sea of transcendent pomp and glory, he who is now dead was hailed with tumultuous applause from uncounted thousands of his fellow citizens, and was inaugurated Chief Magistrate of the United States. The scene was one never to be forgotten by those who beheld it. It was a great day for the nation, glad and proud to do honor to their chosen ruler. It was a glad day for James A. Garfield. It was a glad day for me.

After the election of Republican James Garfield, Frederick Douglass had been appointed as recorder of deeds for Washington, DC. He continued to write and speak, publishing *The Life and Times of Frederick Douglass*. When Democrat Grover Cleveland was elected as President in 1884, Frederick shortly thereafter resigned his position as recorder of deeds. Another trip to, and tour of Europe, was made in 1886. Another tour of the Deep South was made in 1888, touching Frederick's heart and prompting him to make further addresses and writings on behalf of his people. In 1889, Republican president Benjamin Harrison offered Frederick Douglass an appointment as American consul-general to Haiti. By 1891, considerations of health determined the consul-general's resignation. Frederick Douglass returned to his estate at Cedar Hill and to a somewhat quieter life.

Douglass stated, "In the war for the Union I persuaded the colored man to become a soldier. In the peace that followed, I asked the Government to make him a citizen. In the construction of the rebellious States, I urged his enfranchisement."

The career of Frederick Douglass would, come, to a close on February 20, 1895. On that day, he attended a meeting in Washington of women's rights activists. Escorted to the speakers' platform by an old friend, Susan B. Anthony, Douglass acknowledged the cheers of the crowd … That night, while describing the day's events to his wife, Douglass was struck with a heart attack and died at the age of seventy-seven.

In the home of Frederick Douglass at Cedar Hill, now a National Park Historic Site in southeast Washington, DC, are to be found images of angels and Jesus and photos of the Metropolitan African Methodist Episcopal Church. On a fireplace mantel are busts of two philosophers: David Friedrich Strauss, author of *The Life of Jesus*; and Ludwig Feuerbach, author of *The Essence of Christianity*. Frederick Douglass was a lay preacher, licensed by the African Methodist Episcopal Zion Church in New Bedford, Massachusetts.

What might Frederick Douglass preach today?

> It is for freedom that Christ has set us free. Stand firm, then, and do not let yourselves be burdened again by a yoke of slavery. (Galatians: 5:1 NIV)

> Dear friend, do not imitate what is evil but what is good. Anyone who does what is good is from God. Anyone who does what is evil has not seen God. (3 John 11 NIV)

ERIC LIDDELL

A Race

The 1924 Olympics were about to begin. The teams lined up to march into the stadium. The head of the British Olympic Committee, Lord Cadogan, shook hands with the team members, wishing them success. As he came to Eric Liddell, he declared in a loud voice, "To play the game is the only thing in life that matters." Lord Cadogan then looked at Eric. Eric had gotten the point.

Eric Liddell, who would become known as the Flying Scotsman, had set a new British record for the one-hundred-yard dash. He would be entered into the Olympics for both the one-hundred and two-hundred-meter dashes. Eric had earlier received the list of the events he had been entered in with the times and dates. The qualifying heats for the one-hundred-meter dash would be held on a Sunday. Sunday was a day of rest and a day of reverence. Sunday was God's Day. The 4 x 100-meter relays were also to be run on a Sunday.

He would instead run the four-hundred-meter race as a dark horse and qualify with a time slower than the two recent world record holders in that event. Eric would run the two-hundred-meter dash and would receive a bronze medal for third place. Eric had not seen the movie *Chariots of Fire*, and so this would be a life he would need to live.

Most of the schools in the early 1900s emphasized hard study and vigorous exercise. At Eltham, all the boys learned to play rugby, cricket, and track and field. The boys were taught to play by the rules and to be good team players. Eric liked sports more than classwork. At the age of ten, he wrote to his missionary parents, "I don't think much of lessons, but I can run." Eric was also not fond of the school plays, so his drama teacher cast him as a dormouse, which is a shy little creature. Eric really did not have to pretend to be shy. His nickname until graduation was "the Mouse."

In 1914, Eric's mother gave birth to a new baby boy. She and Eric's little sister came to visit and live with him and his older brother Rob for a time. 1914 was also the start of a war with Germany, the Austro-Hungarian Empire, the Ottoman Empire on one side and France, Great Britain, Russia, and, later, the United States on the other — World War I. The senior boys at school volunteered to fight for the British. Before leaving for the front, they proudly returned to the school in their new uniforms. Many would be killed on battlefields, such as Flanders. There were daily readings of the wounded and dead. Eric and his classmates dreaded hearing the names read of the "old boys" they knew. It was like losing one big brother after another. It went on in that way for four years. By 1918, the war had ended, and so instead of off to war brother Robert went to Edinburgh University to become a doctor.

Eric followed his brother to Edinburgh. The Liddells began worshipping at the more ecumenical Morningside Church. Eric became active in the Young People's Union. Eric studied math and science. He was encouraged to try out for university track. The university found their fastest sprinter to be a freshman. If their fast freshman could be coached not to fling back his head or extend his arms forward as if he were boxing, he might be even faster. Try as he may, Eric was unable to change his basic style of running. Eric did win the one-hundred-yard dash at the overall Scottish University Sports Competition. He always shook hands with his competitors and wished them well. Eric also continued playing rugby. He played so well that he found himself on the Scottish international rugby team.

One day, Eric received a visit from a D. P. Thomson. D. P. had received a medical discharge from the Royal Army Service Corps in the autumn of 1917. The doctors were less than optimistic in their report for D. P. The doctors thought D. P. would either die or become a semi-invalid. The war had changed the lives of so many. An older brother of D. P.'s had died at the Somme in 1916. Five cousins had also died in that war. Why did D. P. survive the mud, blood, and gore of that depressing war? He was the weakling. Why did he come home? D. P. became a student at the Glasgow Bible Training Institute. *Life Changers*, a book written by Harold Begbie, was one of D. P.'s favorites. Begbie was best known for being the ghostwriter on Ernest Shackleton's polar explorations. D. P.'s friends said, "D. P." stood for "dynamic personality."

D. P. invited Eric to address some of the young men. On April 6, 1923, Robert Liddell introduced his younger brother. Eric was sincere. He spoke with a "quiet earnestness." In this gathering, he, spoke of the "stature of the perfect man." He described it as having patience, kindness, generosity, humility, courtesy, unselfishness, good temper, gentleness, and most importantly, sincerity. He described sincerity as "the basis of faith, mutual trust and co-operation." The lack of sincerity would negate the other qualities.

On the morning of the Olympic race, Eric was handed a piece of paper from a team supporter. It said, "In the old book it says: 'He that honors me I will honor.' Wishing you the best of success always."

Eric drew the outside lane for the Olympic four-hundred-meter race, rather than a preferred inside lane. As he would start the race ahead of the other runners, he would be unable to see and gauge the speeds of the other runners. As his competitors "were best placed" on the inside, Eric told himself to "Go all out—and don't be behind at the last straight." Fans of Eric Liddell noted that he was known for his slow starts. That day, Eric could say, "I got the perfect start." The standard approach to the four-hundred-meter is to begin at a near sprint, then ease up after about fifty meters while maintaining a fast pace until the final curve has been rounded. Then one sprints full tilt to the finish line.

Eric, in this race, sprinted his first two hundred meters in just six tenths of a second under the winning time of the two-hundred-meter race. "Can I last home?" was the thought bouncing within his head. As Liddell, was running, at least one of his competitors had thought to himself that no one could keep "an all-out sprint" to the finish line.

Horatio Fitch was the favored and predicted winner of the race. Fitch commented that he had begun the race "the way [he] always did—coasting a little." Eric said that the speed at which he ran his first two hundred meters could not have increased "by a fraction of an inch."

It is all out for Eric. Fitch gauged the distance between him and Liddell. Horatio approached the point where he would begin his full sprint to the finish. He had passed every competitor in every race. For Eric, "not till I was at the top of the straight did it suddenly dawn on me that I was several yards in front of the field." With less than one hundred meters to the finish line, Eric began seeing Fitch in his peripheral vision, gaining on him, about to take the lead. In his unorthodox manner, Eric threw back his head and pumped his arms. One observer had been greatly surprised at the initial risk Liddell had taken. He said, "[Liddell] went off at such a terrific pace that it seemed as if he must crack before the end – it seemed impossible that he should last the distance." Eric would later reflect, "A comforting thought flashed into my mind. I could no longer see the second man behind me." "I had no idea he would win it. I couldn't believe a man could set such a pace and finish," said Horatio Fitch. Eric Liddell had set a new world record.

After receiving his new Olympic Gold Medal and the applause of fans, Eric returned to England from France. As he rode the train to Victoria Station, he reminisced his unanticipated victory. His expectations were once more exceeded when he arrived at the station. A crowd of fans cheered and sang "For He's a Jolly Good Fellow." The new BBC Radio broadcasted the good news.

Eric became a minor sensation. He was invited to and spoke at many gatherings. Many offers were sent his way. His Olympic prime could be realized in another four years, at the next Olympics. He returned to Edinburgh and was carried atop a "sedan chair" through the streets of Old Town. On the steps of St. Giles Cathedral, he spoke his thoughts, "There are many men and women who have done their best, but who have not succeeded in gaining the laurels of victory. To them, as much honor is due as to those who have received those laurels."

Eric Liddell could have said to those who showed up that having won the gold medal, his sights were now set on winning others. What

Eric Liddell did say to one congregation was that "the greatest danger was victory," that of "bringing a man up to a level above the strength of his character." He advised to "keep sport free from anything that tends to lower its purity and value" but participate "for the sport's sake alone."

For Eric, the cheering from the crowds offered less satisfaction than the inner knowledge of his religious precepts. Why would he not devote himself to one more Olympic Games? "Because God made me for China," was Eric's reply. Eric returned to his place of birth and where he had lived the first five years of his life. He agreed to teach science and sports lessons at the Anglo-Chinese College at Tientsin. In 1925, Eric's return would be made via the Trans-Siberian Railway. Eric's father had written letters to him, telling him of what had been transpiring over the past eighteen years. His father outlined some of the fighting and disagreements. He wrote, "The grievances of China have been magnified beyond all recognition. So complex is the situation, so varied are the views expressed, so opposite the conclusions reached, so many the solutions suggested, that one staggers beneath the crushing load. A nation is in travail, seeking to reproduce that which will meet all its aspirations. Whether it will do so or not is another question."

The Qing Dynasty which had ruled China for 267 years, collapsed in 1912. A new republic was declared but the political powers devolved into the hands of regional governors and military commanders. Nominal control was exercised by the Nationalist Party and Chiang Kai-shek through the 1920's. The world communist movement started a Chinese Communist Party in 1921.

As a result of World War One and the influence of Wilsonian principles of self-determination, Western powers no longer extended their spheres of influence in China. Internal instability increased. Local warlords prevailed in many areas. Nationalists, supported by big cities, were the largest and most powerful faction. A smaller, but growing number of Communists comprised another group. Local villages could be looted by multiple controlling groups, while the powers-that-be changed hands several times.

One may digress, for a paragraph, into history to the year 1215, when Peking surrendered to Genghis Khan, who conquered half the known world, from China to the Crimea. It is recorded that sixty-thousand girls threw themselves off the walls to their deaths to avoid capture, such was the reputation of Genghis Khan and the Mongols. Coupled with the fall of the Roman Empire and the years known as the Dark Ages, barbarism, by some, for many a century, was a modality and a norm.

The history of the Middle Kingdom—the ancient values with repeated processes of Sinification, buttressed with doctrines of Confucianism—is not to be told within this writing. This history would be challenged by modernity and a mix of external encounters, among them the arrival of the "West Sea barbarians" from as far away as Great Britain.

The secondary and tertiary effects of the Industrial Revolution gave advantages to the Europeans and the other foreign interests within China, chipping away at the old order. The seemingly unnecessary opium wars seemed to highlight the weaknesses of all concerned. China, on the other hand, sided with the Allies in World War I and demanded that foreign powers leave after the war. The import of communism would later challenge the identity of a people as well as their very lives.

After Japan's invasion of China and defeat in World War Two, arrived Mao Zedong's China. By design, it would become a country in permanent crisis. The New State policy would deliberately tear apart Chinese traditions.

Eric's train finally pulled into the train station at Pei-Tia-ho. There were his parents; his sister, Jenny; his younger brother, Ernest; and older brother, Robert, with his new wife to greet him. After a few weeks, James Liddell, Eric's father, traveled by train with his son back to Tientsin, a city of one million. They detoured on rickshaws, passing miles of ports on the way to the Anglo-Chinese College, known as the "Eton of China." Five of the thirty teachers would be from England. Eric taught science. In the afternoons, he began developing an athletic program, and he took Chinese language courses for himself. He said yes to everyone who requested attention or service.

Eric wrote to a Miss Hardie and her Sunday school class in Edinburgh, describing his Christmas fun:

GOOD LEADERS

> Just at Christmas time; Tientsin was being attacked and for two weeks we could hear the guns going just about five or ten miles away. Slowly the attackers were winning their way until on the 23rd of December the fighting was going on in a part of Tientsin city. Then on the 24th Tientsin was taken. It was all quite exciting with the fighting so near. Of course, we were all safe as we live in a part that is ruled by the French ... I wonder how you would like a battle like that to go on just outside Edinburgh?

Eric maintained a fast pace in the classroom, on the sports field, and with members of the Union Church. He also began a weekly after-school Bible study. A few of the members were boys from Christian homes, but many were not. After several months, some of the boys asked to be baptized. Eric needed to know the boys' intentions. He also respected their parents. He visited with them and talked about their sons' requests. He anticipated hearing the parents' anger over their sons' wishes to become Christian. Eric, instead, was surprised in each home he visited. The parents told him their sons were happier and better behaved since attending classes. The parents all approved. Because of the advance of the southern army toward Tientsin in 1927, final exams scheduled for June were postponed till September. Eric had thought he might be invited to the 1928 Olympic Games but did not receive an invitation. He decided to participate in the 1928 South Manchurian Games instead. He ran both the two-hundred-meter and the four-hundred-meter races. His winning times were faster than the gold-medal-winning times held at the Amsterdam Olympics. His final race on British soil was on June 27, 1925, in the Scottish Amateur Athletic Association. A crowd of about fifteen thousand saw him win four first-place finishes.

In February of 1929, Eric and his brother Robert would once again say good-bye to their family as the family left for England, in part because of their father's health. By now Eric was twenty-seven. He had already noticed a young, petite Florence MacKenzie, who had sparkly brown eyes and long, curly black hair. She played the organ at church. She loved laughing and playing practical jokes. There was a problem. Florence was seventeen years old. Eric decided to take her entire graduating class out to a popular café, for a walk, or on a picnic. What to do? Summer vacation rolled around. The MacKenzie family would be staying at Pei-tai-ho. Eric and his roommates would be staying nearby, as this was a popular beach vacation area. In fact, Florence and her family had been there when Eric had first arrived in China. Flo told Eric she would be returning to Toronto to train as a nurse. This would take four years. She would then be twenty-one, which Eric thought was a perfect age to get married. After returning to Tientsin, Eric asked Flo to marry him. "Are you sure you really mean this?" she asked. Soon he was writing his mother to send him a ring for their four-year engagement.

After Flo left for Canada, Eric began preparing for a furlough in Scotland to study to become an ordained minister in the Scottish Congregational Church. His original plan was to request a two-year furlough. However, a fellow science teacher was ambushed and killed. During the first nine months of the year, ninety-seven missionaries were reported to have been kidnapped. Thirty-three were murdered. Eric delayed his leave, taking on additional responsibilities instead.

Finally, while on a one-year furlough, he visited Flo in Canada. His visit would too soon come to an end, and he boarded a ship to Scotland. In August of 1931, a large welcome-home gathering greeted Eric Liddell. People across not only Scotland but also England and Ireland invited the Flying Scotsman to speak. Eric always expressed his genuine concern for every person he met. Back in Edinburgh, he would plainly express, "We are all missionaries. We carry our religion with us, or we allow our religion to carry us. Wherever we go, we either bring people nearer to Christ, or we repel them from Christ. We are working for the great Kingdom of God—the time when all people will turn to Christ as their Leader—and will not be afraid to own Him as such."

At one meeting, he signed his name with a Chinese character behind it. The pastor asked what the character meant. "Keep smiling" replied Eric.

"You know, there is a woman who signs her letters with those same words, keep smiling," the pastor said. He explained that she really did not have a lot to smile about because she had been in a bad accident five years earlier and had suffered considerably since. He explained that she had lost an eye and had gotten some painful skin grafts performed.

"Would she have time for a visit?" asked Eric. Eric visited this woman, Bella Montgomery. She had a surprisingly wonderful attitude. Bella wrote Eric a thank-you note. He received it just before boarding a train.

Perhaps imperfectly written, Bella explained how she found Jesus Christ to be her best friend. At the next station, a young man boarded and sat himself in the same compartment as Eric. The young man was very unhappy—so unhappy he could see no reason to go on living and thought if suicide might be his answer. Eric thought for a moment and then thought of the letter in his pocket. The young man read the letter written by Bella. By the time they reached London, the young man was happier and considering the opportunities he might realize.

Eric paid a visit to his old school at Eltham. He perused the trophies displayed in the trophy case that he and his brother Rob had won. He had been invited to present prizes at the annual sports day. But the boys wanted Eric to win a prize too. Would he run a race as well? Eric had not had the time to stay in shape or practice his running. He wore a tie, jacket, and a regular pair of shoes. He couldn't turn these young men down, could he? He stretched a bit and walked to the starting line. He was running far ahead of his Eltham competitors at the finish line, listening to the boys' cheers and clapping.

Eric would be asked about the political situation in China. Japan saw the situation and had invaded Manchuria in 1931. The initial letters Eric had received simply indicated that life was normal in Tientsin. Later, in his furlough, letters confirmed the Japanese bombing of Shanghai, China's busiest port. Eventually Britain was able to get Japan to stop the attack. However, the Japanese, the Nationalists and the Communists were all now at war with each other.

Toward the end of his furlough, Eric was able to attend the wedding ceremony of his sister to Dr. Charles Somerville. Eric Liddell would be ordained and become the Reverend Eric Liddell. It would soon be time for him to be leaving for China. The London Missionary Society had decided that Eric's father, James Liddell, would retire from missionary work because of his health.

Eric would spend six weeks of treasured time with Flo and her family in Toronto. They talked of weddings and planning for their own wedding. They would plan for a March 1934 wedding in Tientsin.

By September 1932, Eric was back in Tientsin, ready for the start of a new school year. He was made secretary of the Anglo-Chinese College and chairman of the sports committee. Now, as an ordained minister, he would have additional church-related responsibilities. Eric enjoyed keeping busy waiting for Florence's return. In November 1933, Eric received a telegram telling him that his father had suddenly died. Many came by to comfort Eric, as his father had made such a positive impact on so many in and around Tientsin.

The *Empress of Canada*, with fiancée Florence MacKenzie on board, set sail for China. The docking date was set for about March 1, 1934. The ship would encounter bad weather as it entered the Yellow Sea. The next day there were gale-force winds. Eric could see the ship tossing and turning on the high seas, unable to dock. The tide was shifting. The ship could only wait for high tide. Eric set out for home. The wind picked up again, gusting so badly that the boat lunged and plunged. The captain decided there was no choice but to risk docking the ship. As it approached the docks, the tugboats made every maneuver to put the approaching ship in line. Finally, the ship was safely docked.

On March 27, 1934, Florence MacKenzie and Eric Liddell were married at Union Church in Tientsin. Medals and trophies would fill Florence and Eric's apartment, as would laughter and fun and guests. Florence would reflect that Eric's early morning quiet time during his Bible study "was the mainspring of his life."

For the time being, Tientsin would be relatively peaceful. Some of the students were also required to take part in military drills and camps. A letter from Eric to his old friend D. P. Thompson related the thought that the attitude of Christians to the impending wars would be one of the greater challenges of the mission. In 1935, Japanese forces advanced beyond the Great Wall near Peking. Hitler would make plans to hijack the 1936 Olympics in Berlin for his Nazi propaganda.

In July of 1935, Patricia Liddell would come into this world. The words of Eric's favorite hymn would come to mind: "Be still, my soul, the Lord is on thy side." In January of 1937, a second daughter, to be named Heather, would enter the world.

Earlier in the year of 1935, the district council of the LMS had asked Eric to consider assuming a position in rural Siaochang. His brother Rob had also served there as a doctor. Eric and Flo discussed it but decided not at that time. Eric resumed his teaching duties. His fellows at the university rather urged him to remain on the staff and continue using his talents there. Within Eric's sermons was his question "Where does faith come from?" His answer was "… faith comes from hearing, and hearing through the word of Christ."

The summer of 1936 at Pei-tai-ho may have been an especially happy and carefree time in ordinary circumstances. In July, the London Missionary Society decided Eric should be released from college for four months to pursue rural missionary work. In September, Eric left for a trial stay in Siaochang. Along the way, riding in an old mule cart, he saw that the crops were not growing. There were locusts and hunger. There was some form of military everywhere. "Thank you for coming, Li Mu Shi" was the greeting Eric received as he arrived in Siaochang. "Li" for "Liddell." "Mu Shi" for "pastor." They remembered his father well, and a few remembered Eric.

By the time Eric returned to Tientsin, he had made up his mind. Flo also wrote to D. P. Thompson, explaining, "After much prayerful consideration of all the points involved, he felt God was calling him to the country, and I think it was quite obvious he did the right thing. He loved his work, his health improved, and I think he blossomed out in a new way."

Florence and Eric and the girls would also spend time at their summer residence at Pei-tai-ho in the summer of 1937. On July 30, from the roof of MacKenzie Hospital, Eric watched Tientsin fall to the Japanese. Eric assisted refugees pouring into the school and the hospital.

Childhood memories of World War I flooded his brain. Somehow, life returned to something approaching normal under the Japanese.

Eric returned to teaching and his family. In November, a letter was received from the mission in Siaochang, written by Will Rowlands. He described how flooding had destroyed almost everything and that help was needed—especially from Dr. Rob Liddell. The brothers left on November 29 and journeyed to the mission by riverboat for the most part. They would need to learn to negotiate the Japanese, the Nationalists, the Communists, unknown guerillas, and bandits. About eighty people lived at the mission. Many repairs were needed. They discussed the matters at hand. They felt the work at the mission would be conducted with a view that in the long run, China would prevail over the Japanese.

Eric fixed a bicycle. He put on a Red Cross armband and pedaled into the rural countryside. He became a trusted asset to everyone he met, including the militaries. He wrote to his friend D. P. Thompson, "The floods have caused much havoc, but the loss sustained by them forms only a small part of the sorrows of the people. Fear reigns in all their hearts. Bands of irregular soldiers, bandits, etc., are all over the countryside … Repeated demands are made to the villagers to supply grain, money, rifles, and food …"

By June of 1938, Dr. Rob Liddell would be eligible and ready for furlough and would sail home to Scotland with his wife and a sick child. Rob had served many years without taking leave. Rob's own health was not the best at that point either. In July, Eric returned to his family for a month in Pei Tai Ho.

The next month, Eric returned to the mission in Siaochang. Eric turned no one away from the mission or the hospital. "They are neither Japanese nor Chinese, soldier nor civilian. They are all men Christ died for," he would say.

By 1939, the Japanese flag flew over the mission compound. On one morning, the Scottish flag flew over the entrance. It flew for a few hours. Eric explained it as "a joke on honorable matron." Although the Japanese were not pleased with the prank, the matter was forgotten.

Eric would not be deterred from his responsibilities. Per example, whenever the mission ran short of coal, Eric would make the four-hundred-mile trip to Tientsin for money to purchase coal. This would also allow for an opportunity to visit Flo and their children. He would then go to Tehchow to have coal placed on barges for delivery to Siaochang. Should the coal be stolen in full or in part on delivery, he may have to make a trip all over again.

On one trip to Tientsin for medical supplies, as Eric arrived in a village, he was told about a wounded Chinese soldier, not far away. The villagers were afraid to go near. If they approached the man, their homes could be burned, or random adults might be beheaded. Eric and his mule cart driver, who felt safe "near a man of God," found their way to a rather filthy temple. The villagers had sneaked in some rags for the man to sleep on. Eric promised to return the next morning. What should he do? He prayed and opened his Bible to Luke 16:10: "He that is faithful in that which is least is faithful also in much; and he that is unjust in the least is unjust also in much."

The following morning, avoiding the Japanese presence, they helped the wounded soldier into their cart and began a roughly twenty-mile return trip to Siaochang. On their return, a farmer told them about a wounded man in a shed nearby. When they reached him, they noticed rags wrapped around his neck. This man and five others had been dragged from their homes to be questioned and executed. The sword had only slashed the neck. The man was also lifted carefully into the cart. Enemy planes circled overhead on the return to Siaochang. At times, the ground shook with the impact of exploding bombs. Later Eric learned that the peasant was also a gifted artist. Li Hsin Sheng's painting of a peony flower still decorate many homes.

Within a letter to his Dear Family, Eric wrote,

> Often now, when I'm cycling from village to village, what with the frozen ground and the ruts, I have great difficulty in staying on the bicycle and I've a splendid collection of bruises. Nearly everyone is afraid to speak to me in public, but going into their homes, telling

them how so many others are in a similar situation, and getting them to sing hymns, has a wonderfully restorative effect— especially when I sing in English— which makes everyone roar with laughter, even though they don't have much to be cheerful about …

Now, with so many homes vandalized by visiting troops, most people are living crowded together, hungry and prey to disease. At least the National government had outlawed foot-binding. The women and girls are spared that agonizing pain and deformity, but in places where Jesus is scarcely known you find next to nothing is done to help the weak and distressed, especially children and, more especially girls.

Eric would further write to Florence, "Do you remember that little girl, frostbitten as the result of neglect, whose feet had to be taken off, though with care she did grow well and strong? Well, I found out quite recently that she married, and that her children were taught how love can help and heal. We must never forget that Jesus means us to pass on to others His love in deeds of kind thought, remember that what is done for one of His little ones is done for Him …"

Florence, Eric, and the girls left China in the summer of 1939 for Canada and England. They would stand aboard ship's deck, gazing at the beautiful sunsets and sunrises. In September of 1939, the young Liddell family finally arrived in Toronto. Days after their arrival, they heard news of a UK passenger ship, the SS *Athenia* that had been sunk. Germany invaded Poland. France and Great Britain declared war.

The family talked about Eric remaining in Canada for the year. The society was also counting on him to be in the United Kingdom. Once again, Eric would travel by himself across the Atlantic, leaving family behind. The Liddell's had so hoped to visit with Florence and the children as well. Even at a young age, Eric understood the patriotic duty served by his fellows. He, too, felt the need to do something, so he applied to the Royal Air Force to become a pilot. The RAF offered Eric a desk job, considering him too far past his prime to begin flying.

Eric continued to make speaking appearances. A minister wrote, "This simplicity of his was, in truth, that rare gift of the childlike spirit which the Kingdom consists, and before the address ended, the audience was aware of it. As I remember it, Eric did not say a great deal about the more adventurous side of life in Siaochang, but rather spoke as though Japanese armies, Chinese armies, and bandits were the normal background of the day's work."

Eric's furlough was extended, and so Florence and the children joined him and his family in March of 1940. This precious time was so important to them. Just one family story was told in this fashion. The girls had time to, simply and happily, run through the green hills of the countryside. Eric, maybe not surprisingly, caught a small rabbit. He said to the girls, "if you sprinkle a little salt on a rabbit's tail, it slows down, and you can catch them." Patricia turned to Heather with excitement and said, "Hurry! Let's go get some saltshakers!"

Eric and Flo knew World War II had only just begun. Bombing attacks or an invasion from Hitler's Germany was imminent as well. After much prayer and discussion, it was decided that they and their children would head back to China come August. Eric may have only reflected that he had already witnessed a lifetime of war.

Eric and his family left England in a small boat on a convoy of fifty ships. One of the ships was hit by a dud off the Irish coast that evening. Another ship at the back of the convoy was lost the following night. By the next day, the escort accompanying the convoy left. The following morning, another nearby boat was torpedoed and sunk. All on board hurried to the deck, ready to jump into the lifeboats. Around noon, the 'all clear' was given, and then another boat was hit by a torpedo. Eric wrote to his mother about the Atlantic crossing that "[both] kids are well … They weren't scared at all, for they didn't know what it all meant." Five of the fifty ships were sunk along the way. Eighty souls were lost to the sea.

Family time in Toronto and then a train ride across Canada to the Pacific awaited them. The Liddell's found a more peaceful voyage across the Pacific Ocean, arriving in Tientsin in late October of 1940. Eric and Flo were hopeful that it might be a bit safer by this time and they might all be able to move to Siaochang. This would not prove to be possible. Rumors circulated, stating that all foreigners would be sent out of China or detained. Florence and the girls moved into their house in Tientsin.

Eric returned to Siaochang. There, he found that the village had been garrisoned off from any exterior intrusion. Land had been taken and graveyards desecrated while roads were made. Siaochang became a Japanese base. Eric stayed with missionaries in the area and continued to work on his bicycle. He described his work as "giving, giving, all the time, and trying to get to know the people, and trying to leave them a message of encouragement and peace in a time when there is no external peace at all."

A Dr. Ken McAll observed in the hospital, "Our peaceful state is, some of us think, due to an early attitude that Eric Liddell helped us to; one of treating all these soldiers as children of God whom he cares for; and that it was for us, as we showed these over the premises to witness to them, explain why we were here, and try to help them as we ourselves have been helped by the Almighty."

Eric watched Chinese men, now miserable, laboring under the forces of the Japanese. He returned to Florence and his girls for Christmas in Tientsin.

Dr. Ken McAll later recalled about Eric that "he didn't stay put ... And he kept his wife and babies in Tientsin where they were safer, because, it was really, dangerous. We were constantly being shot at or locked up by the communists for identification."

In March of 1941, Eric was able to pop into Tientsin for another visit with Florence. They talked. He shared some thoughts about writing. She was excited for him, and she shared that another baby would be arriving. After putting the girls to bed, they talked in more detail. There were fewer and fewer missionary communities to be seen, as more and more were leaving. Tientsin was becoming less safe. As the days passed, time was of the essence, and a decision was made that Florence and the girls should go to Canada. Perhaps then, in another year, they would be together. They were still young. The safest mode of travel for the voyage would be on a Japanese vessel, and so they all traveled to the port at Kobe, Japan. Eric, Florence, Patricia, and Heather all said their goodbyes as they boarded the *Nita Maru* for their trans-Pacific voyage.

It was difficult for Eric to say good-bye. He somberly returned to the work at the hospital in Siaochang. The hospital, however, would soon be forced to close. Eric thought he would return to Pei-Tai-Ho and there, found the beaches empty and the area vacated. By September, he returned to Tientsin and moved in with A. P. Cullen, who had also sent his family home across the seas. For the first time in a very long time, Eric had time. He decided to follow a dream and put into writing, materials that could be used by Chinese pastors. Cullen described Eric's next fourteen months as "persistent study."

While in study, Eric received a cable from Canada, informing him that he would be a father to a new baby named Nancy Maureen Liddell. Eric completed *The Disciplines of the Christian Life*. Eric also took inspiration from various readings. He read *The Grapes of Wrath*, *All Quiet on the Western Front*, and writings from Aristotle, who Eric said kept "the passion of resentment under control." He also read *Discipleship*, written by Booker T. Washington.

"Why raise your hat when they slight you?" Booker was asked.

"Why should I stoop to be less than a gentleman because others do?" was Booker's reply. Eric followed Booker's advice when encountering the Japanese.

December 7, 1941 - was "a day that will live in infamy," as Franklin Delano Roosevelt said when he spoke, of the bombing of Pearl Harbor. Before most residents had woken, Japanese soldiers had wrapped Tientsin in barbed wire. Eric and Cullen were ordered to the Japanese military headquarters. They were placed under house arrest. The French concession and hospital were closed. Eric and Cullen then moved in with the Smiths in the British concession.

Only gatherings of nine or fewer would be allowed. Ladies could still organize afternoon teas, and so Eric and the other ministers attended many in prayer. Eric also worked on another devotional titled *Prayers for Daily Use*.

During the year Eric lived with the Smiths in their now crowded home, the children enjoyed being taught cricket and tennis. Years later, Reverend Smith said of Eric, "For a year we had the privilege of his sharing our home. I never saw Eric angry. I never heard him say a cross or unkind word. He just went about doing good." Some correspondence was sent and received between Florence and the LMS and Eric regarding the prospect of a rural pastorate in Canada. Late in the summer of 1942, the Japanese suggested a prospect of repatriation.

Eric continued to write long letters to his family. When those were received, the family was left to read letters that had been mostly censored. Magazines published by the London Missionary Society and the China Inland Mission contained some information about the missions and about China. Some quotations from *China's Millions* were as follows:

> We must remind our friends that we are no longer allowed to transmit personal gifts to missionaries in China as in prewar days …

> At the present moment, no British women are allowed to sail for "occupied" China, and we have to suspend, just for the moment, the training of women recruits …

> One of the senior Japanese officers in Kaifeng … has been very friendly during the last few weeks as a result of [a missionary doctor] having located, by means of the hospital X-ray machine, a bullet which had lodged in his chest …

> The Japanese erected electrified barricades around the British concession in Tientsin, stationing sentries and police at the various entrances and exits …

> The Generalissimo [Chiang Kai-shek], speaking in Chunking to a missionary group, said: "We still need and welcome Christians from other lands who will serve

the people. Do not feel that you are guests. You are comrades working with us to serve and save our people and to build a new nation."

Eric called a meeting on March 12, 1943. He informed the others that all foreign nationals would be interned at Weihsien, an American Presbyterian Mission. It was located some four hundred miles away in the Shantung Province. Only "minimum force" should be expected.

Shortly after the attack on Pearl Harbor, the Japanese had taken control of "The Courtyard of the Happy Way," as Weihsien was known. To put it mildly, the mission was trashed. Eighteen hundred internees, half of them children, would be put into the one-hundred-and-fifty-by-two-hundred-yard compound. Within six months, another three hundred children from another missionary school would be added.

The camp was surrounded by electric fences. Searchlights scoured the area at night. Dogs and soldiers patrolled outside. A roll call was held twice daily. Food lines could be three-quarters of a football field in length.

Eric and the others got busy to organize committees to supervise discipline, education, accommodations, supplies, and athletics. Entertainment programs were also scheduled, including Handel's *Messiah* and more. Children would also sing. Games and activities would be organized.

Along with a food scarcity, there were only four showers and little water. Rainwater was caught in buckets. "'Incurvatus in se," or each one's selfish desire to curve inward and live exclusively for his or her own interests, could be considered the biggest of threats. After standing in long lines to wait for half a cup of watered-down stew, those handing out the meager rations would hear the criticisms. The latrines were overflowing. The large contingency of Catholic priests and nuns became the most valuable members of the camp, as they displayed their bravery in the cleanup. A system of plumbing pieced together by the engineering and repairs department was relatively effective.

The general assignment categories were that the missionaries did the washing, the businessmen did the cleaning, and the lawyers were assigned the baking. Eric helped put together a school and a Sunday school. Among Eric's favorite sermon topics were Paul's love letter to the Corinthians and Jesus's Sermon on the Mount.

Another described his arrival at the camp, describing Eric, who he did not know. "[Eric] was wearing the most comical shirt I had ever seen ... I learned later, from a pair of Mrs. Liddell's curtains. But what struck me the most about him was his very ordinary appearance. He didn't look like a famous athlete, or rather he didn't look as if he thought of himself as one. That, I came to know in time, was one of the secrets of his amazing way. He was surely the most modest man who ever breathed."

Liddell was the consummate good neighbor. "He was the man we turned to when personal relationships got just too impossible," said an internee. "He had a gentle, humorous way of ... bringing to one's mind some bygone happiness or the prospect of some future interest just 'round' the corner." "Would you be free to "go for a stroll" was a question Eric always heard. One of the children later said of Eric, "I once saw him unloading supplies from the back of a cart. I said to myself: Why is he doing it? That's someone else's responsibility. Later I realized he did 'everything'. It's said he was worth ten men. I can believe it." Another said, "I was amazed anyone could carry such a timetable."

Camp life was no picnic at a different level. There was never enough food, especially as the war wore on. Some lost from seventy to one hundred pounds. Girls stopped menstruating. The children's teeth began growing without enamel. The Japanese shouted the latest news through the electric fences. Each, and every battle was being won by the Japanese. There were rats and bedbugs, outbreaks of typhoid fever, malaria, dysentery, frostbite, mental breakdowns, and funerals.

Nonetheless, there were also "sports days" on holidays, and times to raise morale. Some of the children played baseball or soccer, and in winter they played hockey. There were races to be run. Eric would teach science and chemistry as well.

Eric thoughtfully mentored young people. Eric delighted in the freedoms of understanding the graces of God. During one prayer session, or gripe session, one of the teenage girls broke down. "Lord,"

Kari Torjesen prayed, "I am willing to stay in this prison for the rest of my life if I can only know you." Years later, Kari said, "I'd planned to go to college. Instead, I went to prison … [but after that prayer] I was free! It was as if the gates had been opened. I was released in my spirit."

As Eric diligently tended to his ministry God produced more fruit. When would the war end? When would the prisoners be free to leave the camp? Those questions persisted.

On one day there was rejoicing for the baptism of a daughter. On another day, a mother stood with her teenage son at roll call. The boy was talking with another boy about whether, or not the perimeter fence was electrified. To win the argument, the boy walked over and grabbed the fence with his hand, only to be electrocuted in front of everyone.

Later the mother said of Eric,

> I recollect the comfort he brought to me in one
> of our meetings, when he taught us that lovely hymn—
>
> Be still my soul; the Lord is on thy side.
>
> Bear patiently, the cross of grief or pain.
>
> Leave to thy God to order and provide.
>
> In every change He faithful will remain.
>
> Be still, my soul, thy best, thy Heavenly Friend
>
> Through thorny ways leads to a joyful end.
>
> Then again, as he spoke from the text, "Be ye reconciled to God," he questioned if we were reconciled to God in all His dealings with us—not only in the initial step of salvation, but day by day in our sorrows and trials, were we reconciled to God. So, my memories of Eric are of one who was quietly and victoriously reconciled to God.

Eric also loved this verse from Corinthians:

> Therefore, if any man be in Christ, he is a new creature: old things are passed- away; behold, all things are become new. And all things are of God, who hath reconciled us to himself by Jesus Christ, and hath given to us the ministry of reconciliation; To wit, that God was in Christ, reconciling the world unto himself, not imputing their trespasses unto them; and hath committed unto us the word of reconciliation. Now then we are ambassadors for Christ, as though God did beseech you by us: we pray you in Christ's stead, be ye reconciled to God. For he hath made him to be sin for us, who knew no sin; that we might be made the righteousness of God in him. (2 Corinthians 5:17–21 KJV)

Eric explains what love is and what it is not in *The Disciplines of the Christian Life*:

> The Christian life should be a life of growth. I believe the secret of growth is to develop the devotional life. God is love. (1 John 4:8)

> By this shall all men know that ye are my disciples, if ye have love one to another. (John 13:35)

> Love is very patient, very kind.
> Love knows neither envy nor jealousy.
> Love is not forward or self-assertive.
> Love is not boastful or conceited, gives itself no airs.
> Love is never rude, never selfish, never irritated.
> Love never broods over wrongs.
> Love thinketh no evil.
> Love is never glad when others go wrong.

> Love finds no pleasure in injustice but rejoices in the truth.
> Love is always slow to expose; it knows how to be silent.
> Love is always eager to believe the best about a person.
> Love is full of hope, full of patient endurance.
> Love never fails.
> (1 Corinthians 13, paraphrase)

Eric would begin to experience headaches. In January of 1945, he would come down with the flu, as would many others. On February 11, 1945, Eric suffered a mild stroke. Doctors suspected an inoperable brain tumor. On February 22, 1945, a silent snow descended from the heavens.

Perhaps as we rise above our own prisons, whatever they may be, we might be blessed to hear in a morning devotion:

> Let all bitterness, and anger, and indignation, and clamor, and blasphemy, be put away from you, with all malice. And be ye kind one to another; merciful, forgiving one another, even as God hath forgiven you in Christ. (Ephesians 4:31–32 RHE)

> Love the Lord your God with all your heart and with all your soul and with all your strength and with all your mind…Love your neighbor as yourself. (Luke 10:27 NIV)

> There is therefore now no condemnation to them which are in Christ Jesus, who walk not after the flesh, but after the Spirit. (Romans 8:1 KJV)

WORKS CITED

Augustine, Saint 'The Confessions' Great Books of the Western World. Robert Maynard Hutchins, Editor in Chief William Benton, Publisher, Encyclopedia Britannica, Inc. 1952

Banks, Adelle M. "5 religious facts you might not know about Frederick Douglass." *Washington Post*, June 19, 2013.

Barr, Stephen M. *The Believing Scientist: Essays on Science and Religion*. Grand Rapids, Michigan: William Eerdmans Publishing Company, 2016.

Bartlett, John. *Familiar Quotations*. Boston: Little, Brown, 1968.

Belmonte, Kevin. *William Wilberforce: A Hero for Humanity*. Zondervan, 2002.

Beltz, Bob, ed. *William Wilberforce: Real Christianity*. Bloomington, Minnesota: Bethany House Publishers, 2006.

Benge, Janet, and Geoff Benge. *Eric Liddell: Something Greater Than Gold*. Christian Heroes: Then & Now. Seattle, Washington: YWAM Publishing, 1998.

Bradstreet, David, and Steve Rabey. *Star Struck: Seeing the Creator in the Wonders of the Cosmos*. Grand Rapids, Michigan: Zondervan, 2016.

Caughey, Ellen. *Eric Liddell, Olympian and Missionary*. Heroes of the Faith. Uhrichsville, Ohio: Barbour Publishing, 2000. Used by permission of Barbour Publishing, Inc.

Chernow, Ron. *Alexander Hamilton*. New York: Penguin Press, 2004.

Collins, Francis. *The Language of God*. New York: Free Press, 2006.

Collins, Francis *Belief: Readings on the Reason for Faith*. New York: Harper One, 2010.

Commager, Henry Steele. Introduction to *The Autobiography of Benjamin Franklin and Selections From His Other Writings*, by Benjamin Franklin. New York: Random House, 1944.

Crutchley, Peter. "Did a prayer meeting really bring down the Berlin Wall And end the Cold War?" BBC Religion & Ethics. October 9, 2015.

De Hartog, Leo. *Ghengis Khan, Conqueror of the World*. New York: Barnes & Noble Books, 1989.

de Tocqueville, Alexis. *Democracy in America*. Chicago: University of Chicago Press, 2002.

Douglass, Frederick. *Douglass: Autobiographies: Narrative of the Life of Frederick Douglass, an American Slave / My Bondage and My Freedom / Life and Times of Frederick Douglass*. New York: Library of America, 1994.

Dupont, Christian. *Declaring Independence: The Origin and Influence of America's Founding Document*. Charlottesville, Virginia: University of Virginia Library, 2008.

Egan, Eileen. Such A Vision Of The Street: Mother Teresa—The Spirit and the Work. New York: Doubleday & Company, Inc., 1985.

Eichinger, Eric T., and Eva Marie Everson. *The Final Race: The Incredible World War II Story of the Olympian Who Inspired Chariots of Fire.* Carol Stream, Illinois: Tyndale House Publishers, 2018.

Elvers-Guyot, Julia. "Peace prayers helped bring down the Wall, says Leipzig pastor." Interview with Christian Führer. DW. January 7, 2009.

Federer, William J. *America's God and Country: Encyclopedia of Quotations.* Coppel, Texas: Fame Pub, 1996.

Federer, William J. *George Washington Carver: His Life & Faith in His Own Words.* St. Louis, Missouri: Amerisearch, 2002.

Fellows, Lawrence. The Gentle War: The Story of the Salvation Army. New York: Macmillan, 1979.

Fleming, Thomas. *Liberty: The American Revolution.* New York: Viking, 1997.

Fleming, Thomas. *The Man from Monticello: An Intimate Life of Thomas Jefferson.* New York: Morrow, 1969.

Folwell, William Watts. *A History of Minnesota in Four Volumes.* St. Paul, Minnesota: Minnesota Historical Society, 1924.

Free Press. Mankatofreepress.com. civilwarsaga.com/Albert Woolson: The Last Civil War Veteran.

Führer, Christian. *Protestant Lutheran Church of St. Nikolai in Leipzig: A Spiritual Church Guide.* Regensburg, Germany: Schnell & Steiner GMBH 2011.

Führer, Christian: *Und wir sind dabei gewesen* (And We Were There). Berlin, Germany: Ullstein, 2009.

Geisler, Norman L. and Frank Turek. *I Don't Have Enough Faith to be an Atheist*. Wheaton, Illinois: Crossway, 2004.

Gill, Gillian. *Nightingales*. New York: Ballantine Books, 2004.

Glover, Jane. *Handel in London: The Making of a Genius*. New York: Pegasus Books, 2018.

Goodwin, Doris Kearns. *Team of Rivals: The Political Genius of Abraham Lincoln*. Waterville, Maine: Thorndike Press 2013.

Hamilton, Duncan. *For The Glory: The Untold and Inspiring Story of Eric Liddell, Hero of Chariots of Fire*. London: Penguin Books, 2017.

Harris, Ellen T. *George Frideric Handel: A Life with Friends*. New York: W. W. Norton and Company, 2014.

Haugen, Brenda. *Alexander Hamilton: Founding Father and Statesman*. Minneapolis: Compass Point Books, 2005.

Herbstrith, Waltraud. *Edith Stein: A Biography*. San Francisco: Harper & Row, 1985.

Hill, Brennan R. *8 Spiritual Heroes: Their Search for God*. Cincinnati, Ohio: St. Anthony Messenger Press, 2002.

Huxley, Elspeth. Florence Nightingale. London: Weidenfeld and Nicolson, 1975.

Jefferson, Thomas. *Basic Writings of Thomas Jefferson*. Edited by Philip Sheldon Foner. New York: Willey Book Co., 1944.

Jefferson, Thomas. *Writings: Autobiography / Notes on the State of Virginia / Public and Private Papers / Addresses / Letters*. Edited by Merril Peterson. New York: Library of America, 1984.

John Paul II. *Crossing the Threshold of Hope*. New York: Knopf, 1994.

John Paul II. *Rise, Let Us Be On Our Way*. New York: Warner Books, 2004.

Kaplan, Fred. *John Quincy Adams: American Visionary*. New York: Harper Collins, 2014.

Keates, Jonathan. *Handel: The Man & His Music*. London: The Bodley Head, 1988.

Kelly, Regina Z. *Henry Clay: Statesman and Patriot*. Boston: Houghton Mifflin, 1960.

Kengor, Paul. *A Pope and a President: John Paul II, Ronald Reagan, and the Extraordinary Untold Story of the 20th Century*. Wilmington, Delaware: ISI Books, 2017.

Kennedy, John F. *Profiles in Courage*. New York: Harper, 1961.

King Jr., Martin Luther. *I Have a Dream: Writings and Speeches that Changed the World*. Edited by James Melvin Washington. San Francisco, California: Harper San Francisco, 1992.

Kissinger, Henry. *Kissinger on China*. New York: Penguin Press, 2011.

Kline, Mary-Jo, ed. *Alexander Hamilton: A Biography in His Own Words*. The Founding Fathers, volume 2. New York: Newsweek, 1973.

Kynge, James. *China Shakes the World*. Boston: Houghton Mifflin Company, 2006.

Lambert, Dominique. *The Atom and the Universe: The life and work of Georges Lemaitre*. Translated by Luc Ampleman. Edited by Karl Van Bibber. Brussels: Copernicus Center Press, 2015.

Landa, Pauline. *Georges Lemaitre*. Translated by Jessica Foster. Middleton, Delaware: 50 Minutes, 2019

Leidner, Gordon, ed. Abraham Lincoln: Quotes, Quips and Speeches. Nashville, Tennessee: Cumberland House, 2000.

Levin, Phyllis Lee. *Abigail Adams: A Biography*. New York: Ballantine Books, 1987

Lewis, C. S. *Mere Christianity*. New York: MacMillan Publishing Co., Inc., 1977.

Lian Xi. *Blood Letters: The Untold Story of Lin Zhao, A Martyr in Mao's China*. New York: Basic Books, 2018. Excerpts from *Blood Letters* by Lian Xi copyright 2018 Reprinted by permission of Basic Books, an imprint of Hachette Book Group, Inc.

Liddell, Eric. *The Disciplines of the Christian Life*. Escondido, California: eChristian Books, 2011.

Lincoln, Abraham. Speeches and Writings 1859–1865. New York: Literary Classics of the United States, 1989.

Ludwig, Charles. *George Frideric Handel*. Illustrations by Arthur Schneider. Fenton, Michigan: Mott Media, 1987.

McCullough, David. *John Adams*. New York: Simon & Schuster, 2001.

McDonald, Lynn. *Florence Nightingale at First Hand*. Continuum, 2010.

McGee, Dorothy Horton. *Framers of the Constitution*. New York: Dodd Mead, 1968.

Metaxas, Eric. *Amazing Grace: William Wilberforce and the Heroic Campaign to End Slavery*. New York: Harper Collins Publishers, 2007.

Miller, William Robert. *Martin Luther King Jr.: His Life, Martyrdom and Meaning for the World*. New York: Weybright and Tailey, 1968.

Monk, Linda R. *The Words We Live By: Your Annotated Guide to the Constitution*. New York: Hyperion, 2003.

Mother Teresa and Fr. Brian Kolodiejchuk. *Mother Teresa: Come Be My Light: The Private Writings of the Saint of Calcutta*. Edited by Fr. Brian Kolodiejchuk. New York: Doubleday Broadway Publishing Group, 2007.

Mother Teresa. *The writings of Mother Teresa of Calcutta*. San Diego, California: The Mother Teresa Center, exclusive licensee throughout the world of the Missionaries of Charity for the works of Mother Teresa. Used with permission.

Muggeridge, Malcom. *Something Beautiful for God: Mother Teresa of Calcutta*. Harper & Row, 1977.

Munson, Daniel C. Malice Toward None: A Minnesota History. St. Cloud, Minnesota: North Star Press, 2014.

Newell, Roger *Contemporary Church History Quarterly* 20. September 2014. Reflection on Pastor Christian Fuhrer of the Nikolai Church in Leipzig.

Nightingale, Florence. *Notes on Nursing: What It Is, and What It Is Not*. Dover Publications, 1969

Perry, John. *Unshakable Faith: Booker T. Washington & George Washington Carver: A Biography*. Sisters, Oregon: Multnomah Publishers, 1999.

Perry, John. *George Washington Carver*. Thomas Nelson, 2011.

Piper, John. *Amazing Grace in the Life of William Wilberforce.* Wheaton Illinois: Crossway Books, 2006.

Pollock, John. *Amazing Grace: The Dramatic Life Story of John Newton.* San Francisco: Harper & Row, 1981.

Roberts, J. A. G. *A Concise History of China.* Cambridge, Massachusetts: Harvard University Press, 1999.

Roth, David E. The Illustrated History of the Civil War, 1861–1865. New York: Smithmark Publishing, 1992.

Russell, Sharman Apt. *Frederick Douglass: Abolitionist Editor.* Black Americans of Achievement. Philadelphia: Chelsea House, 2005.

Salvation Army USA. salvationarmyusa.org. December 2019.

Sebba, Anne. Mother Teresa: Beyond the Image. New York: Doubleday, 1997.

Spink, Kathryn. Mother Teresa: A Complete Authorized Biography.

San Francisco, California: Harper San Francisco, 1997.

Spitzer, Robert J. *Evidence for God from Physics and Philosophy: Extending the Legacy of Monsignor Georges Lemaitre and St. Thomas Aquinas.* South Bend, Indiana: St. Augustine Press, 2015.

Srodes, James. *Franklin, the Essential Founding Father.* Washington, DC: Regnery Publishing, Inc., 2002.

Stapert, Calvin R. *Handel's Messiah: Comfort for God's People.* Grand Rapids, Michigan: William B. Eerdmans Publishing Company, 2010.